A FAITH FOR

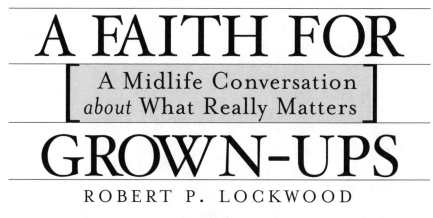

A Midlife Conversation
about What Really Matters

GROWN-UPS

ROBERT P. LOCKWOOD

LOYOLAPRESS.

CHICAGO

LOYOLAPRESS.
3441 N. ASHLAND AVENUE
CHICAGO, ILLINOIS 60657
(800) 621-1008
WWW.LOYOLABOOKS.ORG

Cover photo: © Stone/Erik Dreyer
Cover and interior design by Megan Duffy Rostan

Library of Congress Cataloging-in-Publication Data
Lockwood, Robert.
  A faith for grown-ups : a midlife conversation about what really
matters / Robert Lockwood.
    p. cm.
  ISBN 0-8294-1647-1
  1. Catholic Church—Doctrines. 2. Christian life—Catholic authors.
3. Middle aged persons—Religious life. 4. Baby boom generation—
Religious life. I. Title.
BX1751.3.L63 2004
248.8'4—dc22

2003026383

Printed in the United States of America
04 05 06 07 08 09 10 Versa 10 9 8 7 6 5 4 3 2 1

CONTENTS

A Story, Not an Argument

What is a sacrament?
A sacrament is an outward sign instituted
by Christ to give grace.

It was a gray and cold Hoosier Sunday in February; not that there's any other kind in northern Indiana. We ducked straight into the wind as it bounced off the crust of ice on the church parking lot. We were doing the Hoosier winter-walk, leaning into the wind with the head leading the way for the feet, eyes always on the ground to catch the slick spot before it catches you. Hoosiers take enormous pride in making it through a winter without one fall on the ice. They mark the years by notorious slips. "Winter of '57? That's when Aunt Flo took a tumble down the back steps after the ice storm and landed on the cat."

We were winter-walking to a small neighborhood parish for a baptism. My son's good friend had fathered a child and we were invited to witness the sacrament. We had known the kid and his parents since his freshman year in high school. He was one of the uncounted numbers of young nomads who had wandered in and out of our house over the last eight years. And now he was a father, without benefit of marriage. He and mom had been living together since shortly after their mutual conception became mutually known. Both were raised and schooled Catholic, so baptism was the thing to do. Things are pretty murky out there at times, but I try to keep a stiff upper lip. Baptisms help renew the faith.

The church was filled with the usual mix. I am sure the new grandparents on both sides—and the pastor—hoped that the sacrament might not only welcome a new soul to Christ, but also help make tepid faith a bit more fervent. There were assuredly a good deal of Catholics on both sides of the little church who might make the rounds on Easter, Christmas, and special events. But they mostly observe the command of Sabbath rest by sleeping in. One father leaned over to his adult son and whispered, "I said you wouldn't be struck down by lightning at the church door."

The couple's buddies, all in their early twenties, had the spit and vinegar of new adults. The fact that a baby had been sired by one of their own was just another confirmation that they were no longer just marking time. The parents of the new parents were baby boomers, getting a bit long in the tooth. That's where I find myself. Back in the 1960s and 1970s, we worried about becoming our parents. Now we are becoming our grandparents.

All these musings went away in the miracle of the sacrament's ritual. A little one was baptized in the name of the Father, and the Son, and the Holy Spirit. Cameras flashed, baby wailed at the anointing with holy oil, smiles and laughter were everywhere. "Baptism is the seal of eternal life," St. Irenaeus told us, and with it, we will be able to depart this world marked with the sign of faith. The week-old grandfather approached me from behind and gave my sleeve a tug. "Thanks for coming," he said, then added with a smile, "keep this a secret for twenty-four hours, but he's going to propose to her tomorrow. Birth, baptism, marriage. The order seems to have changed since we were kids." He was a happy guy. It was a good day.

Marked with the Sign of Faith

The next day—a gray and cold Hoosier Monday in February—there was a funeral Mass at another little church. A friend's mother had died in her sleep. The friend, my age almost to the day, had been the eldest son in a large brood. His mother had gone to sleep at home in the evening and didn't wake up in the morning. The suddenness of it left her large family to cope not only with the fact of her death, but also with the shock of it. Her adult children had the look of things meant to be said but never said. It was a sad day.

She was a good woman, and the pastor rightly praised a life of faith lived well in service to God and man. An old priest once referred to her kind as the leaven of the Lord. With good humor, as well as abiding, prayerful, and active faith, these people touch more souls than they ever realize. They evangelize without knowing the word.

The funeral liturgy was ripe with baptismal imagery. "For surely you know that when we were baptized into union with Christ Jesus, we were baptized into union with his death. By our baptism, then, we were buried with him and shared his death, in order that, just as Christ was raised from death by the glorious power of the Father, so also we might live a new life" (Romans 6:3–4). As I sat in the pew, I wondered about the baptism of my friend's mother nearly seven decades ago. Back then, I imagine a little baby had been brought to church by parents carefully dressed for the occasion. In a tiny white outfit, she was received into the church; she was washed with the waters of baptism as solemn godparents looked on. And now she is gone, departing from this world marked with the sign of faith. The casket was blessed and the pastor reminded us once again that in baptism, she had put on the life of the Lord. Then the body was taken out to be buried.

Bookends

Baby boomers seem to be caught between baptisms and funerals. Our kids are raising kids; our parents are either gone or going; friends are beginning to take their leave naturally, rather than by surprise or accident. We are that great demographic bulge, the subject of eager marketers, philosophical navel-gazing, and our own self-awareness. We are the children of the "greatest generation," born after the last world war, nurtured in the 1950s, educated—in more ways than one—in the 1960s, newlyweds, then parents, in the 1970s, 1980s, and the early 1990s. Strictly defined, we were born sometime between 1946 and 1965. We are near forty, and many of us are post-fifty and climbing. What was Paul Simon telling us in "Old Friends"? Could we even imagine back in our callow youth how strange it would be at age seventy, sitting on a bench in the park? That was then and this is now. Seventy is not too hard to imagine anymore.

Of course, we are in the driver's seat now. Instead of electing presidents, we are the presidents. The generations between our children and the Boomers can't stand us, while we have already taken most of the jobs of the generation before ours. We sit on boards, run the schools, keep the power going, haul the freight, complain about the government. Yet, we also hear the whispering that "all this shall pass." We are just about at the point where we are taking that as a promise rather than a warning. Old ambitions—met or unmet—seem less important. The drive is still there, but we want to steer it in another direction. We have come to realize that we are on a pilgrimage, though we are not sure where it ends, and maybe not even quite sure of the purpose.

A healthy part of us—estimates run as high as 30 percent—were baptized and raised Catholic. More than half of those raised Catholic had their salad days in the church before Vatican II. We remember the Mass in Latin, Friday abstinence from meat, tortuous regulations for celebrating the Lenten season, confessions-in-a-box. If we attended Catholic grammar school in that period before everything changed, even our very language betrays our upbringing. Words float to the surface that we may not be able to define anymore but are a living part of us: rogation and ember days, transubstantiation, the Angelus, Sabatine privilege, decades to number beads not years, introit, nocturnal adoration, the poor souls in purgatory, the church militant and the church triumphant. We vaguely remember Pope Pius XII, we definitely recall the portly John XXIII, but the twenty-five-year pontificate of Pope Paul VI is the pope of our youth and early maturity. We were taught our faith out of the *Baltimore Catechism,* and it was a part of our childhood like breathing out and breathing in. The coffee table had Catholic magazines like *Maryknoll, Ave Maria,* and *Our Sunday Visitor.* We had crucifixes on the walls at home, statues of Mary in the backyard, palms from Palm Sunday on picture frames; we said grace before meals and knelt for our night prayers ("If I should die before I wake, I pray the Lord my soul to take."). The list goes on and on, relics of a time and a faith from our childhood—as Garry Wills quoted Shakespeare, "bare ruin'd choirs, where once the sweet bird sang."

Even those boomers born toward the end of the boom, and who never attended Catholic grammar schools, know that world pretty well. From World War II until the assassination of John F. Kennedy in 1963, Catholicism and American culture had coalesced in a heady brew that remained as a hangover until the 1970s. In *American Catholic* (Random House, 1997), Charles Morris explained that the "Catholic impulse was perfectly in accord with the powerful forces that were transforming American culture in the 1940s and 1950s. . . . Catholics were becoming Everyman." Catholic kitsch was spreading throughout popular culture and affected everything from the movies to nascent television. Morris writes: "It is not likely that anyone looking at America with a stranger's eye during [the 1950s], and examining much of the rest of popular culture and social mores, would have concluded that Catholicism was an alien religion . . . or that the Church was anything less than a dominant, possibly the dominant, religious and cultural influence in the country."

And then Catholicism seemed to go away, and many of the baby boomers went away as well. Come the birth of the cultural revolution in the late 1960s and its victory in the 1970s, the faith of our childhood seemed to lose its hold on us. If our timing was just right, when we ducked out in the late 1960s and took another look ten years later, we didn't even recognize it anyway. The church of our childhood was gone.

Slabs of Talking Meat

For any number of boomers, this was hardly cause for grief. While some found the old memories and the old ways appealing, a lot of Catholic boomers had rejected that whole childhood faith. (I started to lose mine the first time I saw a miniskirt. At the very least, that was the end of any thoughts I might have had of a priestly vocation.) They dropped out after recurring nightmares of tyrannical nuns of indeterminate age exaggerated by memory and years. They didn't like Catholic grammar school, or they hated CCD classes, at least in retrospect. Grouchy and inflexible priests chewing kids out for lousy Latin responses at Mass didn't help either. Authority, women's rights, institutionalism, perceived sexual anachronisms over birth control and abortion, or just sheer boredom with a faith that seemed dry, rigid, and, yes, childish pushed any number of Boomers away. Marital problems, contemporary gnosticism, the designated hitter rule—it didn't matter what was put on the list. It wasn't so much theological disagreement as theological apathy. It just didn't matter anymore, even if we boomers tried to dress it all up in pop psychology of our injured inner child or in cultural, political, and philosophical disagreements. Pulling out an old cliché from the 1960s, we just didn't find much "relevance" in something that spoke to us of days gone by. We outgrew Catholicism in the 1960s and 1970s, just like we outgrew Mickey Mantle, Bugs Bunny, and that crush on Annette Funicello.

But as time went by, some of us came back. A lot of us, in fact. We didn't come back to recapture childhood innocence, like watching *The Honeymooners* reruns on late-night television. We didn't come back to escape the quiet desperation; we didn't come back because we discovered our own mortality; we didn't come back for our kids. At least none of that for the long haul. We came back because we couldn't find a better Truth in all the little truths we had been toying with for twenty years, give or take. We first peeked back in the door just to see if something was there that we had left behind. We discovered that there was so much more than we ever knew.

I was home for Christmas during my sophomore year at college. Christmas of 1968. My older brother and I had been busy bonding. We had spent one night up until three in the morning drinking beer and cackling like idiots reading a *National Lampoon* parody called "Nancy Reagan's Dating Manual." I can't remember a line from it but it must have been a classic because I still get sympathy pains in the gut from laughing whenever I remember that night. For some reason, my brother had two goals that holiday season over and above exposing me to *National Lampoon* magazine. He wanted me to get my hair cut, the golden locks having been untouched by shaver or scissors since my father had bribed me the previous June. The other goal was to get me to go to Mass on Christmas. I passed on the haircut and argued religion. At one point, my brother slurred, "Are we just slabs of meat that talk?" For some reason, that question got to me. I attended Mass for the first time since high-school graduation. And I got absolutely nothing out of it once the choir laid off the Christmas carols. Or at least that was what I thought. It was actually the first step back to the church. Amazing grace.

This book is about our collective pilgrimage and about trying to understand that Truth the church embraces. It's looking at the Catholic faith as an adult. It's for my brother and sister baby boomers, particularly those raised in the church who took a hike once Dylan explained that the times they are a changing. It's a story, not an argument; a plot, not a textbook.

* * *

I fled Him, down the nights and days;
I fled Him, down the arches of the years;
I fled him, down the labyrinthine ways
Of my own mind; and in the midst of tears
I hid from Him, and under running laughter.
Up vistaed hopes I sped;
And shot, precipitated,
Adown Titanic glooms of chastened fears,
From those string Feet that followed, followed after.
But unhurrying chase,
And unperturbed pace,
Deliberate speed, majestic instancy,

They beat—and a Voice beat

More instant than the Feet—

"All things betray thee, who betrayest Me."

   from "The Hound of Heaven" by Francis Thompson (1859–1907)

CHAPTER 1

When All Was Right with the World

What is a mystery?
A mystery is a truth which we
cannot fully understand.

The kid heading toward me had that seedy look. A line flashed in my head, like something from an old Ray Chandler mystery: "He could spit fear." I don't know what that meant exactly, but it fit the moment.

I was out for an evening walk with the dog. I never thought the time would come when I would consider a stroll through the neighborhood exercise, but that's what happens as the hair gets grayer and the waistline stretches. All the exercise and all the fad diets can't combine to beat the years, though men in particular like to think so. A diet to start next Monday, a few weeks of sit-ups and we'll be thirty again. Of such things great lies are built over a rare steak and a cold beer.

The kid wore a baseball cap brim backward and a floppy old jacket hanging low in the night drizzle. Baggy tan pants and black sneakers finished the sartorial splendor. When he finally walked past harmlessly, I let out a little breath and sucked the night air in deeply.

What was that smell? When he went by, he left a brief but very distinct odor, like a cigar burning in a mattress. No, it wasn't an illegal substance. It was something else. I racked my brain, the memory triggered like hearing an old song on the radio. Something from the past. As if to help the memory, my thighs began to itch in sympathy.

And suddenly I was back. Twenty-four eleven-year-old boys sitting on one side of the aisle of Christ the King Church in Yonkers, New York. Thirty-two girls in blue jumpers and skirts are across from us. It's a rainy March morning and we have trekked in from various parts of the neighborhood to begin a Lenten school day with prayer and devotions. Nobody got a ride to school in 1959. Buses were for the public-school kids. The Old Man had the car anyway, and nobody was rich enough for two cars. If it rained you were outfitted in hat and rubbers. Puddles formed under the pews, mixing in with about a thousand coats of pine wax to create its own unique aroma. But that wasn't what I had just smelled.

Wet corduroy pants!

Take fifteen mangy mutts, soak, and they don't smell nearly as bad as one pair of wet corduroy pants. Our blue corduroy pants were part of the school winter uniform, worn for extra warmth. The fall and spring pants were made of some thin faux substance that tore in the knees if they got a whiff of the asphalt of a Catholic school playground. But we took them any day over the corduroys that introduced us to a lifetime of jock itch. Years later and we're still scratching. The blue pants went with the white shirts and blue ties with the "CK" logo stitched on them in white, though by March most of us would have colored that over in blue ink from our fountain pens in an act of desperate boredom during arithmetic.

With the stench of corduroy overpowering the lingering smell of incense, hundreds of us jammed into the pews, class by class, for a Lenten prayer service during which we would be reminded that each of our sins pressed a thorn deeper into the forehead of Christ. That "told-a-lie-twice" that we rattled off in the confessional on Saturday afternoons was not some small affair. It was part of an eternal understanding. The knowledge that Christ died for our sins was explained very personally. This was not sin in the abstract. Christ did not suffer solely for what Hitler and Stalin had done; He suffered because you clobbered your little brother for touching your stuff and because you talked in line yesterday afternoon when heading back to class after recess.

Bookshelves are filled with baby-boomer recollections of growing up in the postwar Catholic Church in the years prior to and just after the Second Vatican Council. Some are funny, others are desperate. Most are cynical. It is a curiosity that, as far as I know, there are no fictionalized memoirs of growing up in a public elementary school at the same period. Stuff like *Blackboard Jungle* doesn't count because the theme was "juvenile delinquents" in high school, rather than the allegedly stultifying atmosphere of elementary school. That was an age where every kid feared the neighborhood "JDs" and we were warned that if we followed a certain disreputable path, we would end up with "JD cards." I never saw a JD card, though there were more than enough juvenile delinquents where I hung around.

The difference, of course, between the public-school environment and the parochial schools was that central linking of faith and education. Arithmetic was just arithmetic over at Public School 16 in my neighborhood. At Christ the King—and thousands of Catholic grammar schools across the country—arithmetic was only a part of the whole. There was a thread intertwining with spelling, geography, history, and reading that held it all together. It was our faith. Our Catholicism was never confined to the religion class that usually started the morning's education. It was not solely the prayers that would mark the transition of one class to the next, the Angelus at Noon (when kids would freeze in place at the sound of the church bells: "The angel of the Lord declared unto Mary. And she conceived of the Holy Ghost. Hail Mary, full of grace . . ."), the saints days celebrated, the steady pace of the liturgical year from September through June. The faith pervaded every moment of the day, making phonics not merely a drudge of endless sounding-out, but a part of the eternal cosmos: "When you see WH together," Sister explained, "it produces a 'whe' sound, as in *whip*. Like the WHips that lashed Jesus on Good Friday." Public school kids back then were being introduced to a vague and flattened civic religion that identified George Washington with a White Anglo-Saxon Protestant culture, as bland as an Episcopalian box social. Even the Jewish kids weren't offended. It was a white-bread experience without texture or taste that no one bothers to recall. Love it or hate it, accept it or reject it, praise it or blame it, no one who experienced eight years of Catholic grammar school in the 1950s, 1960s, or early 1970s could find it forgettable. I mean, their school was named after a number. Our school was named Christ the King.

And that can be the essential problem. The grammar-school experience of those three decades was so inextricably bound to the faith that one is simply identified with the other. When the nun told us that Jesus was disappointed that we spoke in class, she was playing an ace to maintain her sanity, not trying to present the Catholic faith. Too many of us have never much gone past it. Most of what a generation or two identified with Catholicism was a nun's attempt to exercise crowd control over a bunch of kids more interested in being home watching *Three Stooges* reruns. It was a childish presentation of the faith for childish minds. No harm done, except if we never get past that.

That said, there was something clearly overwhelming in the faith of our youth. And therein lies the contradiction. The faith some of us avoid now has little to do with the faith as it is to be lived and known as an adult. Yet, at the same time, that introduction to the faith in the church of our childhood was powerful. It lingers with us. Kenneth Woodward, religion editor at *Newsweek* for many years, described Catholicism—and particularly the Catholicism of a baby boomer's youth—as a sensual religion. By that he didn't mean sexy. God forbid. When I graduated in 1963 from grammar school, I couldn't be screwed-up by sex. Sex hadn't been invented yet. Woodward meant that it was an experience that appealed to each of the senses. As the smell of wet corduroy can put me back in a cramped pew in Yonkers, New York, four decades earlier, there are sights, sounds, and textures that are an integral part of that immersion in mid-twentieth-century American Catholic culture that was our elementary education. It was a heady brew.

Confessions of a Saturday Past

If you planned on receiving communion on Sunday, late Saturday afternoon was reserved for confession. Under a gray autumn sky four of us were hanging around the park named for a soldier killed in a war, which war we were not sure. Mike, Tom, Ralph, and myself. Eleven years old and moving up the ranks in sixth grade at Christ the King. Ralph was an edgy kind of kid who had all the telltale marks of an early "JD": he had hair long enough to comb with a healthy dose of Vitalis, rather than the ubiquitous crew cut. He was in our class after being left back a grade, yet was still lingering at the bottom of the ranks. He had already begun littering the air with profanities, mild but with a promising future. In our teens he would have the largest individual collection of *Playboy* magazines in North Yonkers, which he kept hidden in a closet behind an old Electric Football game. Mike was what we all wanted to be—tall, good-looking, athletic, and friendly. The priests would have pressured him for a vocation except for the rarity that his parents lived apart. It was a Catholic divorce, meaning no legalities dictated by a court, no ladies on the side, but separate living quarters with Mike in a house with his mom and siblings. Dad showed up on Sundays for Mass and a family meal. Mike didn't talk about it so neither did we.

Tom was my best friend. He wished only to be as good in baseball as he was in school, and never came remotely close. With perfect diction and an expansive vocabulary, he came from white-collar money and was the only kid who said "trousers" instead of "pants." I was "Lockwood," forever called solely by my last name for reasons I can't recall. I was shorter than anyone in my class—boys and girls—and had been hit by a car in fifth grade. There was no permanent damage, but the braking tire had left an indentation on the street that made for a perfect first base in punchball games. That was the sum and substance of my identity among peers.

"You serving tomorrow?" I asked Tom. "Yeah, nine o'clock." That was the kids' Mass. Every kid in the school was required to attend. You sat with your class. It was like a half day of school thrown in on the weekends. Mike had a Sunday Mass as well, as he was tall enough that he could serve as an altar boy at the ten-thirty. High Mass was usually reserved for seventh and eighth graders only. Ralph was not an altar boy. None of the Sisters ever asked him if he was considering the priesthood. They envisioned his vocation, if not in prison, as siring future Catholics while working the line at the elevator plant downtown.

"Well, I'm receiving so we should go over," I said. "Receiving" meant going to communion on Sunday. It had to be planned ahead back then as it involved the practical necessity of confession—you wouldn't dare receive communion with a soul stained by sins, of which there were many and varied—and of maintaining a complete fast from food and water from midnight on. People who went to Mass at 12:30 p.m. on Sunday rarely received communion. A friend recalled a girl in his class just before their first Holy Communion Mass. Dressed to the nines in her white outfit, they were already in line to process over to the church when, out of simple habit, she leaned over and took a swig from the water fountain. The nun reacted as if she had just taken a chicken out from under her petticoats and throttled it. She dragged the kid, who was now blubbering all over the place, out of line and hauled her out to the pastor. He rolled his eyes, announced that he would give her a retroactive dispensation, then put her back in line. The masses were less forgiving. Her thirsty classmates eyed her as if she were wearing rouge and red lipstick.

The walk to church took us from the park to what was collectively known as "The End of the Line." That was our neighborhood. It was first called the End of the Line because it was where the trolley cars that came up from downtown had the last stop before turning around. Though I have only a dim memory of the trolley cars, it was still the last stop for the buses that replaced them. When the bus route eventually moved a few miles farther north, the End of the Line was still the End of the Line. It was about two blocks of small groceries, a pharmacy, a bakery, barbers, and a butcher shop, a pizza place, a couple of bars, and a Chinese laundry where we would shout "no tickee, no shirtee" to see if we could get the owner to chase us. (There was no sensitivity to ethnicity back then, and the sole political correctness in speech involved a reluctance to swear in front of women and small children.) There was a small apartment building where Dirty Ernie and Crazy Frankie lived—two adults of unclear resources whose nicknames described the mental state of both. There was the convent that housed the Sisters who taught us. The most important place was Baum's, a combination newspaper, paperback, toy, candy, and soda shop that was the neighborhood hangout for every kid in the parish from first grade through high school. It was run by two Jewish fellows and serviced hundreds of Irish, Polish, and Italian Catholic kids. They liked us, we liked them. They refused to carry dirty books and detective magazines, so they got along fine with the powers that be at Christ the King. Like most of my generation at the End of the Line, I bought my first pack of Luckies at Baum's and would volunteer for the early morning shift putting the Sunday *New York Times* together in exchange for free sodas until they closed for the day after the late Mass.

An alley off the End of the Line led to the playground, school, church, and rectory of Christ the King. As we talked about the last episode of *The Untouchables* and began to develop plans for Halloween night, we headed over to confession. The school yard, which doubled as the church parking lot, had about thirty cars in it, and people were coming and going from the weekly shrove. As we entered the church, we naturally dipped our fingers into the cool holy water, touching forehead, heart, and shoulders in the sign of the cross. It was darker than we usually saw it, the altar unlit, with the focus on the confessionals in back. The votive candles were a red twinkle and provided the only light from the sacristy, and their odor reached the back of the church. The dim light cast small shadows from the stations of the cross that hung between a series of stained-glass windows adorned with saints, scenes from the life of Mary, and the deaths of the martyrs. Each bore the engraved name of a donor family, each window dedicated in memory of a loved one long dead. I had been in the church a thousand times, but I always found something new in one of those windows each time I looked at them.

We knelt together, feigning an examination of conscience as we had a fairly set list of sins that varied only in number rather than occurrence. We were still a bit too young to venture into mortal sin though Ralph swore he had done it once, but wouldn't reveal the nature of the abomination. We didn't have a grasp yet on sexual sins, though we were becoming fascinated with certain noticeable developments among the taller girls in class. We assumed Ralph either stole something big from a grocery store in another neighborhood or deliberately ate a hamburger on Friday. Ralph had notions. A mortal sin was completely out of my league, and I was pretty well convinced that Tom and Mike never really told a lie twice, even if they said so in the confessional. The organ was playing that afternoon, as someone was practicing for tomorrow's High Mass. It gave a certain majesty to the moment, as we could finally hear the notes as they were supposed to sound, uncluttered by boys of varying pitch trying to keep up with nuns who had falsetto voices. We generally sounded like scalded cats, so it was good on that Saturday to just hear the music played gently, as we tried to recall exactly how many times we had disobeyed our parents.

The actual procedure was quick: a few minutes in the pew with head bowed, the wait on line, a minute in the darkened confessional alone until you heard the swish of the grate opening between you and the priest, the litany of sins, a comment or two from the priest, an Act of Contrition, and the words of absolution. We'd kneel in the pews to say our penitential prayers, then rush back out into the late afternoon sun. That evening after dinner I mentioned that I was receiving tomorrow and asked that a few Sunday doughnuts be reserved for after Mass.

Sometimes our memories recall the ordinary as crystal-clearly as the extraordinary. That was one confession among hundreds when I was a kid. But somehow my brain has latched onto it and never let it go. There is a laundry list of reasons for the near disappearance of confession since the 1960s: a decline in an understanding of sin, the renewed liturgy with emphasis on the penitential rite at Mass, confession as allegedly part of the "clerical culture" that offended women, and the very success of pre-Vatican II confession that made the sacrament seem an assembly line rather than a grace-filled encounter with divine forgiveness. All of the above or none of the above. Pick your choice or add to it depending on your perspective or prejudices.

I try to recall what I felt about confession as an eleven-year-old kid generally more focused on stickball and Bugs Bunny cartoons than sacramental matters. I remember no embarrassment because I was too young for embarrassing sins. I wouldn't have thought of the theology of the sacrament. I don't even remember—as I would later as things got more serious—any great sense of being shriven. I was just a kid. I sinned according to the definitions taught to us by nuns, parents, priests, and neighbors; I confessed, was forgiven, and "received" the next day. It was part of the ordinary rhythm of life, as natural as breathing out and breathing in. And yet the memory sticks with me like a defining moment. It's a mystery.

But as the old catechism used to tell us, a mystery is just a truth we cannot fully understand. Perhaps it was that sensual nature that Woodward described. It was touch and taste, sight and sound. It was the spoken word, mumbled prayer, candles, and organ. It was art and architecture, the smell of incense, and the sound of the grate in the confessional moving slowly open. An eleven-year-old could never break all this down into its component parts. I could barely diagram a five-word sentence. But it washed over us like waves on the beach. It was grace.

Catholicism has always been red wine and cold beer: rich in culture, but as common as the front stoop on a city street. It motivated the greatest philosophers in Western thought. But it was just as real in the taverns, playgrounds, and seedier apartments at the End of the Line. Even Dirty Ernie never missed Mass. It is a sacramental faith where grace comes through the ordinary works of creation—water, wheat, oil, and wine. It can raise us up, but it is most comfortably lived in the muck and mire of quiet desperation that is the life we are all slogging through. It is a faith where the ordinary person can become extraordinary without even realizing it. Perhaps that was the part of the all-embracing culture of our Catholic youth that we never recognized.

The Massacre of Nicky Alfostarino

Of course, scratch the surface and the problem that lots of boomers have with their childhood faith usually isn't confession or the stations of the cross during Lent. It might have been a particularly lousy experience at the hands of somebody representing the church. So let's get it out of the way. Let me tell you my worst story, even though I was just in the background.

In seventh grade, we were having the usual day. After morning catechism, the Sister had hauled up a few toady girls to hang around her desk to help her with "an assignment." The rest of the drones were given ten math problems to solve. This would go on for about two hours. Naturally, we entertained ourselves. Harry Clapigen tried to dislodge a tile from the floor with his compass. Tom finished his math problems in ten minutes, then worked up elaborate written rules for a three-man tennis game that he was certain they would be playing any day at Forest Hills. I drew endless pictures of Japanese Zeros attacking Nazi Panzers. Good fun, weak history. I don't know what the rest of the girls did to entertain themselves. I barely knew they existed. October in Catholic grammar school, circa 1960.

Nicky Alfostarino sat like he always did, a great Italian Bhudda. A smile on his face and a daydream in his heart, Nicky was one of the invisible ones. He never caused any trouble, never answered a question or asked one, never hung around Baum's after school or the park on the weekends. Nothing ever happened to him or because of him. For all we knew, he went home at the end of school, stepped into a closet, and didn't come out until the next morning's oatmeal. He just existed with a perennially lopsided smile that advertised harmless for all the world to see.

For two hours, Nicky had been engaged in his favorite mission: doing absolutely nothing. At 11:30 A.M., the Sister decided to check how we did on the math problems. For some reason, she called on Nicky first, and he shook his head from his two-hour reverie.

"Mr. Alfostarino. What's the first answer?"

Nicky just sat there. "Dunno, Sister," he finally mumbled.

"You mean you couldn't solve it, Mr. Alfostarino?"

Buddha smiled, sensing an out. "That's it, Sister. I couldn't get it."

"Then tell me what you could get, Mr. Alfostarino."

"Not much, Sister." And somebody giggled. It was a girl, and we never picked her out of the herd, but she was as much to blame for what happened next. The giggle set the nun off.

"QUIET!" she bellowed, then headed up the aisle toward Nicky's desk. "LET ME SEE WHAT YOU HAVE DONE, MR. ALFOSTARINO!!!" She grabbed his paper, peered at it through pinched "granny glasses," which would become quite hip in fewer years than we expected. She then held up Nicky's paper for each of us to see, turning dramatically toward every corner of the classroom.

On the lined paper she showed us from Nicky's desk was the usual cross with J.M.J. at the top, standing for the Holy Family—Jesus, Mary, and Joseph. On the left-hand side was a carefully scrawled "Nicholas Alfostarino." On the right-hand side was the date. Under that, on the first line, was the number 1 with a circle around it. Two hours of work, and that's what Nicky had accomplished. I'm looking down at my paper, and I hadn't circled the 1 yet. And I had the date wrong. Nervous. Very nervous.

Nicky sat there like a fat tick, waiting for whatever hell was about to befall him. Like war, grammar school was relentless boredom interrupted by a few moments of outright terror. The Sister had a nub of a red pencil in her hand, and she started poking at Nicky's head, emphasizing every phrase. "What do YOU (poke) think this class is all ABOUT (poke)? Do the good SISTERS (poke) work to save your SOUL (poke) so that you can just SIT (poke) here and do NOTHING (splash) . . . " It was the "nothing" that did it. She somehow hit a soft spot with that red pencil, and it jabbed right into Nicky's skull. It stuck for a second or two, then popped out.

The blood streamed down the side of Nicky's face right onto that white Christ the King shirt. Dorothy Abacolini screamed. She actually screamed.

"EVERYBODY STAY IN YOUR SEATS!" Sister yelled, looking like Crazy Frankie when someone stole one of his deposit bottles from his old shopping cart. Nicky just sat there, staring at the blood soaking into his shirt, no doubt wondering how he was going to explain this one when he got home. Sister grabbed him up from his chair and pushed him toward the door. "MISS O'NEIL, WATCH THE CLASS! TAKE NAMES!" And normally she would. She was one of those who would carefully jot down the identity of anyone fooling around when Sister left the room. But it wasn't necessary that day. We just sat there, stunned. As far as we knew, there was no rule against the nuns killing us, and we assumed our parents would go along with it: "We are sorry, Mrs. Lockwood. Your son was running in the playground once too often and we had to kill him." My mom would nod, and say simply, "I understand. I promise you, Sister, he'll get killed even more when his father gets home."

Nicky never came back to school. His parents yanked him out and put him in P.S. 16. Our nun never returned either. They say she just broke down and never went back to teaching. That happened every once in a while. A nun would just disappear during the school year, sent back to the motherhouse. We always thought they made us miserable. In listing their sins of the past, we don't give too much thought to how miserable we must have made some of them.

Of course, that's how these stories always end. There is barely a kid who went through Catholic grammar school in the 1950s, 1960s, or 1970s that doesn't have his or her tale of woe. Somewhere in this world, Nicky Alfostarino—now called "Nick"—sits at a bar and regales the boys with his story about the nun who stabbed him in the head with a red pencil. And then everyone else chimes in with something: hit in the mouth with an eraser, jabbed with a pointer, knocked around by a nun the size of Dick Butkus. I certainly don't have any Ingrid Bergman memories of the nuns. None of them ever taught me how to swing a baseball bat or throw a punch, they never offered sage advice for a personal problem (as if any kid would have ever approached a nun with anything personal, other than saying, "I gotta go to the can" or "I think I'm going to throw up!"). They handled things differently in those days, and the relationship of adult to child was one of more or less studied indifference going both ways, nun or no nun. Most of those nuns were from a hardscrabble childhood, and they viewed us as slightly on the spoiled side, as we were all guaranteed three squares a day, clean clothes, and an education. A lot of them had grown up with a lot less. Their job was to somehow force a connection of faith to life in our goofy heads, teach us to read and write, and introduce us to some sense of personal responsibility, human decency, and a fundamental Christian morality.

That said, the good Lord, for whatever reason, decided that the faith would be lived and passed on through human beings. Human beings are a notoriously messy creation—ignorant, nasty, short-tempered, crude, and even cruel at times. If you are not careful, sometimes they'll even stick a pencil in your head. But a lousy experience when we were kids is just a lousy experience with a representative of God's messy creation. We can't make it a judgment on faith, even if it came at the hands of someone who represented the faith to us.

Of course, if the truth be told, more times than not the nuns did a better job of it than we would like to admit.

Johnny O'Brien's mother was invisible. It was just understood: Never go to Johnny's door, never ring the bell, never call on the phone. We hung around with Johnny, even though he was now a class behind us. He had been with us in first and second grade, but he was held back along with a few others that year. We wouldn't see him much during the week, but weekends and summers it was like he was part of our class. Johnny showed up when he showed up. He might be there on his front porch when we went by, and he'd head to the park with us. Or, we could hang around the sidewalk in front of his house to wait and see if he would come out. But you never went inside. None of us ever ate peanut butter sandwiches in his kitchen or got yelled at by his parents for messing around too loudly down in the basement, as we had in every other kid's house. The reason was that Johnny's mother was "sick"—always sick, day in and day out. Looking back, I guess it might have been the bottle. There was a lot of that in those days. The men who drank hung around O'Toole's Tavern at the End of the Line convincing themselves that they didn't have a problem. The ones with a problem were those who could be seen every morning scampering out the door of O'Toole's and across the street to catch the 7:20 A.M. bus into the city for work. But the women who boozed generally did it alone in their homes, a ritual that might begin with a shot in the early morning cup of coffee.

I rang Johnny's doorbell one time. He was supposed to be at an altar boys' meeting and I decided to go get him. Johnny's mother answered the door and I can still see her. Gaunt, sunken eyes rimmed in near black, yellowed teeth that stuck out too far from pinkish gums. I knew she was younger than my mom, but she looked twenty years older. I asked for Johnny. "Not here," was all she said, then quietly closed the door. She sounded so tired. So very tired. As I headed back to the walk, I saw Johnny peeking out an upstairs window. We both looked away. When I got to school, I told the nun that Johnny wasn't coming. When she asked how I knew, her face reddened as I answered. "Don't you ever disturb that house again, young man. Do you hear me?!" "Yes, Sister."

About a year later, when we were in seventh grade, Johnny's mother died. We felt kind of bad for Johnny, but not too bad for his mother. We didn't know her. But Petey Grantz had an idea.

"You guys do your arithmetic homework?" he asked us. He might as well have asked us if we knocked over a bank on the way to school that morning.

"So, here's how to get out of trouble," he continued, without pausing for the obvious answer to such a question. "Just ask Sister if you could be excused to go over to the Requiem Mass. The sixth grade class would all be going, but if you say you were Johnny's friends, you could get out of morning classes, too." Petey was no dope, and it sounded good to us. We approached the nun right after morning prayer and made our case. She just glared at us, and our little speech was pretty quickly reduced to mumbles. When we finished, there was a moment of silence. Then: "Did any of you visit the funeral home last night to pray for her immortal soul?" she asked.

Another question that didn't need an obvious answer. We had all been home watching *Dennis the Menace* and avoiding arithmetic homework. "Did you pray for her soul and for poor Johnny last night?" We mumbled our collective, "No, Sister," and she paused an extra moment for a little drama, as she eyed us up and down. "You couldn't pray for Johnny's poor mother last night when you were too busy watching television, but you would gladly offer up class for her this morning, is that right?" "Yes, Sister," the dummies responded. "Sit down," she said, "and be glad that I don't keep you for an hour after school in prayer for the repose of her soul." We were glad.

The Sisters had their eccentricities, like any teachers who ever taught any kids in any school in any generation. The difficulty is that we identified them with far more than just geography and spelling. They were the most dramatic symbol we had of the faith. Their faults were exaggerated—as are those of any teacher—and their offenses, such as they were, overblown. Being a kid in grammar school is a catholic experience, meaning that it is fairly universal. The problem is that too many of us have equated those universals with a Catholic experience. And we never went beyond that.

How They Explained It All to You

I did not have many academic achievements at Christ the King school. I remember instead the small victories, like those rare days when I could remain in my seat when the nun said, "All those who didn't do their homework last night, stand up!" And I would swirl around in my desk and eyeball them like the slackers they were. In a class of fifty-six students, I hit the median at report-card time with stunning regularity—half the kids did better, half the kids did worse. Frankly, I thought I was doing pretty well considering that most of my time was devoted to Rocky and Bullwinkle cartoons rather than any serious academic pursuits.

There was one shining moment, however.

In second grade, I won a catechism bee. The nun had divided us into those who had received communion last spring (having reached the "Age of Reason" by then, about which we thought that if Mike Gardener—who spent most of his time studying what his finger had mined from his nostrils—was representative of the Age of Reason, we wanted no part of it) and those who would receive the coming spring. Naturally, it was anticipated that those who had already received would be further along the path of sanctity and should win hands down. But I was a pro when it came to the *Baltimore Catechism*. Something about its basic logic, its cool black-and-white answers, its no-nonsense approach that made the world perfectly reasonable, held a certain charm for me. Plus, as a totally unoriginal thinker, I was a whiz at memorization, which, more than faith, was the key to success with the *Baltimore Catechism*. I was not supposed to win things like this. The catechism bee title was reserved for two or three boys who hadn't colored in the "CK" on their ties, or for the taller girls who cleaned up the classroom for the nun at the end of the day. I was simply one of the great unwashed and was aiming above my station in being there at the end.

After a grueling morning, there were only three of us left. The first was asked, "What is the 'matter' of baptism." He answered "coffee" and was gone. (The nun had said in one class that in an emergency you could use coffee to baptize if straight water was not available. The nuns always created these kinds of sacramental emergencies, then got mad when we only remembered that stuff.) The next kid fell to that mystery that would flummox St. Thomas Aquinas, the Trinity. The nun had lobbed a soft one at him, realizing that the balance of nature could be permanently altered if Lockwood came out of this on top: "Who made Eve from the rib of Adam?" He answered: "Jesus." And he went down in flames, the nun refusing to get into a thorny theological discussion about that one. I answered "God," then had to get another one right to be crowned Emperor of the Faith. She decided to give me a trick question not in the Catechism. With a name like Lockwood, she figured I'd never know it. "Who drove the snakes from Ireland?" "St. Patrick," I said immediately, making happy untold generations of my mother's Irish ancestors, part of the Church Triumphant in heaven. I picked up a little statue of the Infant of Prague for my efforts. Except for my eighth-grade diploma and a written comment on a barely passed test in fifth grade—"Your handwriting is improving"—that statue was the only physical evidence of academic achievement that I earned in eight years at Christ the King school.

The nuns and the Catechism were a spicy brew just meant for each other. The nuns had a black-and-white answer for everything, and the Catechism put it all in print. Life's greatest mysteries were reduced to ironclad syllogisms. The *Baltimore Catechism* was a creation of genius in the Catholic Church in America. While revised on a number of occasions, the *Baltimore Catechism* remained the standard text for teaching the faith to children throughout the United States from the 1890s through the mid-1960s. Though it's worth many a chuckle now, the simple question-and-answer

format grounded untold millions of Catholic kids in a clear understanding of fundamental Catholic beliefs. Since it has been abandoned, generations have been freed from endless memorization,
but also from a foundational understanding of Catholicism.
Nothing has been developed since that has done a better job.

Yet the weaknesses of the old *Baltimore Catechism* are also pretty
clear in retrospect, particularly for Catholics growing up in the
post–World War II era. It was developed in an age of fierce apolo-
getics, when Catholics were a defensive minority drowning in a sea
of straitlaced American Protestantism. Its arguments for the faith
were built against the Reformation and the pseudo-scientific
rationalism of the nineteenth century. Finally, its self-assurance did
not offer much in the way of an understanding of how our faith
might develop as we grew. With most kids never moving on to any
true adult catechesis, growth in knowledge of the faith ended with
the last installment of the *Baltimore Catechism* in the eighth grade.
Catholics with doctorates, but with an intellectual understanding
of the faith that hadn't deepened since memorization of the difference between the particular judgment and the general judgment,
were easy pickings when the late 1960s rolled around. Game, set,
and match for miniskirts, pot, garbled Eastern philosophies, and
the Rolling Stones. So it goes.

Per omnia secula seculorum, roughly translated from the Latin,
means "for always and everywhere." If there was a phrase that
defined our early collective Catholic education, it was that. And if
there was something that undermined the faith as we grew to
adulthood, it might have been that phrase as well. With everything
presented in such infallible fashion—with life spelled out as if

every mystery could be answered with a few memorized phrases that were designed for kids to understand—there was bound to be a reaction when things got more complicated. But, of course, that catechesis was meant for an uncomplicated time in our lives. In sixth, seventh, or eighth grade, there is not much of a past and the future can hardly be envisioned. Every moment is lived in the moment when you are that age. As Stephen King wrote, if change needed permission from junior high-school students, it would cease to exist. It was easy to believe in teachings for always and everywhere when you were going to be a kid forever. But the *Baltimore Catechism* was meant to provide an understanding that was part of a process, not an end point. It wasn't often presented that way, unfortunately, and a lot of people ended up rejecting what they never really experienced.

Leavings

Rejection is probably too strong a word. Many of us just drifted away from the faith, a sojourn begun late in high school or early in college, and never thought of as a permanent break. It just knocked an obligation out of our lives when we didn't need any more obligations. If the faith was distasteful, it was a distaste brought on by a desire to get on with it, to get rid of the things from childhood that cluttered our lives and our thinking, including a faith that we connected to grammar school.

I ceased to act like I believed when I no longer practiced the faith as if I believed—not the other way around. To rebuild the faith, I had to try to understand it as an adult, not as a kid being force-fed nostrums so I wouldn't act up while standing in line. Looking at the faith through adult eyes opened up something so much greater than the habits of childhood. But ironically, it was taking another look at my childhood that made me better understand the foundation on which my adult faith rests. Along with the daily grind of memorization and regurgitation, something more was going on. As I began to try to understand the faith of my childhood, I realized that grace comes in unpredictable ways. Sometimes it is there all along. But sometimes it comes only in the reexamination.

So here is our task: to take an adult look at the faith. To do it, we have to begin at the beginning, then proceed on the pilgrimage accordingly. We start with the Apostles' Creed—the prayer we memorized to begin the rosary. The creed is an ancient expression of the faith that goes back to early Rome. It presents four fundamental tenets of the faith: belief in God, belief in Christ, belief in the Holy Spirit received through the grace of the sacraments that open a new life for us, and belief in the church that is one, holy, catholic, and apostolic. It begins with these words: "I believe in God, the Father Almighty, creator of heaven and earth."

*   *   *

It's a sunny late-spring day in eighth grade, May 1963. Graduation can't be too far away. We are hanging around by the fence at the end of the school yard—eighth-grade territory, though the girls aren't there. There is a strictly enforced, though unmarked, line down the middle of the playground that separates the boys

from the girls. The little kids are over to the side playing marbles
in the dirt. We are the lords of the playground, the eighth-grade
masters of all we survey. It's a Friday (meatless lunch, of course)
and we will have a CYO baseball game down at the park near the
Hudson River an hour after school. Some of the girls have started
to come to the games to watch us play. We will look sharp in our
baseball uniforms; they will look decidedly different—and more
interesting—in clothes other than uniforms. The white blossoms
on the apple tree in the yard next to the school are dropping slowly
on our side of the fence. We are talking that day of *that day*—nothing more, nothing less. At noon, the bells for the Angelus ring at
Christ the King church. The kids in the playground instantly
freeze, no matter what they had been doing. The dull roar ceases.
Heads bow, and we begin to say the Angelus in unison. God's in
his heaven, and all is right with the world.

* * *

V: The angel of the Lord declared unto Mary.
R: And she conceived of the Holy Spirit.
Hail Mary, full of grace, the Lord is with thee. Blessed art
thou among women, and blessed is the fruit of thy womb,
Jesus. Holy Mary, Mother of God, pray for us sinners, now
and at the hour of our death. Amen
V: Behold the handmaid of the Lord.
R: Be it done unto me according to thy word.
Hail Mary, full of grace . . .
V: And the Word was made flesh,

R: And dwelt among us.

Hail Mary, full of grace . . .

V: Pray for us, O holy Mother of God.

R: That we may be made worthy of the promises of Christ.

Let us pray. Pour forth, we beseech Thee, O Lord, Thy grace into our hearts; that we, to whom the Incarnation of Christ, Thy Son, was made known by the message of an angel, may by His Passion and Cross be brought to the glory of his resurrection. Through the same Christ, our Lord. Amen.

CHAPTER 2

A Little Help from My Friends

Who made us?

God made us.

Why did God make us?

God made us to show forth His goodness
and to share with us His everlasting
happiness in Heaven.

A t Fairfield University in the fall of 1967, things hadn't gone quite nuts yet. Most of the incoming freshman class at this small Jesuit-run university in Connecticut were middle-class Catholic kids expecting a middle-class Catholic education. No feminist poetry, no women's studies program, primarily because no one had thought of such stuff at that time, at least not at Fairfield where freshmen actually were fresh men. Even if they had thought of that stuff, there were no women on the campus, except for a few teachers of indeterminate age and the ladies who served lunch and dinner at the cafeteria. Upperclassmen said that around mid-semester when those cafeteria women set the mind to thinking of high-school girlfriends, it was time to get home for a weekend. A 1957 graduate would have recognized the school ten years later. There was mandatory check-in every night, a freshman retreat, ritual hazing, and priest-monitors living on every floor of the dorms. Back in those days, the Jesuits had priests to burn. No booze was allowed on campus, though you could smoke every-where but the chapel in the basement of one of the dormitories. Girls were permitted to visit the dorms every other Sunday between 2:00 and 4:00 P.M., during which time every door to every room had to remain open, whether you had a female guest or not. Freshmen could not have cars, and only seniors could live off cam-pus. It was the calm before the storm that was only a matter of months away. Fairfield University was an all-male world back then and quietly content, like a T-Rex not seeing the approaching asteroid in the night sky.

Our education was based on the traditional Jesuit model, and the only choice we had freshman year was whether we were arts or science majors. After that, every course was assigned, and students in arts, like me, were expected to begin a rather rigorous training in theology and philosophy. It made no difference to us. We were vet-erans of the Catholic-school system and "religion class" had been a given since first grade. We wouldn't have been surprised to discover that a college-level edition of the *Baltimore Catechism* was required reading. Instead, we got an introduction to the new theological twists and turns that were beginning to trickle down after Vatican II. The professor who taught my freshman theology class was a layman who wanted to expose the great-grandchildren of immigrants to some new theological thinking. Being the sons of a simple faith, we dubbed the course "Heresy 101." Our theology professor would eventually quit his teaching career and move on to write popular biographies. He did one on Marilyn Monroe.

I don't remember too much about the course, except that I got a "B" when I expected an "A." The professor was offended because I cut the maximum allowance of six classes, so he knocked me down a grade. I viewed those cuts as my due, particularly since it was an 8:00 A.M. class three days a week. That's how one begins to learn about life during college—as Woody Allen said, a lot of it depends on just showing up. He assigned a ton of reading as real work was expected in undergraduate theology back then. Only one of those books made an impression. It was called *Your God Is Too Small,* by J. B. Phillips, a British Anglican priest. I devoured that book, as the author kindly instructed us to expand our view of what it means when we say, "I believe in God."

The Great Unknown

God. The Creator. The Prime Mover. The Word. The Chief Architect. The Great Unknown. The Mysterious Silence. That is really where the process begins. At some point in our lives—more likely at a lot of points—we revisit that process. A just man sins seven times a day. A just man also experiences a moment of doubt at least as often. The entire question of faith, the entire question of Catholicity, rises and falls on that very simple question: Does God exist? Before we can conceive of a God too small, or a God so large that he becomes irrelevant, we have to wrestle with the fundamental concept of his existence.

It was easy to believe in God when you were a kid. It fit into the natural order of things and seemed a most reasonable answer to what you understood of the world. In fact, it would be infinitely harder for a kid not to believe in God. The possibility of senselessness is an adult concept. To a kid, the existence of God gave sense to the world and sense to his or her place in it. In some ways, that's still not a bad motivation for belief and not a few learned philosophers and theologians have reverted to such an argument after years studying the issue. The church itself argues that belief in God is natural to mankind. It can be reasoned. That's where you get into concepts like the prime mover that tickled our fancy back in sophomore year in high school. God as the summit and source of creation, tracing back all matter to its original movement. Creation is a matter of fact and, if so, creation must have a Creator, the logic tells us.

There is the philosophical argument for God's existence based on the logic of first cause. It is easy to see that nothing in the world exists without being caused by something else, including us. People exist because of their parents, their parents because of grandparents, and back through the generations. The same holds true for animals, inanimate objects, as well as the heavens itself. But at some point, there was a first cause, or a prime mover that is uncreated creation. Or, the Creator. Philosophically, we've found God, though not much of an appealing one all things considered. It's of little comfort to cry out to a first cause when the bus is going through the guardrail or our daughter's first date shows up in leather riding a Harley.

A more personal philosophical construct is God as the great designer. We meditate on the beauty that exists in the natural order—a sunset at First Encounter Beach on Cape Cod in September, the eyes we have that can take it in, the magic of a thumb that can comfort a little child or allow Shakespeare to grasp a pen to write *King Lear,* the movement of the tides or the grace of a bird in flight. These are matters unexplainable that cannot be created by any action of man or woman. They hint broadly of design, beauty, and purpose, rather than a random bumping and burping of atoms. Even the chaos and meanness of the created world tells us of this perfection mutated, not contradicted. We know what is good because we can recognize wrong. The beauty of creation sings to a Great Designer with a purpose, not simply a random harvest of disassociated remnants of a cosmic explosion. That tickles the fancy a bit better than first cause.

There is also the argument that is based on our endless longing. We seek goodness and are naturally attracted to it. Even the darkest soul feels the ache of longing and incompleteness in his or her life. Our attraction to goodness and beauty is never perfectly met and tells us that there is something more. Maybe it is Pure Beauty. A Pure Completeness exists somewhere, but not in this life. It is found beyond. It is found in God, and our lives are a pilgrimage toward it.

All of these philosophical constructs are swell but collectively make a kind of "'Bleeding Gums' Murphy" argument for God. "Bleeding Gums" was a character on *The Simpsons,* a blues man who meets up with little Lisa. He explains to her the meaning of the blues: It's not to make the blues player feel better, but for the listeners to feel worse. There is a vaguely depressing aspect to all these philosophical constructs as God simply is logically proven to exist, but is not proven particularly personal in the way we would like to get to know him. Semantically reasoned proofs of the existence of God don't light much of a fire as we get older. They seem like just so much wordplay, one-upmanship, like Immanuel Kant trying to show in set mathematical categories how the mind thinks. It might impress a sophomore after a few beers, but it gets to be too much of a construct, too much of a philosophical game to treat it seriously once we have been down the road a piece. Once we have outgrown the cheap thrills of word games, we are back to square one: God.

Screaming at the Almighty

I heard a television minister tell the story of encountering a fellow standing in the middle of the sidewalk pointing his finger skyward and shouting long and loudly at God. He was complaining about what he saw as bad treatment from eternal hands. The minister interrupted him, aghast at his invective aimed directly at the Almighty. "You can't speak to God that way!" the minister shouted. "Look buddy," the fellow responded, "at least I'm still talking to him!"

It's that kind of assurance we want, a faith so deep in the existence of God that we can shout at him when the quiet desperation can't be quiet any longer. I had that when I was a kid. So did most of us, I imagine. God fit comfortably in the back pocket of daily life, all wise, all knowing, always there. As a kid hanging around the End of the Line in Yonkers, I acknowledged intellectually that God was everywhere. But I generally felt that he must have had a place somewhere within the confines of Christ the King parish, preferably in the apartment building at the End of the Line that housed Dirty Ernie and Crazy Frankie. Because he was so close.

Even in college, where I took on an atheistic affectation, I never really ceased to consciously believe in God. We were just not very involved. And many of us stay at that point, even after dropping the atheistic affectation. Americans by a large majority profess belief in God. Even when the bell-bottoms were at their widest and the hair at its longest in our misspent youth, God was real to us when we were alone, scared, or in trouble . . . which was a good deal of the time. But he had ceased to mean much in how we lived our lives and made our decisions. We acknowledged God's existence, but lived as if he didn't exist. That's the rut we often find ourselves in now, especially late at night when the demons come and we wonder if he exists at all.

A God Too Small

In *Your God Is Too Small,* J. B. Phillips argued that a lot of us conceive God based on childhood impressions. Perhaps that's why the book appealed to me so much as a freshman in college. It was my first real venture into a more adult understanding. And that is what strikes me now as the problem most of us have with the concept of God. The God we ignore—or even reject—is the abridged God; it's the idea of God made comprehensible for children. We never grow into a deeper understanding of what it means when we speak of "God" but, rather, base our image of God on childish notions.

I took a little cruise on the Internet and found that *Your God Is Too Small* is still in print. A Touchstone Book edition was published in paperback in 1997. It's a little book, and I must have had a different concept of hefty reading assignments in 1967. Back then, before I graduated to the *National Lampoon, Mad Magazine* was my idea of an afternoon's reading. Phillips's book still holds up, though it's definitely a creature of the early 1960s. But like an old song, Phillips still has some things to say long after his day is done. He describes some common images of God that he calls destructive, that make God "too small," a "God not big enough to account for life." Here are a few examples.

God as Policeman. This is identifying God as the eternal—and internal—nag. God is perceived as the cop-on-the-beat waiting to nail us for expired parking meters. He's ready to pounce on every fault, and is undoubtedly displeased with anything that strikes us as funny.

God as Our Parents. Here Phillips slips on a Freudian banana peel, but it still holds up for some of us. This is where we picture God as some kind of wrathful parent—or tyrannical nun from the third grade—whom we have to please. As a result of this image, we develop a concept of God to be held in fear and near loathing, or our inner rebellious teen takes over and we snub our noses at his authority.

God as Grand Old Man. Thanks to Michelangelo, a lot of us have an image of God as a majestic old man with a flowing beard. The practical result of all this, as Phillips points out, is that we fail to grasp an "ideal of God operating with unimpaired energy in the present." Instead, we have God as revealed to Charlton Heston, an old man thundering commandments to a wayward people in *The Ten Commandments*. This is God as a meandering old crank who is more the almighty curmudgeon.

God as Manager. This is when we begin to philosophically create God as "lofty principle." God is complete truth; God is unconditional love; God is absolute beauty. Maybe this is where God is too big. We create an image of him so lofty that he becomes a depersonalized abstract, pretty but irrelevant. He certainly cannot be pictured as caring for an individual soul. This is also the flaw of imagery in the prime mover argument. There is a "so what?" reaction to this image of God, because he is so far removed from human existence. This is God as infinite dullness, a perfect philosophical or aesthetic image that is essentially meaningless. It's like when the nuns told us about the "beatific vision," where we would spend all eternity in heaven staring at the infinite wonderfulness of God. It was both an incomprehensible picture and an incredibly boring concept. The nuns seemed enthused; we found it a little depressing. It made hell look like where the action is.

God as a Better Us. Phillips includes under his description of "God as Manager" a more fatal flaw to our own era. This is an image of God as an infinitely expanded person. This is God as superman, taking all the common traits of man and making them very right. It is making a God of mankind, simply enlarging our small understandings of ourselves and identifying them with the deity.

God as a Really Good Us

Phillips goes on with other ways we limit our understanding of God, but you get the drift. It's actually a very similar process—except we're going down the food chain—to the animals in Walt Disney cartoons. There, we impute to animals human characteristics, reactions, and thought. Big deal—kids like it. But in essence, we often are guilty of the same thing in reference to the image we create of God. We simply take human characteristics and bounce them back up the food chain. God becomes a really good *us* that thinks a lot better and has all the answers.

Looking back over the last thirty years, we can see in our own day the "false Gods" that have been created. There is Jesus-as-hippie, supplanted in the 1970s by Jesus-as-sensitive-guy. We have God-as-drinking-buddy. This is God sitting at the bar listening to us cry in our beer and patting us on the back and saying, "There, there. Everything is okay." We have God-as-happy-uncle, a God who condemns nothing that we enjoy and buys every rationalization for anything we want to do as long as nobody ends up directly dead (though we can get around that as well if we have a really good reason). And we have God-as-tolerance, a God who wants or expects nothing and smiles benignly on everyone but cigarette smokers and those who eat a lot of red meat. The list goes on and on.

All these concepts of God, from policeman to therapist, are not God. They are concepts of small gods that often don't even measure up to what the Greeks invented for their Parthenon. These gods are man-made images that make God too small and make a god that no one would worship, that offers no answers, that is never really real. We turn around and find that God is just us, maybe in more appealing fashion, but still us. The problem is that while that might work when the sun shines, it begins to fail us in the darkness. As we mature—and life gives us a few kicks and we begin to settle in to a better understanding of what we will never know—these images of God become more and more mundane, more and more useless.

When we come back to that essential question—"Does God exist?"—we often find that our doubts come from these images. As we put in the years, we begin to reject these small gods—or ignore them. Once we have made God into these small images, we discover that we can no longer believe in him. All we are really rejecting is the small gods that never made a lot of sense anyway.

My favorite rant from the pulpit is the claim that we have created false gods of materialism, or sex, or physical beauty, or whatever has the righteous indignation going that day. Those are the sins of the young and they grow out of it. Nobody feels dumber today than the person who put in his office back in his salad days the poster proclaiming, "Whoever dies with the most toys wins."

We haven't built up immunity to human temptations, but we have matured enough to know when we are stupid and sinful—perhaps that's the best definition of maturity.

The serious problem is not material substitutions for God, at least not for us and not any longer. The serious problem is living our lives as if God does not exist, whether we acknowledge his existence or not. And that problem generally comes about because we have created a false image of God and—rightly—find that image unworthy of active worship and involvement in our lives, and eventually unworthy of belief. In the end, I really don't think our stumbling block is the question of whether or not God exists. It's whether the God we have created in our minds—or retained in images from our childhood—is worthy of our belief.

Submit and Die (and Other Happy Thoughts)

I liked that God of my childhood. He was familiar, knowable, touchable, and believable. He was a good start in my coming to know God. But he was just a start. If I failed to grow in my understanding of him—to develop an image of God bigger than my world—I would eventually outgrow him, or my image of him. And that's what happens to a lot of us.

The argument is made by the church that belief in God comes naturally to mankind. Even the most primitive culture embraces belief in some kind of deity, and there has never been a part of the human tribe with an unforced atheism. Faith comes naturally to people and people naturally to faith. We see reflections of an understanding of God in the beauty of creation, whether it is marveling at the stars, the mountains, the forests, and the seas, or the miracle of new life. We see it as well in the goodness of people, and the qualities we admire in others as reflections not only of an ordered pattern to life, but of a perfection that exists in its Creator. We even find an understanding of God within the consciousness of our being: I think, therefore I believe.

Yet, unbelief can come just as naturally, particularly as we put on the years. Sad and senseless things happen almost routinely, and, after a while, these can have a deadening effect on belief in much of anything.

It is believed that Europe began to lose its faith at 9:40 A.M. on All Saints' Day, 1755. An earthquake struck in Lisbon, Portugal. In a matter of six minutes, thirty churches filled with devout souls celebrating the ancient feast were killed, along with thousands of homes destroyed. It was claimed at the time that 15,000 died outright, another 15,000 fatally injured. It was a catastrophe that chilled the continent. The Lisbon earthquake took on special meaning in the salons of the philosophers. Among intellectuals in Western Europe, the Christian faith was under attack from the "new learning." In response to the agony of Lisbon, the ultimate questions were asked: How did such scenes of horror speak of a God that is good, a God that cares at all? Why would God strike down the devout honoring his saints? The French philosopher Voltaire, in a poem on Lisbon, responded to the God who would allow such a meaningless catastrophe the only way he saw possible: "What must we do, O Mortals? Mortals, we must suffer, submit in silence, adore, and die." It was a deadening pessimistic answer that would undermine a faith already shaken by intellectual doubt.

With the Lisbon catastrophe, doubt entered the mind of Europe, some say, and would lead to the Age of Unbelief in revolutionary France. Of course, that is historical simplification on a grand scale. But centuries later, the questions haven't changed much. Books are still being sold that ask the eternal questions of why bad things happen to good people, and why, if there is a God at all, he allows evil to thrive.

Of course, while the theologians and pop philosophers try to explain it, things eventually return to the question of faith. Belief in God and a purpose to each life do not mean a surrender of intellect. But it can mean an unwillingness to surrender to senselessness. Senselessness is simply a barometer of our own ignorance and human limitations. In the Old Testament, Job reached out to God from the dunghill: "I know that you can do all things, / and that no purpose of yours can be hindered. / I have dealt with great things that I do not understand; / things too wonderful for me, which I cannot know. / I had heard of you by word of mouth, / but now my eye has seen you. / Therefore I disown what I have said, / and repent in dust and ashes" (Job 42:1–6). Good stuff, but it still sounds perilously close to Voltaire's advice that we suffer, submit in silence, adore, and die.

There is a better scriptural verse, of course, one that offers a statement of belief and the beginnings of an answer to senselessness, and a picture of God that is no longer too small or too large for our understanding: "I am the resurrection and the life; whoever believes in me, even if he dies, will live, and everyone who lives and believes in me will never die" (John 11:25–26). Now, I am not the type who likes to shout scriptural proof texts from the mountaintop. My mother, God bless her, would argue the Vietnam War with me by referring to what the Blessed Mother had told the children at Fatima, and it drove me nuts. Yet, that central passage from Scripture is God assuring us of his existence, and that life has meaning and purpose. We find our knowledge of God through Christ, and that begins our path toward an adult understanding of God. Scripture is the story of revelation. If we express a belief that God is real, if we acknowledge at some point or many points in our lives that God exists, it leads us reasonably to the conclusion that it is likely then that he would make himself known to us. He is not some withdrawn Prime Mover, some infinite Prime Beauty. He is God, he is living, and he has revealed himself to us.

The Psychic Hotline and the "Evil Eye"

We can argue proofs for the existence of God, but at some point the term *faith* has to come up. A step in faith has to be taken, though others have called it a leap (if you remember your Kierkegaard). St. Augustine said, "Seek not to understand that you may believe, but believe that you may understand." My fifth grade nun put it more succinctly: "Act as if you have faith, and faith you will have."

There was a report that analyzed the status of faith among Italians, generally considered a Catholic people. It was depressing. According to the report, fewer than half of contemporary citizens of Rome believe in an afterlife or that Christianity could represent the true faith. The story portrayed Romans as functioning agnostics at best. Yet, at the same time, their belief in superstition was firm. The survey found that 37 percent of Romans believe in the influence of the stars over human destiny. Seventeen percent acknowledged the particular benefit of palm reading, while 27 percent believed in the effectiveness of the "evil eye." I had heard of horoscopes and palm reading, but the "evil eye" threw me. Old horror movies seemed to have something to say about it, and I remember witches would give the evil eye, resulting in illness, bad luck, or an encounter with Larry Talbot after he had been transformed into the Wolfman. But in Roman culture, the evil eye is apparently a bit more generic, involving certain hand or finger gestures to ward off troublesome influences. The basic concept is that there is some lingering malevolence out there, and by making the proper gesture you can save yourself a lot of trouble. Romans use these gestures when walking by cemeteries or encountering a particularly nasty individual.

Where faith no longer exists, a hundred foolish things rush in to fill the void. And certainly such a vacuum can exist in contemporary American culture, as well as our own lives. Aspects of New Age hocus-pocus brought nonsensical belief to the mass market. People who deem Catholicism unworthy of credence will babble on and on about healing vibrations from crystals or finding out all about their inner needs or their boyfriend's cheating through a psychic hotline.

It's odd, isn't it? Faith in God is very hard; believing that we must avoid gerbils for the next seven days due to the predictions of a stranger during a brief phone call is easy. The reason is simple, of course. Fashionable beliefs—or old-fashioned superstitions like the evil eye—do not demand a conversion. They are easy to believe and give some sense of certainty and control in an uncertain, uncontrollable world. (I won't buy that gerbil after all!) To live a belief that requires nothing more than hand gestures to ward off evil or a good credit line on a charge card to ring up my psychic friend, is easy stuff. It does not require that a life be changed or that fundamental truths be confronted. To believe in God and to make that belief fundamental to life is difficult. Flannery O'Connor wrote, "What people don't realize is how much faith costs. They think faith is a big electric blanket, when of course it is the cross. It is much harder to believe than not to believe. . . . Don't expect faith to clear things up for you. It is trust, not certainty."

The creed said at Mass actually speaks little of God the Father: "We believe in one God, the Father, the Almighty, maker of heaven and earth, of all that is seen and unseen." That's it. But without that first and essential acknowledgment of that core belief in the existence of God, the whole story of Christ and his church crumbles into the meaningless void. If Christ is not the revelation of God to us, then he is nothing; and God remains an infinite mystery whose very existence is mere speculation. But it is through Jesus that we find God, and we find Christ in his church.

"Lord I believe. Help my unbelief."

*   *   *

Fairfield University would be exclusively male until my senior year when a handful of coeds were accepted for the first time. That year we were at the first day of class with a favorite history professor who liked to tell ribald stories about historical personages. He was describing what actually happened at the famous "Defenestration of Prague" that began the Thirty Years' War in the

Holy Roman Empire. The emperor's representatives had been tossed from a window in a show of defiance. They survived only because they landed in a heap of human waste. We loved that stuff. Then the door opened and a young woman stuck her head in. Dead silence. She looked at us and we looked at her. "This can't be freshman math," she said to the professor. "Two doors down," he answered, and she backed out with a little wave. The sigh of relief broke a vacuum created by twenty seniors holding their collective breath. I swear the walls had almost bowed in.

We were dinosaurs. We might as well have had targets on our back for the approaching comet.

* * *

Let nothing trouble you
Let nothing frighten you.
Everything passes
God never changes
Patience
Obtains all
Whoever has God
Wants for nothing
God alone is enough.
St. Teresa of Ávila

CHAPTER 3

In the Beginning

On what day was the Son of God conceived and made man?

The Son of God was conceived and made man on Annunciation Day—the day on which the Angel Gabriel announced to the Blessed Virgin Mary that she was to be the mother of God.

On what day was Christ born?

Christ was born on Christmas day in a stable at Bethlehem, over nineteen hundred years ago.

Okay, explain this one to me. What exactly are you doing in this picture?"

My wife had picked up my 1965 yearbook from Manhattan Prep, my sophomore year. There I was in the class photo. I appeared in only one other picture in the yearbook, lumped with five other losers in madras sports jackets. They took those second small-group pictures of us with the kids that we hung around with for two reasons. First, it let our parents get a visual of the rough-necks that we associated with so the school couldn't be blamed if we turned out rotten. And second, since it assured we were in the yearbook at least twice, the folks would buy a copy. The stars of the class showed up everywhere, of course—with the group shots of the English Club, the newspaper staff, Advanced Math, the various sports teams. They were also caught in spontaneous shots at the dances, ball games, and devotional events, as well as comfort-ably conversing around the lockers, missing only pipes and ascots while they discussed the markets, politics, and what is wrong with young people today. The schnooks and losers showed up twice—class photo and the one with their buddies. I showed up twice.

The wife was looking at our class shot and noticed that with my right hand at my side I was forming a circle with my thumb and forefinger, like I was giving somebody the "A-Okay" sign.

I answered her question: "Look closer at the other kids." There were only about sixty-five kids in the class. And she noticed that at least twelve were making the same sign with their hands.

"What's that all about?" she asked.

"Goofin'," I responded.

"What's goofin'?" she asked.

"I have no idea—didn't then. Don't now," I said.

There. I admitted it at long last. In sophomore year, "goofin'" was all the rage among the less intellectually encumbered at Manhattan Prep. The idea was to lure a kid into an unintentional glance at your circled thumb and forefinger. "Hey, is this your pencil?" a guy would ask, and when you looked over, he'd have the pencil between his thumb and forefinger. "Goofed ya!" he'd say, then cackle uproariously, and you would be suitably shamed. The "goof" gesture was supposed to be obscene, but 99 percent of the kids, at least in sophomore year, had no idea what it meant. Like most of life at the time, we just went along with it, laughed at inappropriate moments, and never understood a thing.

Manhattan Prep was a Christian Brothers school on the campus of Manhattan College in the Bronx. It doesn't exist anymore, closing just a few years after I graduated. So I have no permanent record and every five years I don't have to figure out ways to duck a high-school reunion. But it was my halfway house in Catholic education from Christ the King at the End of the Line to the Jesuits at Fairfield University. There were a few kids from the End of the Line—Mike was there, along with a few other ne'er-do-wells from Christ the King—in my freshman year. But the student body came from all over the Archdiocese of New York, and my horizons in sophomoric behavior were accordingly expanded over the mere tomfoolery of the End of the Line. Like Fairfield University, Manhattan Prep was all male. I didn't know it at the time, but I had seen my last female in an educational setting as a student when Millicent Mogarty closed out the final class in eighth grade with a prayer. From then on, it was education in full testosterone.

Every class at Manhattan Prep began the same way. The Brother walked in and announced with world-weariness, "Stand." And we stood, dressed in our khakis, yellow or white button-down collar shirts, paisley ties, penny loafers, and sports jackets that by the end of the term issued an odor that would offend a maggot. The only change in four years was that as freshmen in 1963 we all had crew cuts; by senior year Brother John—the dean of discipline who we called "The Bear"—was on the lookout for hair reaching below the back collar.

The Brother would then begin the litany:

Brother: "Saint John Baptiste de la Salle . . . "

Response: "Pray for us."

Brother: "Live Jesus in our hearts . . ."

Response: "Forever."

Brother: "Sit down idiots."

Response: We sat down.

For the most part the brothers were good souls, and we generally liked them. They were ordinary guys with a masculine faith, perfectly comfortable coaching baseball or leading a rosary. Of course, we knew not to push it in class where physical discipline was not only ferocious but casual. One Brother who taught sophomore world history specialized in "noogies." That's where one knuckle was extended in an inverted "V" from a closed fist and applied forcefully to the top of the head around the center of the cranium. Most of us did it to other guys rather routinely, and it was considered almost playful. When Brother Joseph performed his specialty your teeth would vibrate for about a week. But we didn't much resent it. This was a time when physical assault was a part of life, like the basic elements of earth, wind, and fire. A day didn't go by when someone didn't slug you—a brother, a sibling, a best friend, or a perfect stranger. Life was a free-for-all existence in high school in the mid-1960s.

It was a tradition at Manhattan Prep that students in the upper classes take part in a "closed" retreat. This meant that they took us on buses to an old mansion out on Long Island where the Jesuits lectured us for a couple of days. The Jesuits treated us like men, even though we didn't deserve it. One priest talked about how, whenever he was starting a retreat, he prayed that he would not be plagued by doubts of his faith. This was pretty heady stuff for seniors in Catholic high school in the mid-1960s.

It was at my senior closed retreat that a Jesuit introduced us to the Shroud of Turin. The Shroud of Turin, said to be the burial cloth of Christ, first appeared in the fourteenth century. Theologians and church officials pronounced it a hoax. Further, a document was discovered at the turn of the last century stating that a bishop formally declared it a fraud after an artist confessed that he had painted it. Carbon dating tests in 1988 seemed to prove that the cloth itself was from the fourteenth century.

But every story has another side. Some question the sample taken for the carbon dating tests, while others claim that pollens from the cloth could only have come from first-century Palestine. Others bring up the remarkable photos of the shroud taken in 1898 in which the negative provided a positive image of a man—something no artist from the Middle Ages could have produced. They also claim that the image on the shroud could not have been painted onto the cloth. In any case, the church has never proclaimed it a genuine relic and simply presents it as an object of veneration, like any marvelous devotional piece of art.

The Jesuit at our senior retreat gave a slide show presentation of the shroud. He gave us the basics on the history but didn't try to convince us of its authenticity. It wasn't really part of his story. Instead, he used the representation on the shroud to discuss a crucifixion—any crucifixion—in the first century under the Romans. He pointed here and there on the shroud, explaining why the Romans did what they did. And then he tied it all together with the Passion accounts from Scripture, showing the similarity to what we know of crucifixion historically, and the story told on the shroud as well. At the end he said to keep those things in mind during the stations of the cross planned for the afternoon devotional.

And I think we did. I know I did. Because Christ now seemed different to me than the ethereal image in childlike prayers and picture books. Christ was no longer the "meek and mild," but a man who walked among us, preached, suffered, died, and rose. It was an event in history, and Christ was a reality in time. He died that we might have eternal life. And he taught so that we might know God. If I believed him to be the Son of God, then what he taught contained fundamental truth. I had been told that, of course, but something in the young Jesuit's presentation made it all come together for a bunch of wise-guy seniors convinced they not only knew all, but simply were all. Jesus had suddenly become more real in a world previously filled with the Beatles, miniskirts, and a budding little war in Southeast Asia. It was a moment when an understanding of faith began its pilgrimage from a child's eyes to those of an adult.

Of course we headed out after the last lecture the next day, and I won 75 cents on the bus back to school playing three-card monte. No deeds to do, no promises to keep. The stuff that's going to last doesn't stay with us right away when we are seventeen and fancy-free. But it can come back to us. Eventually.

Scripture 101

Catholicism has a very simple premise. It is grounded in the fundamental belief defined in the opening sentences of the Apostles' Creed: "I believe in God, the Father almighty, creator of heaven and earth. I believe in Jesus Christ, his only Son, our Lord . . ." We believe in God, and we believe that in Jesus Christ there is the revelation of God in real time. From those essential beliefs all else flows. That revelation comes from a source as real as the ground beneath us and the sky above us. The New Testament is not *King Lear* or the *Star Wars* trilogy, delightful inventions that teach us a lesson. Jesus Christ was born, he lived, taught, died, and was raised in a place we can see, and in a time in history that we can study.

Deny those fundamental beliefs, and you don't have to worry about anything. At least in this life. Accept them, and there is work to be done. As Pascal, the great seventeenth-century French philosopher, explained, that is the fundamental gamble—if there is no God, do as we please, for life ends at the grave. But if there is a God, you are gambling eternity. At the same time, if we believe that Jesus Christ was simply a swell fellow, or a prophet, or just another man who said good things, nothing is required of us. If we believe that he is the Son of man in whose life, death, and resurrection hang the tale of our salvation, and who reveals God to us and how we are meant to live through this vale of tears, we can't simply nod our heads then turn to the Cubs game. Assenting to belief in God and belief in Jesus has to demand some changes in the way we think and the way we go about the business of our lives.

It is fashionable to dismiss the Gospel accounts as mere creations of a postapostolic age with its own agenda. But the facts belie the wishful thinking. The Dead Sea Scrolls, long rumored to have secret content that would destroy the alleged myth of the Gospels, have been studied in their entirety and do nothing to subvert the Gospels. In fact, they tend to reinforce the historicity of the Gospel accounts. Despite a few decades of scholarly deconstruction, the New Testament and the accounts of the life and teachings of Christ contained therein remain the clearest presentation we have. We know more of Christ reliably through the Gospels than we know of the Greek Peloponnesian War, yet one is accepted as history, the other doubted. That's probably because the Peloponnesian War makes few demands on us if we take it seriously.

Let's look at the forest, rather than the trees—let's take one of the Gospels and follow the story from start to finish to try to get a sense of the whole. To get a sense of Christ, his life, and his teachings. We'll start this time around with the infancy narratives.

The Beloved Physician

It was St. Paul who described Luke as "the beloved physician." They knew each other well, as Luke apparently accompanied Paul on various missionary journeys and was with him during his captivity in Rome. Luke is credited with authoring the Gospel named for him, and it is generally agreed that it was written around 85 A.D., roughly fifty or sixty years after the Crucifixion. He is also named as the author of the Acts of the Apostles. Luke was a gentile of Greek origin, usually assumed to have been born in Antioch. He is said to have died peacefully at the age of eighty-four, though early traditions had him dying a martyr.

It was the "beloved physician" who gave us the most beloved Gospel account of the life of Jesus. It is in Luke's Gospel that we find Jesus in our midst. This is Jesus sharing creation with us. More than any of the other Gospel accounts, Luke names names and tells the stories in a simple narrative. It is from Luke that we receive the account of the birth of Jesus with all the description that has captured hearts: the inn with no room, the birth in a manger, the shepherds in the fields, the heavenly host. But it is also Luke who grounds it all in a time, in a place, in history: "In those days a decree went out from Caesar Augustus that the whole world should be enrolled. This was the first enrollment, when Quirinius was governor of Syria. So all went to be enrolled, each to his own town. And Joseph too went up from Galilee from the town of Nazareth to Judea, to the city of David that is called Bethlehem, because he was of the house and family of David, to be enrolled with Mary, his betrothed, who was with child" (Luke 2:1–5).

His Gospel begins with the birth of John the Baptist—the prophet whose story must end for the public ministry of Jesus to begin. Again, Luke places matters in the context of time, place, and people: "In the days of Herod, King of Judea, there was a priest named Zechariah of the priestly division of Abijah; his wife was from the daughters of Aaron, and her name was Elizabeth" (Luke 1:5). He describes Zechariah and Elizabeth in words that would make most of us a bit envious: "righteous in the eyes of God, observing all the commandments and ordinances of the Lord blamelessly" (Luke 1:6). The blameless ones of Luke's history are old and childless. Zechariah was offering incense in the temple when an angel appeared, announcing that his prayers had been heard. His wife would have a son "in the spirit and power of Elijah" who would "prepare a people fit for the Lord" (Luke 1:17).

Later, the angel appears to Mary, a cousin of Elizabeth, who is engaged to Joseph. He greets her with the words that would become the source of a prayer ever on the lips of Catholics: "Hail, favored one! The Lord is with you." He announces that she will have a Son who will "rule over the house of Jacob forever, and of his kingdom there will be no end." He tells her of Elizabeth's pregnancy and that "nothing will be impossible for God." She answers: "I am the handmaid of the Lord. May it be done to me according to your word" (Luke 1:28, 33, 37, 38). And that's the Annunciation, remembered in the Joyful Mysteries of the rosary, countless works of art, and a feast celebrated on March 25, nine months before Christmas.

Mary runs to find Elizabeth. Her cousin greets her with those familiar words: "Blessed are you among women, and blessed is the fruit of your womb" (Luke 1:42). Mary responds to the miracle of what has happened to her in a prayer that has come down through the ages, a traditional favorite lifted from the text of Luke's Gospel. It is traditionally called the Canticle of Mary, or the Magnificat, and it is said today as part of the church's Liturgy of the Hours. It is a song of pure joy:

> My soul proclaims the greatness of the Lord, my spirit rejoices in God my Savior; for he has looked with favor on his lowly servant. From this day all generations will call me blessed: the Almighty has done great things for me, and holy is his Name. He has mercy on those who fear him in every

generation. He has shown the strength of his arm, he has scattered the proud in their conceit. He has cast down the mighty from their thrones, and has lifted up the lowly. He has filled the hungry with good things, and the rich he has sent away empty. He has come to the help of his servant Israel for he has remembered his promise of mercy, the promise he made to our fathers, to Abraham and his children for ever.

The second chapter of Luke outlines the birth of Jesus. The narrative of the Nativity begins with Caesar Augustus and ends with shepherds coming down from the hills to see the child in a manger. Luke tells of the infant's circumcision, and then Mary's purification and the rite of the presentation in the temple. Purification was necessary under Mosaic law for women who had given birth, as it was also that first-born males be presented at the temple. Luke then introduces one of his great portraits: Simeon, who was "righteous and devout" (Luke 2:25). Simeon was part of a sect within Judaism that lived and prayed in solitude for the coming of the Messiah, the "consolation of Israel." Luke tells us that Simeon had been promised that "he should not see death before he had seen the Messiah of the Lord" (Luke 2:26). When Joseph and Mary arrived with the infant Jesus, Simeon took the child in his arms, and his blessing—traditionally called the Nunc Dimittis in Latin—is another prayer that Luke gave to generations: "Now, Master, you may let your servant go / in peace, according to your word, / for my eyes have seen your salvation, / which you prepared in sight of all the peoples, / a light for revelation to the Gentiles, / and glory for your people Israel" (Luke 2:29–32).

Luke tells us that the family then returned home. And then he gives us one more portrait from the childhood of Jesus. At the age of twelve, Jesus and his parents went to Jerusalem for the celebration of the Passover, as they did each year. As they went back home, they assumed he was with the general company of travelers. Discovering that he was missing, they returned to Jerusalem the next day, where they found him in the temple "sitting in the midst of the teachers, listening to them and asking them questions, and all who heard him were astounded at his understanding and his answers" (Luke 2:46–47). When they asked him why he had stayed behind, Luke tells us he answered: "Why were you looking for me? Did you not know I must be in my Father's house?" (Luke 2:49). He then returned with them to Nazareth where he "advanced [in] wisdom and age and favor before God and man" (Luke 2:52).

A Hijacked Riddle?

Bright guys will tell us that these infancy narratives are myths and legends created by the early Christian community to justify the messianic claims that they would attach to Jesus. Did Luke describe real events in history—angels and shepherds, a pious old prophet, a prodigy in the temple astounding the learned with his grasp of Scripture? Some will argue that these are well-intentioned inventions from an early Christian community attempting to prove that Jesus crucified was, in fact, the long-awaited Messiah. The stories of the infancy narratives were created, they say, to link the

Old Testament with the New in order to see Jesus as the fulfillment of the prophecies. The thesis is that the New Testament evolved out of the complex historical circumstances in the church's infancy, rather than as an actual reflection of the life and teachings of Jesus.

So the curious today have to ask if it is all a hoax or, at best, a hijacked riddle. But then again, perhaps they don't have to ask. The undeniable fact of history is that the New Testament was composed by those of the first generation that had faith in Jesus. As Luke notes, his sources were the original eyewitnesses and ministers of the faith. Written within the life span of those who knew Jesus, the general facts of his life and teachings were widely known. The books of the New Testament, composed so early in the Christian tradition, were an attempt by those first faithful to share that faith with others. Certainly, there was the attempt in Luke and all the Gospels to somehow present the mystery of Christ in all his earthly life. That does not mean, however, that the stories from Luke surrounding his birth are theological narratives, but rather they are narratives with a theological purpose. They were conveyed to us in the New Testament by men of faith attempting to explain their faith. The infancy narratives of Luke were the stories of Jesus passed on to him by the very first believers. They were retold by Luke as a vital means to explain who Jesus was and who Jesus is. The mystery of Jesus is conveyed through these infancy narratives.

Arguing historicity is a fool's game. The infancy narratives come from the earliest era in the life of the Christian community. If pure invention, then Christianity is pure invention. And that leads to the second point that is always fundamental to a Christian understanding of the New Testament in its entirety. No final proof will answer every question, confirm every doubt. At some point, a response in faith is eventually necessary, eventually demanded. The infancy narratives convey the truth of who we understand Jesus to be. At some point in the whole mystery of Jesus, a response in faith is needed to the narrative of his life and teachings. And that, by the way, is the eternal beauty of the narrative of the Annunciation—Mary's response, and acceptance, in faith.

In the Nicene Creed, Catholic belief is spelled out: "For us men and for our salvation he came down from Heaven: by the power of the Holy Spirit, he was born of the Virgin Mary, and became man."

Which leads to a fundamental question: Why? If true, what was the purpose of this amazing event? The answers to the big "why" of Jesus Christ are conveyed in Luke's narrative and throughout the New Testament. But let us begin with the general principles first.

The Great Abstraction Becomes Real

Why did Jesus come among us? For two thousand years believers in Jesus Christ have understood that the mystery of the birth of Jesus is centered on a few essential beliefs.

Jesus came for the salvation of mankind, to reconcile us with God. The one article of faith that has been and always will be unarguably true is original sin. There is a fundamental flaw in humanity caused by a primordial flaw, a primordial sin. Each generation wants to deny original sin, and inevitably has the results of it smack them square in the face: the horror of Verdun; the rise of Hitler, Stalinism, Pol Pot; or beginning the new millenium with September 11, 2001.

There is a fundamental flaw in humanity. Yet, "For God so loved the world that he gave his only Son, so that everyone who believes in him might not perish but might have eternal life" (John 3:16). Jesus, the only Son of God, was the ultimate sacrifice for the sins of mankind. Through his death humanity was reconciled with the Creator.

At the same time, he came to save us from death. The belief of the church is simple. In Christ, death is defeated, death has lost its sting. John quotes Jesus, just before he raised Lazarus from the dead: "I am the resurrection and the life; whoever believes in me, even if he dies, will live, and everyone who lives and believes in me will never die" (John 11:25–26). Which brings us back to another issue. We can't really say that we accept Jesus as a good man, a prophet, a great moral teacher, like a Buddha or a Ghandi, because he did not describe himself in that fashion. His claims were infinitely more than that, without the pun intended. Uttering that last quote from John, he is either the Savior or insane. There isn't much of a middle ground. Jesus either meant what he said, or he is meaningless. Perhaps St. Paul put it best: "If there is no resurrection of the dead, then neither has Christ been raised, and if Christ has not been raised, your faith is vain; you are still in your sins. Then those who have fallen asleep in Christ have perished. If for this life only we have hoped in Christ, we are the most pitiable people of all" (1 Corinthians 15:13–19).

Jesus became man that we might know God's love for us. Depending on when your religious education took place, the idea

of God's infinite love is either a revelation or a reminder of a sappy
poster that decorated a back wall in the classroom. To those educated in the faith prior to Vatican II, the concept of God's love for
us was usually reduced to a warning. It was described within the
context of not only the infinite, but the infinitely easy to offend:
"God loves you, and his Son suffered the torments of the cross so
you can squirm in your pew during Benediction? Is that what you
think young man?" We were constantly under the impression that
God was an elderly aunt put off by the slightest social contretemps.
The real love of God for each of us is fierce. It flaunts conventional
correctness because the closest analogy that we do have is the love
a good parent has for a child: impassioned, powerful, strong, and
dynamic. It is this love of God for us that makes us real. The entire
social teaching of the church is based on the infinite love that is
God, and that God has for each created being. That is why every
human life is sacred; that is why every human life has infinite dignity.
Of all Scripture, there is probably none so comforting for each of
us personally: "For God so loved the world that he gave his only
Son, so that everyone who believes in him might not perish but
might have eternal life" (John 3:16). There isn't anything sappy
about that.

Jesus became man so that we might know how to live. Jesus as man
provides a working guide on how to live. The key to understanding
the Gospels is to understand that they teach us how to live in this
life. Certainly, the Gospels point the way to salvation and the con-
quest of death, but the message of the Gospels also points the way to
happiness in this life. At some time in the game, we begin to realize

by ourselves what the Gospels have been teaching us all along. Life can stink if we do not view it from the perspective of eternity. It is nasty, brutish, and short. No collection of finer things can make it finer. But when we view life from the perspective of eternity, when we see serenity as its own reward, we begin to get a peek at the mystery. If you believe this is your only chance at happiness, then you are bound to despair. But if you believe that we are on one side of eternity, the perspective changes. And you find that a decent life decently lived in the spirit of the Gospels has rewards of its own on this side of eternity. The message of the Gospels is not to dismiss this life, but to understand it; to have life, and have it abundantly. It is through the teachings of Christ that we discover how to live. As Gregory of Nyssa, an early bishop, put it: "We had lost the possession of the good; it was necessary for it to be given back to us."

Jesus became man so that we might know God. We are right back where we started. The revelation of Jesus is the revelation of God, our view of the mystery of the Creator. It is the fundamental Christian belief. That Great Abstraction beyond our comprehension becomes knowable in Christ. And what is the answer to the question, Who is this God? He is "Our Father." Through Christ, God has given us the path to him and all we need to know of him. If this is not true, if this is not the meaning of the life of Christ, then there really isn't much point to it. It is just another story, a two-millennium legend with less poetry than the Aeneid, less glamour than the Iliad and the Odyssey. The nativity narratives become bedtime tales for children if there is no truth to the claims of Jesus. But if there is truth—and he is Truth—then the revelation begins with Christ surrendering to our humanity as an infant in a manger, born of a virgin, whose presence was announced to shepherds in the fields. Without understanding Christ as the revelation of God, the Gospels are just old stories that will eventually be simple curiosities. But if we believe that Jesus is who he claims to be, then the Gospels become much more than sweet stories. They become urgent: "You belong to what is below, I belong to what is above. You belong to this world, but I do not belong to this world. That is why I told you that you will die in your sins. For if you do not believe that I AM, you will die in your sins" (John 8:23–24).

And in the End . . .

According to the meticulous historical records of Manhattan Prep, "goofin'" was the invention of Nathan Gander, better known as "Golly" Gander by both teachers and students. Golly was a year ahead of us and received his nickname in freshman year. He had brought to school a copy of *Fanny Hill*—a notorious, if incomprehensible, example of nineteenth-century Victorian pornography—and was doing a public reading of it in the boys' room. Brother Vincent had apparently overheard and barged in the door. "What's that you're reading?" he demanded. Gander answered that he had found it on the floor and was trying to discover just that. "Golly, Brother, I think it might be a dirty book!" he said in mock horror. "Golly, do you think I'm stupid!" the Brother answered. And Nathan Gander was Golly Gander forevermore.

Like many kids at the time, Golly Gander was fairly certain he would end up a music star. He had learned a few chords on the guitar and together with his fellow band members—"The Baileys"—would be playing Yankee Stadium in front of tens of thousands of screaming girls. (They named themselves The Baileys, Golly explained, as a riff on the "Beetles" from *Beetle Bailey*. They were undeterred when they discovered that the other group spelled it "Beatles" and it had nothing to do with the comic strip.)

Hearing of Gander's alleged skill, Brother Mike—one of the younger brothers infected with the adventurous spirit creeping over everything by then—decided that he would put on a "guitar Mass" for the school. This was a new thing, one of the early changes in Catholic life coming out of Vatican II, still a year from conclusion in the fall of 1964. Allegedly "hip" Masses that used a few old folk music standards in place of a thousand hymns from our grammar school days were popping up here and there. It would make the Mass "relevant" to our young minds (that appeared to be the theory), and thus more entertaining. It was an odd theory, as none of us ever considered the Mass entertaining, nor thought it was supposed to be. It was the Mass, after all.

This goal of relevancy was new to us, as well as to the adult world just trying it on for size. We had spent our entire grammar school experience being grilled that whatever we said, thought, or did was essentially meaningless unless it parroted adult experience. Suddenly, there was a new school of thought that wanted to pander to us. Generally, we hated when adults attempted this. Nothing seemed more condescending—even to kids who spent their lives at the receiving end of condescension—than Brother Mike in a crew cut with white sox and loafers quoting Beach Boys lyrics while trying to make a theological point. Fortunately, enough of the Brothers felt no great need for relevancy. Brother Mike was on his own.

We filed into the oversized chapel on campus and there was Brother Mike with Golly and his fellow "Baileys." Brother Mike said we needed to practice the songs before we got started. We did a couple of "Brothers Four" numbers, including "Michael Row the Boat Ashore." The Brothers Four were a bit too clean-cut for us. If he had thrown in a little Kingston Trio—they always seemed a bit more subversive—we might have reacted more positively. But then he hit us with "Kumbaya," which, even on first hearing, gave all new meaning to the word "cloying" to our young ears.

I'm not sure which kid started it, but at some point it began from the back of the chapel during Mass: "Someone's thankful Lord, *kumbayaaaaa*." And we began to insert "dum-dee-dum, dum-dee-dum" after the drawn out note on "kumbaya."

Brother Mike freaked out, especially when Golly and the boys started plucking chords for the added dum-dee-dums and we started snickering. He stopped everything and screamed at us for insulting the beauty of the Mass and a sacred song from a different culture. The priest at the altar just stared at him, while Brother Gregory, the principal, bounded up the aisle and immediately ordered Golly and The Baileys to leave the sanctuary. Rock fame was fleeting. "This Mass," Brother Gregory announced, "will continue in sacred silence." It did.

Thus the beginning—and end—of guitar Masses at Manhattan Prep, at least during my tenure.

Golly sat next to me after his expulsion from the sanctuary. "Did you see?" he asked. "See what?" I said. "When I was playing the guitar," he explained, as he circled thumb and forefinger on the fat end of the guitar pick, "I was goofin' everybody!"

* * *

Glory be to the Father, and to the Son, and to the
   Holy Spirit.
As it was in the beginning, is now, and ever shall be,
   world without end.
Amen.

CHAPTER 4

Travels with Luke

How long did Christ live on earth?

Christ lived on earth about thirty-three years, and led a most holy life in poverty and suffering.

Why did Christ live on earth so long?

Christ lived so long on earth to show us the way to heaven by His teachings and example.

It was seventh grade at Christ the King School. Mike and I were stuck doing our full hour of adoration in front of the Blessed Sacrament. It was part of the parish's Forty Hours, a devotion to Christ in the Eucharist. The Eucharist would be "exposed" on the altar for forty hours. At least a couple of people were supposed to be there the whole time. The older kids in the grammar school were expected to do their part during the school day when the men were at work. We couldn't imagine who pulled the 3:00 A.M. shift, but you can bet somebody was there. Christ the King geared up for these kinds of things.

The nun had sent us over to the church with the usual admonitions: "You are to go there, kneel in the first row, face the Blessed Sacrament, pray, and meditate on the mystery of the Most Holy Eucharist. You are to remain silent. You are to remain until relieved. Remember: You are in the presence of Jesus, who will be watching over you. He will not tolerate your foolishness, but will be pleased with your sincere piety. Questions?"

"What if I gotta go to the can?"

"Hold it."

And that was that. We walked over to the church on a dark, chilly Yonkers morning. It seemed in those days that it was semidark during the winter until about noon. "I hate this," Mike said. "I can't pray that long." I hadn't thought about that. I was actually kind of upbeat. I hadn't done arithmetic homework the night before, of course, and I figured if Sister didn't get too carried away with catechism I'd still be in church when she did the "all-those-who-didn't-do-their-homework-stand-up" routine. You took your wins anyway you could get them as a kid back then.

We stepped out of the semidark morning into the semidark church and headed up to the front. We were replacing Ralph and Tom, who turned from their front-row pews to watch us approach. We got to the front, took a knee, made a sign of the cross, and headed into the pew. "What took you eight balls so long?" Ralph whispered, though there was no one there but the four of us. You always whispered in church then, just like you always took a knee and made a sign of the cross in front of the sanctuary. "Hey, we're on time," Mike answered, and showed him his watch. "Jeez," Ralph responded, "I coulda sworn you were an hour late. The nuns'll never scare me with eternity anymore. I just had it."

They took off and we took their place. We knelt in the pew, made another sign of the cross, and stared at the altar with the exposed Eucharist. I started with a silent Our Father, then threw in a few Hail Marys, an Apostles' Creed, and then the starting lineup for the Yankees, first by batting order, then by position. After that, I was on to thinking about why Mike the Cop didn't like Costello, and what Mr. Fields charged for rent in those crummy apartments, and why Abbot called Costello his partner when they didn't really do anything to earn a living, and the fundamental mystery: Was Costello supposed to be a grown-up or a kid? And what in God's name was with Costello's friend Stinky— a grown man dressed like a six-year-old? And then I looked over at a painting on the wall above the door that led to a place where the choir stood. It showed a cloud with a big hand coming down from it. That was all. Nobody told us what it meant because we never asked, but what did it mean? I thought about that. And then I whispered to Mike, "We almost done?" And he looked at his watch and said, "We only got here five minutes ago." And then I knew what Ralph meant. When two big eighth graders finally came to replace us—"Beat it punks" was their faith-filled salutation to fellow Christians—I was fairly certain that my shoes would be out of style when I went outside. But I felt pretty good anyway. We had remained until relieved.

Travels with Luke

The difficulty was that sometimes all the stuff we did that involved faith when we were kids was geared for adults. They didn't dumb much down for us, and we were dumb enough that it should have been dumbed down. For a kid, a lot of it unintentionally obscured what was really the main point—the mystery of Jesus. A lot of us have carried that forward to adult life. We remember kneeling at Forty Hours and rehashing old Abbot and Costello television shows, but we don't remember what it was supposed to be all about. To understand the faith as an adult, we really should begin with Jesus. It should always begin with Jesus.

Luke begins the story of the public ministry of Jesus with John the Baptist, a cousin of the Lord. We pick up the story in the third chapter of the Gospel. Once again, Luke puts it all in a historical context: "In the fifteenth year of the reign of Tiberius Caesar, when Pontius Pilate was governor of Judea . . . " Luke sets the world's stage for a prophet who would announce the coming of a Savior meant for the world. (Historians calculate by Luke's description that John's mission was between 27 and 29 A.D.) John "went throughout [the] whole region of the Jordan, proclaiming a baptism of repentance for the forgiveness of sins" (Luke 3:3). He did so rather indelicately: "You brood of vipers! Who warned you to flee from the coming wrath? Produce good fruits as evidence of your repentance" (Luke 3:7–8). He would demand action: for the man with means to give to the poor, for the tax collector to be honest, for the soldier to cease his bullying. When the people asked him whether he was the Messiah, he responded: "I am baptizing you with water, but one mightier than I is coming. I am not worthy to loosen the thongs of his sandals. He will baptize you with the holy Spirit and fire" (Luke 3:16). Luke then tells us that John's sharp tongue landed him in prison. He had publicly castigated Herod Antipas, the tetrarch of Galilee. Herod had seduced and married his stepbrother's wife, who also happened to be his niece. It was quite the public scandal and outraged the Jewish population.

Jesus, Luke reports, was baptized along with so many others who had heard John's call to conversion. And "the holy Spirit descended upon him in bodily form like a dove. And a voice came from heaven, 'You are my beloved Son, with you I am well pleased.'" Luke says that at this point Jesus was about thirty years of age. He concludes this chapter with a genealogy of Jesus: "He was the son—as was thought—of Joseph." He traces his line back through "David, the son of Jesse" and Jacob, Isaac, Abraham, Noah, Methuselah, and finally "Adam, the son of God."

After his baptism by John, Jesus retreated to the desert for forty days of fasting (note the connection to Forty Hours devotion—no matter what we thought, those devotions were not just picked out of the air, you know). Luke then tells the story of his temptation by the devil. The devil asked why, if Jesus was hungry, he could not turn stone to bread. He then offered him kingship over all the world, if he would bow down to him. From the top of the temple in Jerusalem, he dared him to throw himself down, for surely, as Scripture promised, angels would save him. Jesus responded with Scripture: "It also says, 'You shall not put the Lord, your God, to the test.' When the devil had finished every temptation, he departed from him for a time" (Luke 4:12–13).

Old-time preachers who buy space on late-night television have a field day with the story of the temptation of Jesus. They especially like that part where the devil shows him the kingdoms of the world and promises it all to him, if he simply pays homage. Take from it what you will. Personally, I see it as Luke presents it. There is a reality to the devil, and the reality is evil. Evil is real in this world and will tempt even Jesus. And Jesus conquers evil. Evil tempts the body, tempts with power, tempts with mockery and grandiosity. It can even tempt by twisting the good, as the devil can quote Scripture to suit his purposes. This was another thing the nuns used to tell us that seemed pretty stupid until we encountered the real world.

Jesus returned from the desert and began to preach, gaining a powerful reputation. Luke then tells the critical story of the return of Jesus to Nazareth, where he had grown up. He arrived at the temple, and before the assembly read from the prophecy of Isaiah on the coming of the Messiah. That was what the crowd wanted to hear. It was a time of urgency and oppression. The Scripture reading told of hope and liberation. But Luke describes what happened next: Rolling up the scroll he gave it back to the assistant and sat down. All in the synagogue had their eyes fixed on him. Then he stood up and said, "Today this Scripture passage is fulfilled in your hearing" (Luke 4:21). They wondered what this was all about, remembering him simply as the son of Joseph. Then Jesus told them that a prophet will never be accepted in his own home, reciting those times in Scripture when the people rejected the prophets. Now they will reject him. They got the point. He was announcing himself as Messiah. And they reacted with rage at the blasphemy, taking him to the cliff on the edge of town to throw him off. But Jesus "passed through the midst of them and went away" (Luke 4:30).

We can take from this a simple message that "you can't go home again." They will always egg you where they knew you when, like the successful CEO returning to the high-school reunion and finding himself no higher or lower on that unique teen social ladder than the day he graduated. And we can nod our heads and walk away from it. But there is so much more here. Christ is announcing himself. He is publicly stating to the boys from the hometown that the prophecies of the Old Testament—the prophecies that give meaning, faith, and hope to their lives—are fulfilled in him, the carpenter's son. They are scandalized, ready to throw him off a cliff for his blasphemy. The message that comes to us from this narrative is that Jesus isn't just that swell fellow, that friendly uncle. He is the Promised One of God, the Messiah. The revelation of God will be in him and to us, and our lives can never be the same.

After his encounter with the boys of Nazareth, Jesus went down to Capernaum, a town in Galilee, where he continued to teach. In the synagogue at Capernaum, he cured a man possessed, and Luke explains that the demons he expelled recognized him as the Messiah.

Jesus Calls Disciples

The fifth chapter of Luke begins with Jesus calling his disciples. The call Luke eloquently describes is the same call to discipleship that comes to each of us. And what a set of lives Luke tells us about. These are the ordinary men of their times, the popular and the not so popular. He called a tax collector, fishermen, even a traitor. They will be his closest followers in his public ministry, following him to what they thought was a bitter end. Their story begins here, and they are us in all our weaknesses. They join him because he calls them. Jesus wants humanity up close, in all our messiness.

Here we meet Simon Peter, the larger-than-life apostle who almost always manages to bring a smile in Luke's Gospel. Simon Peter was always the one to open his mouth wide, and often insert his foot. If someone was about to overdo it, that someone was usually Simon Peter. It is his sheer humanity that so captures us. When Jesus encountered Simon Peter, he was a commercial fisherman, a life as rugged and dangerous then as it is now. The day's fishing was done and Simon and his companions were cleaning their nets. Jesus had been preaching, and the crowds were beginning to close in on him. He climbed into Simon's boat and asked that he row him out a bit so that he could continue to address the crowd. Simon Peter agreed, and when Jesus was done speaking, he asked to go out further, and that the men lower their nets for a bit of fishing. Of course, in his first words reported in Luke's Gospel, Simon Peter explained to Jesus why he is wrong: "Master, we have worked hard all night and have caught nothing." But then, having immediate second thoughts, he added, "but at your command I will lower the nets" (Luke 5:5). After lowering the nets, they haul so many fish that the load nearly swamps his and his mates' boats. Then Simon fell to his knees and said, "Depart from me, Lord, for I am a sinful man" (Luke 5:8).

At that moment, Simon Peter catches us. Here is someone who speaks down the generations. A tough man who works hard and long, this is no plaster saint with a perfect past. To send political correctness flying, Simon Peter is a man's man. Perhaps that is what Jesus saw in him. Of course, Jesus ignored his outburst and, addressing Simon Peter and his mates, James and John, he says simply: "Do not be afraid. From now on you will be catching men" (Luke 5:10). They brought their boats in, left all behind, and followed him.

Jesus approached Levi, a tax collector, whose profession, much as in our own times, is despised. Jesus simply said, "Follow me," and Levi became a follower. He hosted a great banquet for Jesus and invited his friends—including his fellow tax collectors. That set the tongues to wagging again, complaining that Levi and his friends were sinners. Jesus answered, "Those who are healthy do not need a physician, but the sick do. I have not come to call the righteous to repentance but sinners" (Luke 5:31–32). There are two very appealing parts to this narrative. First, of course, is the idea of Jesus moving comfortably among the sinners of his day. It gives most of us a bit of hope. But the second telling point is that his comfort is not just in being with us. He expects to bring about a change in our hearts. That's the catch. Luke's entire Gospel is telling us that a conversion is necessary. His Gospel was written to change lives. It was written in the understanding that once Jesus is encountered in Scripture, we can't go on living the same old way. The Messiah has come, and we have got to be about the business of change.

The Sabbath was rigorously kept in the time of Jesus, so rigorously by some that it could squeeze the life out of faith. It's a constant danger, the desire of the overzealous pilgrim to live faith as if it is a ball-and-chain of rules rather than a liberating conversion of heart. St. Teresa of Ávila prayed that she be free of gloomy saints. The traditions, practices, and devotions of the faith—from the meatless Fridays of our youth to the Lenten practices of today—were never meant to be mindless actions observed for the sake of being observed. The devotions and practices of faith are meant to be acts of conversion, not mindless rubric. They are useless if done without thought to the meaning behind the devotion, such as a basketball player making the sign of the cross before a foul shot.

On the Sabbath in the time of Jesus, no work was allowed whatsoever. The spirit of the tradition was to set aside a day for rest, a day to celebrate in the glory of God. Jewish tradition had it that when the Sabbath was finally celebrated in perfect joy and harmony, the Promised One would come. But to some, the day was not a search for perfect joy, but a leaden series of obligations carried out for the sake of meeting the norms.

Luke tells how one Sabbath the disciples were hungry, and they picked a few grains from the fields to prepare a meal. This was seen as labor, and a violation of the law. When the Pharisees grumbled, Jesus related a story from Scripture, describing how David had taken food from the temple to feed his hungry men. He concluded that the Sabbath rest was made for the good of people, not to deprive people. Another time, a man with a withered hand approached him for a cure on the Sabbath. The Pharisees waited to catch Jesus at work on the Sabbath. Jesus healed the man's hand to show that the law was never meant to preclude mercy.

How to Live

Luke follows the calling of the disciples with the story of the "Sermon on the Plain." This is a shortened version of the Sermon on the Mount related in the Gospel of Matthew, presenting what we call the Beatitudes. The Beatitudes are, simply, the demands of the converted life. Though demanding, they are the keys to happiness in this life. In Luke's version, Jesus begins with the Beatitudes, then provides an outline of a life worth living:

Love your enemies and do good to those who hate you.

Do to others what you would have them do to you.

Be compassionate, as your Father is compassionate.

Do not judge, and you will not be judged.

Do not condemn, and you will not be condemned.

Pardon, and you shall be pardoned.

Give, and it shall be given to you.

For the measure you measure with will be measured back to you.

Why look at the speck in your brother's eye when you miss the plank in your own?

A good man produces goodness from the good in his heart; an evil man produces evil out of his store of evil. Each man speaks from his heart's abundance.

Any man who desires to come to me will hear my words and put them into practice. (Luke 6:27–49)

Luke moves from the Sermon on the Plain to Capernaum, where Jewish friends of a Roman centurion approached Jesus. First tax collectors, now a Roman soldier. The centurion, who had been kind to the Jews, had a favorite servant who was dying. He asked Jewish friends to approach Jesus on his behalf. Jesus went with them toward his home. He was greeted by servants who said in his name, "Lord, do not trouble yourself, for I am not worthy to have you enter under my roof . . . say the word and let my servant be healed" (Luke 7:6–7). (This is the prayer echoed at Mass just prior to receiving the Eucharist: "Lord, I am not worthy to receive you, but say the word, and I shall be healed.") Luke describes Jesus as amazed at such faith from a man who was, after all, both a pagan and the representative of an occupying force. The servant was healed. Scripture scholars describe the story as Luke's way of relating that Christianity was universal in its appeal. I read it as a simple act of faith and humility that echoes pretty well down through the centuries. Faith must be fundamental if a life is to be lived as described in the Beatitudes.

Luke tells the story of the penitent woman. One of the Pharisees invited Jesus to eat with him. A woman—who had a reputation around town—barged in and stood over him, crying. She used her hair to wipe the tears from his feet, then washed his feet with oil. His friend complained that if Jesus was any kind of prophet, he would know the past this woman brought to the table. Jesus said to him that if a man forgave a large debt and a small debt, which of the debtors would be more grateful? The one who owed more, the Pharisee replied. Then Jesus explained what the woman had just done—and the Pharisee had not done—to show her contrition and her love. An old Bible of mine has the verse as: "I tell you, that is why her many sins are forgiven—because of her great love. Little is forgiven the one whose love is small." Then, after forgiving her sins, Jesus said quietly to the woman: "Your faith has saved you; go in peace" (Luke 7:50). In the story, everyone assumes the woman was a prostitute, though Luke never wrote exactly what she had done. Of course, the importance to Luke was that she was saved through her faith and her "great love." And the importance as well is in the warning: Little is forgiven of those whose love is small.

From there, Luke writes, Jesus went with his apostles from town to town, "preaching and proclaiming the good news of the kingdom of God," healing many along the way. Again, Luke names names—he cured "Mary, called Magdalene" (in popular literature she was often confused with the rumored prostitute), Joanna, and Susanna. Luke then relates a "parable"—a story with a lesson—of Jesus. He told the crowd of a farmer planting seed. The seed lands all around, but will only grow on the good soil. Then Luke parses the meaning of the parable, with the seed being the word of God and how we react to it: For some, faith is stolen by the devil, Luke says. Simply enough, some just give in to evil. Others hear the Good News and welcome it, but after a while they lose their enthusiasm for it, as sin seems more attractive. Some hear, but are carried away with their own concerns or the pursuit of wealth and the good times, "and they do not mature." That one sure sticks. "But as for the seed that fell on rich soil, they are the ones who, when they have heard the word, embrace it with a generous and good heart, and bear fruit through perseverance"

(Luke 8:15). In its simplest terms, Jesus was telling the story of
faith and life.

Healings and the Eucharist

Luke relates one of the odder stories in Scripture—a story of possession. In Gerasa, along the shore of Galilee, a man wandered naked
and lived in the graveyard. As Jesus approached, the demons pos-
sessing the man screamed out in fear. Jesus drove the demons into a
nearby herd of pigs that then drowned themselves in a lake. Oddly
enough, the people then react by asking Jesus to get out of town. The
miracle frightened them. When the man who had been cured asked
if he could come with Jesus, he responded no, and told him to stay
in the town and to report "what God has done for you" (Luke 8:39).

One of life's curiosities is that the miracle of faith can sometimes
be a scary proposition. We want to keep things on an even keel.
Those moments in life when we see, really see, that more is going
on than what we can touch or reason, can generate just a little bit
of fear that everything we thought to be so reasonably true, may
just not be quite true after all. The benign agnosticism of the ordinary can be more appealing than the demands of the miraculous.
Maybe that's the point of the miraculous cure of the demoniac of
Gerasa. Perhaps the people of Gerasa were fearful of what having
faith would mean to their lives. They didn't want miracles. They
wanted the ordinary. The ordinary is easy. Miracles mean that we
have work to do.

The story that follows the demoniac in Luke is about the child
of Jairus. She was the dying daughter of a chief of the synagogue.

He approached Jesus and begged him to come to his home. As they walked, the crowds pressed in on him. A woman in the crowd who had suffered for years from bleeding, reached out and touched a tassel from Jesus' cloak. She was cured. Jesus kept asking who had touched him, and the woman finally came forward. She described what happened, and Jesus told her, "your faith has saved you; go in peace" (Luke 8:48). When they arrived at the house, Jairus was told that his daughter had already died. Jesus then went into the dead child's room with only the parents and his apostles Peter, James, and John. He told them not to cry, "for she is not dead, but sleeping" (Luke 8:52). He then took her hand and told her to get up, and "her breath returned and she immediately rose" (Luke 8:55). With that, Luke concludes the eighth chapter, leaving astounded parents told by Jesus not to tell anyone what had happened.

The ninth chapter begins with Jesus sending out the apostles "to proclaim the kingdom of God and to heal [the sick]" (Luke 9:2). He tells them to take nothing with them, and, if they are not well received "when you leave that town, shake the dust from your feet" (Luke 9:5) for there are many more who will need to hear.

Luke then recounts the story of the multiplication of the loaves. The early Christian community saw in this story the reflection of their celebration of the Eucharist. The crowds had followed Jesus once again, and, as evening came, they needed to be fed. The apostles wanted to send them on their way, but Jesus responded that they should feed them. They had nothing, they said—only a few loaves and two fish. "Then taking the five loaves and the two fish, and looking up to heaven, he said the blessing over them, broke them, and gave them to the disciples to set before the crowd" (Luke 9:16). This Eucharist fed the entire crowd.

Following Jesus

After feeding the people with this Eucharist, Jesus asks the apostles how the crowds described him. The apostles told him that some thought he was John the Baptist or a prophet returned from the dead. But it is Peter who responded with an extraordinary confession of faith, announcing that Jesus is "The Messiah of God." And Jesus, predicting his coming passion, tells them not to reveal this to anyone. Jesus gives the conditions for those who would follow him:

> If anyone wishes to come after me, he must deny himself and take up his cross daily and follow me. For whoever wishes to save his life will lose it, but whoever loses his life for my sake will save it. What profit is there for one to gain the whole world yet lose or forfeit himself? Whoever is ashamed of me and of my words, the Son of man will be ashamed of when he comes in his glory and in the glory of the Father and of the holy angels. (Luke 9:23–26)

What does this mean? The conditions of discipleship are: understanding that life is a pilgrimage, that one should live a life of self-denial, and never search for the material as a substitute for the spiritual. One must also have faith. Simple. So simple, it only takes a lifetime to get it.

Eight days later, Luke relates, came the Transfiguration. This was a critical moment for the apostles, particularly Peter, James, and John. It was at this point that the teaching of Jesus would become the reality of Jesus. As Luke tells it, Jesus took the three apostles with him up a mountain. While in prayer, Jesus was transformed: "His face changed in appearance and his clothing became dazzling white." The apostles "had been overcome by sleep" but then woke up to see Jesus speaking with Moses and Elijah. Peter, of course, announces that they should erect three shrines to remember the event. Luke tells us that he didn't know what he was talking about. Then a cloud enveloped them and they heard a voice saying, "This is my chosen Son; listen to him." And then Jesus was with them, alone, as before.

Scripture scholars have had a field day with this one over time. Of course, the idea is that in Jesus the Law (Moses) and the Prophets (Elijah) come together. This is the fundamental announcement to the three apostles that Jesus is the Messiah, the Son of God. A short time later, Jesus tells his apostles that soon "the Son of Man is to be handed over to men." There is a clear connection here in understanding this mystical event. For a brief moment, Jesus confirms to the apostles that he is the Chosen One, then he adds that the cross will be necessary. But they did not understand that teaching.

As in chapter 9, Luke begins the tenth chapter with Jesus sending out seventy-two disciples to evangelize the countryside, reminding them that "I am sending you like lambs among wolves" (Luke 10:3). Again, he advises them to take nothing. When they return with stories of their success, Jesus offers a prayer: "I give you praise, Father, Lord of heaven and earth, for although you have hidden these things from the wise and the learned you have revealed them to the childlike" (Luke 10:21). This sending out of the disciples is, in a sense, the precursor of the mission of the church. Evangelization and mission are at the heart of the faith: We are never meant to hide our beliefs, to refuse to share the joy and meaning of the life of Christ. It is a message meant for everyone in every age.

Luke then tells the story of the Good Samaritan, the universally loved parable that teaches us that everyone is our neighbor. Jesus was asked what one must do to gain heaven. He replies by asking what the person thinks. The scholar answers with a combination of material from the Old Testament books of Leviticus and Deuteronomy: Love God, love your neighbor. Jesus answered: "Do this and you will live" (Luke 10:28). But then the man asked, "And who is my neighbor?" Seems rather obvious, but he was referring to a common enough Jewish understanding that "neighbor" meant only those of the Jewish covenant. Jesus then set a story along a dangerous route between Jerusalem and Jericho. A man was beaten, robbed, and left to die. Two faithful Jews passed him by in turn, then along came a Samaritan. The Samaritans had intermarried with the pagans and were generally dismissed as inferiors, much like the Irish "Soupers" of the nineteenth century who converted to Protestantism during the famine in return for a bowl of soup. But the Samaritan stopped, cared for the man, took him to a place, and paid for his keeping. Jesus then asked which of the men was a neighbor to the injured man? When the man answers, Jesus says, "Go and do likewise." Our neighbor is universal.

Luke begins the eleventh chapter with a defining moment. Jesus was in prayer and when he finished, the disciples asked that he teach them how to pray. He said to them, "When you pray, say:

> Father, hallowed be your name,
> your kingdom come.
> Give us each day our daily bread
> and forgive us our sins
> for we ourselves forgive everyone in debt to us,
> and do not subject us to the final test. (Luke 11:2)

The "Our Father" is considered to be the perfect Christian prayer. It is very simple: It recognizes God and our hope to be with him for all eternity. It petitions for our basic human needs—not more than we need but what we need; it asks forgiveness of our sins as we promise to forgive those who have wronged us; and we ask, finally, not to be subject to the "final test." This is not a plea that we won't be tempted, but that we will have the faith to overcome temptation, knowing that God never gives us anything that we cannot survive. That covers an awful lot of bases. It is a prayer, and it is a simple rule for living. It is a guide to Christian happiness in this life, which is the point of so many of the teachings of Jesus.

Luke then proceeds to relate various stories of Jesus' preaching to the crowds and his parables and miracles. They are a sampling of the sayings of Jesus that give us a greater insight into his mystery, divine providence, and the way of Christian life.

> "And I tell you, ask and you will receive; seek and you will find; knock and the door will be opened." (Luke 11:9)

> "If you then, who are wicked, know how to give good gifts to your children, how much more will the Father in heaven give the holy Spirit to those who ask him?" (Luke 11:13)

> "Blessed are those who hear the word of God and observe it." (Luke 11:28)

> "Whatever you have said in the darkness will be heard in the light, and what you have whispered behind closed doors will be proclaimed on the housetops." (Luke 12:3)

> "Take care to guard against all greed, for though one may be rich, one's life does not consist of possessions." (Luke 12:15)

> "If even the smallest things are beyond your control, why are you anxious about the rest?" (Luke 12:26)

> "Notice how the flowers grow. They do not toil or spin. But I tell you, not even Solomon in all his splendor was dressed like one of them." (Luke 12:27)

> "Do not worry anymore." (Luke 12:29)

> "For where your treasure is, there also will your heart be." (Luke 12:34)

"Much will be required of the person entrusted with much, and still more will be demanded of the person entrusted with more." (Luke 12:48)

"I tell you, in just the same way there will be more joy in heaven over one sinner who repents than over ninety-nine righteous people who have no need of repentance." (Luke 15:7)

"The person who is trustworthy in very small matters is also trustworthy in great ones; and the person who is dishonest in very small matters is also dishonest in great ones." (Luke 16:10)

"No servant can serve two masters. He will either hate one and love the other, or be devoted to one and despise the other. You cannot serve God and mammon." (Luke 16:13)

"Things that cause sin will inevitably occur, but woe to the person through whom they occur. It would be better for him if a millstone were put around his neck and he be thrown into the sea than for him to cause one of these little ones to sin." (Luke 17:1–2)

"If your brother sins, rebuke him; and if he repents, forgive him. And if he wrongs you seven times in one day and returns to you seven times saying, 'I am sorry,' you should forgive him." (Luke 17:3–4)

"What is impossible for human beings is possible for God." (Luke 18:27)

Luke will then take his story to the end: the entry of Jesus into Jerusalem, his final Passover meal, his arrest, trial, crucifixion, and resurrection. That needs a bit more of a look than just a brief dipping.

At some point, all this has to mean something or mean nothing. It is not a story that will respect indifference. But that's the clumsy kind of position we often find ourselves facing. It's not that we don't believe—what we don't believe is what was presented to a child for a child's understanding. It's that we haven't quite figured out what it means to believe. We not only need to believe, but also to discover that we want to believe.

* * *

The Apostles' Creed

I believe in God, the Father almighty, creator of heaven
 and earth.

I believe in Jesus Christ, his only Son, our Lord.

He was conceived by the power of the Holy Spirit and born
 of the Virgin Mary.

He suffered under Pontius Pilate, was crucified, died, and
 was buried.

He descended to the dead. On the third day he arose again.

He ascended into heaven, and is seated at the right hand of
 the Father.

He will come again to judge the living and the dead.

I believe in the Holy Spirit, the holy catholic church, the
 communion of saints, the forgiveness of sins, the resurrection of the body, and the life everlasting. Amen.

CHAPTER 5

Here Comes the Sun

What were the ends for which the sacrifice of the Cross was offered?

The ends for which the sacrifice of the cross was offered were: to honor and glorify God; to thank Him for all graces bestowed on the whole world; to satisfy God's justice for the sins of men; to obtain all graces and blessings.

A t the End of the Line, a fellow named Mike ran a delicatessen of an old-fashioned kind that hardly exists any more. Today's delicatessen is actually a "deli section," a small part of a huge grocery store that could swallow up the entire grounds of Christ the King School. You can stand for an hour in a "deli section" and never really smell anything. It was different at Mike's. Sure, there were canned goods, soda, candy bars, laundry detergent, beer by the six-pack, paper towels, and clothespins for sale. But the heart of Mike's went straight back on the wooden floors. Mike would be there, behind the cash register, ready to take your order. There was no sandwich board, no menu with cute little names like "Sammy's Hammy Hoagie" or "What's Your Beef on Rye." You asked Mike for a sandwich and he made it for you. Nothing fancy. Under glass there were gobs of freshly cooked meats—ham, turkey, roast beef, pastrami. Then there was the potato salad and the cole slaw that his wife made from scratch. And waiting to embrace it all were the breads, still in the brown bags delivered at the crack of dawn from the bakery across the street—marble rye, long French loaves, and the hard rolls with a crust so crunchy you could cut a gum on them if you weren't careful, yet so rich and light on the inside where there were always little pockets of air in them.

Four of us would walk into Mike's, when we were of an age where paper routes put a little change in our pockets. All the smells mixed together, and our stomachs would offer a rumbled salute to Mike and his skills. Ralph would go for a pastrami sandwich on a loaf of french bread, with lettuce, tomato, and a little salad oil. Our Mike looked for a ham-and-swiss on seeded rye, slathered in mustard. I was a turkey guy—thin-sliced, mayo oozing out the sides of a hard roll, crunchy lettuce sitting on the turkey pretty as a picture. Mike would make each of the sandwiches individually. These things took time and care. Slicing the meat carefully—with a sharp-edged knife rather than any mechanical contraption—cutting the bread, pulling the lettuce by hand from a fresh head. We'd watch him, an artist at work, like Michelangelo painting the Sistine Chapel. Then it was Tom's turn: "Roast beef, please. On Wonder Bread. Just a little butter with that." And Mike would blink for a minute. "Wonder Bread?" he'd ask him every time. "Plain white bread from a factory?" And Tom would nod. He explained each time to us that he didn't like the way all the food was handled, and was just sitting out there. He trusted it more if it came from a factory. He thought that way until he was eighteen and got a summer job working in a plant that made a popular candy bar.

The Word Became Flesh

Too often, like Tom, we are content with a "white-bread" faith. That is a shame. Our faith is amazing. The astounding thing at the very center of the Christian mystery is that God became one of us. As Scripture puts it, "The Word became flesh, / and made his dwelling among us, / and we saw his glory, / the glory as of the Father's only Son, / full of grace and truth" (John 1: 14). The central Christian belief is that, in Jesus, God became man. In nun talk, it is "the mystery of the Incarnation" that Divine Love could walk among us and be one of us. The Incarnation describes the singular and extraordinary belief fundamental to a Christian understanding of Jesus. Jesus is truly man, and at one and the same time, he is truly God. To understand Jesus only as man is to profoundly—astoundingly—understate the miracle of the Incarnation and miss the entire meaning of the New Testament. But to deny that he is also fully and truly man is to miss the full glory of the Incarnation: He is one of us.

Now hold that thought, then understand what it means, as much as we can understand any mystery (if we think of "mystery" meaning "a truth we cannot understand"). "The Son of God . . .

worked with human hands; he thought with a human mind. He acted with a human will, and with a human heart he loved. Born of the Virgin Mary, he was truly made one of us, like to us in all things except sin" (Documents of Vatican II, cited in the *Catechism of the Catholic Church*, 470). We could add to the list: he got cold, he got hungry, he got thirsty. He laughed, he cried, he enjoyed the company of friends. And he could be alone.

And in the End

Two themes, among others, run endlessly through Luke's Gospel: that Jesus is the Son of man; and that the cross awaits him. Jesus has been telling us through Luke how to live as his disciple. It is a challenging agenda. But now, the message goes much deeper: the triumvirate of our faith. We believe in his passion. We believe in his resurrection from the dead. And we believe that he will come again.

We pick up the story in the nineteenth chapter of Luke. It was time for his entry into Jerusalem, a dramatic public acknowledgment that he was the Anointed One of God. There is no mistaking, no denying that message now. His supporters cry out: "Blessed is the king who comes / in the name of the Lord. / Peace in heaven / and glory in the highest" (Luke 19:38). Their cries will come down through the ages as the Sanctus, the prayer said at Mass as the eucharistic prayer—the consecration—which begins, "Holy, Holy, Holy, Lord! God of power and might. Heaven and earth are full of your glory. Hosanna in the highest! Blessed is he who comes in the name of the Lord. Hosanna in the highest!" The Pharisees, shocked by such blasphemous adulation, told Jesus that he should silence his followers. He responded: "I tell you, if they keep silent, the stones will cry out" (Luke 19: 40). All creation understands the Incarnation.

Jesus now becomes a thorn in the side of those offended by his message. He tossed out the "traders" at the temple, people who sold overpriced animals to the worshippers for sacrifice. He would preach there daily. The high priests, elders, and Pharisees approached him, demanding to know by whose authority he taught at the temple. Jesus responded with his own question, recalling the dead John the Baptist: "Was John's baptism of heavenly or human origin?" (Luke 20:4). It was a trick question, for they knew that if they said "from God," Jesus would want to know why they did not believe in him. If they answered "from men" the crowds would probably stone them, as John remained enormously popular. So they said they didn't know the answer, and Jesus replied: "In that case, neither will I tell you by what authority I do these things" (Luke 20:8).

His enemies then tried to trick him. They asked, for example, if they should pay taxes to the Romans. Jesus took a Roman coin from them, and asked whose face was on it. When they answered Caesar, he said, "Then repay to Caesar what belongs to Caesar and to God what belongs to God" (Luke 20:25). They also approached him with a riddle. According to the Law of Moses, if a husband died childless, his brother should marry her so the children will be of the husband's family. His questioners built up an elaborate case of a woman widowed over and over again with the brothers of her original husband, each of whom dies in turn leaving her childless. In the afterlife, they asked Jesus, which of the men will be her husband?

Jesus answered that those who are "deemed worthy . . . neither marry nor are given in marriage. They can no longer die, for they are like angels; and they are the children of God because they are the ones who will rise. That the dead will rise even Moses made known in the passage about the bush, when he called 'Lord' the God of Abraham, the God of Isaac, and the God of Jacob; and he is not God of the dead, but of the living, for to him all are alive" (Luke 20:35–38).

Over and over again in the four Gospels and in Paul's letters and the Acts of the Apostles, that teaching is there: God is not the God of the dead. The meaning is there for anyone to see. If we accept the teaching of Christ, we accept that there is an eternal life after this life. That is the promise in the death and resurrection of Christ. Death is no more, because God is the God of the living, and that means that how we live our lives must change as well, as Jesus has been telling us throughout Luke. Which is how we find ourselves stuck with Flannery O'Connor again: Faith doesn't make life easy. It makes it hard. It means that we can never accept the ordinary again.

Luke relates Jesus' prophecies of the persecution of believers, the destruction of Jerusalem, and the second coming of the Son of man. Jesus once again predicts that the temple and the city will be destroyed. He reminds his followers that the years ahead will be a time of persecution. He promises them that by "perseverance you will secure your lives" (Luke 21:19). But by that he does not mean that they will necessarily survive persecution. They will "secure their lives" in the understanding that God is not the God of the dead. That is the promise he gives to his disciples. It is a promise that lives today.

Central to this prophetic message is that Jesus will come again. He is not dead and gone; he is alive and risen and will come again. He uses language that is also seen in the Book of Revelation, the last book of the New Testament, to describe this second coming: "There will be signs in the sun, the moon, and the stars, and on earth nations will be in dismay, perplexed by the roaring of the sea and the waves. People will die of fright in anticipation of what is coming upon the world. . . . And then they will see the Son of Man coming in a cloud with power and great glory. But when these signs begin to happen, stand erect and raise your heads because your redemption is at hand" (Luke 21:25–28). He then promises them that "this generation will not pass away until all these things have taken place. Heaven and earth will pass away, but my words will not pass away" (Luke 21:32–33).

There are a number of things going on here. First, on a literal level, Christ is speaking of the destruction of Jerusalem, just a few decades away. He is also speaking of the early days of the Christian community. There is more: He is also telling his disciples that the world is not eternal and, in the end, he will return. But at the same time, Jesus is also telling them that they must live each day as if it is their last. Despite a spate of books and fundamentalist tracts predicting various end-time scenarios, no one knows the day or the hour. But we do know as an absolute certainty that each of us will have our own particular end-times.

The Passion

Most of us know the narrative of the Passion, even if it has been years since we darkened a church. It begins with the time of the

Traitor. "Then Satan entered into Judas, the one surnamed Iscariot, who was counted among the Twelve" (Luke 22:3).

Then, a drama in three acts. Let's follow it, beginning in Luke's twenty-second chapter.

Act I

It is Passover day. Jesus sends out Peter and John to find a large room in the city for the Passover meal. That evening, Jesus tells his apostles assembled together for the traditional Passover meal that very soon he will suffer. "Then he took the bread, said the blessing, broke it, and gave it to them saying, 'This is my body, which will be given for you; do this in memory of me.' And likewise the cup after they had eaten, saying, 'This cup is the new covenant in my blood, which will be shed for you'" (Luke 22:19–20).

It is the institution of the Great Sacrament, the Bread of Life that he has promised, that left some of his followers unwilling to believe that "hard saying" when he first revealed it. Now, at the Last Supper, the meaning becomes clear. Through this Eucharist, he will remain a living presence in his church and institute a vital intimacy with his followers from that evening forward. This central miracle of Catholic life is followed by a story of humanity so simple and telling that it is perhaps the most human moment in Scripture. Jesus declares that one will betray him, and the apostles respond with a heated dispute of who among them will occupy the greatest position when Jesus comes into his kingdom. Almost with a sigh, Jesus tells them to "let the greatest among you be as the youngest, and the leader as the servant" (Luke 22:26). He then turns quietly to Peter, reminding him that he must "strengthen his brothers" (Luke 22:32).

Peter puffs up his chest to announce that "I am prepared to go to prison and to die with you." Jesus tells him that "before the cock crows this day, you will deny three times that you know me."

After the Passover meal, Jesus goes out to the Mount of Olives to pray, as he did most evenings. The apostles come with him. Luke tells us earlier that he would normally come to the city at dawn to begin to preach, then return to the Mount of Olives in the evening for prayer. He leaves the apostles to pray alone: "Father, if you are willing, take this cup away from me; still, not my will but yours be done" (Luke 22:42). When he returns, he finds them sleeping. He wakes them, and, as he is speaking, a crowd approaches, led by Judas. It is the traitor's moment. One of the apostles lashes out with a sword, cutting off the ear of a servant. Jesus says, "Enough!" and heals the servant's ear. He then turns to the temple leadership and says: "Day after day I was with you in the temple area, and you did not seize me; but this is your hour, the time for the power of darkness" (Luke 22:53).

He is arrested and taken for trial to the house of the high priest. Peter trails behind and joins a group sitting by a fire in the courtyard. A servant girl accuses him of being a follower of Jesus. Three times, Peter denies knowing the man. Once. Twice. Three times. And the cock crows.

Peter will return to strengthen his brothers. Judas will not. In anguish over his sin, he kills himself. Peter and the apostles seek forgiveness in the love of the Lord. Failure and sin are never gone from our lives; but in and through him, the ultimate failure of a hopelessness that denies the love of God and the power of the Holy Spirit need never be.

Act II

Beaten by his guards, Jesus is tried the next morning in front of the temple leadership. They demand to know if he is the Messiah, the Son of God. "You say so," Jesus answers (Luke 23:3). It is blasphemy. He is taken to Pilate, as the Romans are the only ones with the authority to execute a man. Pilate shrugs the matter off as one of the endless religious disputes of the area that is no business of the Empire, unless they disturb the peace of the Empire. He sends him on to Herod. Herod, Luke reports, "had been wanting to see him for a long time, for he had heard about him and had been hoping to see him perform some sign" (Luke 23:8). He questions Jesus, but receives no answer. Angry and insulted, he sends him back to Pilate for the Romans to deal with. And Luke tells us a strange result of all this: "Herod and Pilate," Luke writes, "became friends that very day, even though they had been enemies formerly" (Luke 23:12).

Jesus stands once again before Pilate. The Roman says to the crowds that neither he nor Herod found any reason to put Jesus to death. But the crowds shout back that Jesus should be crucified. They want Barabbas freed, a man who had led an uprising in the city and killed another. In the act of ultimate cynicism, Pilate agrees. Barabbas is let go, and Jesus is led off for crucifixion.

There are two other criminals led away with Jesus. They come finally to "the place called the Skull" (Luke 23:33). There, Jesus is crucified between two thieves. He offers a final prayer: "Father, forgive them; they know not what they do" (Luke 23:34). The crowds jeer and even one of the thieves hanging from a cross joins the chorus. The other thief says, "Jesus, remember me when you come into your kingdom." And Jesus replies, "Amen, I say to you, today you will be with me in Paradise" (Luke 23:42–43).

At midday, Jesus cries out: "Father, into your hands I commend my spirit" (Luke 23:46). And he dies.

Act III

His body was taken down by Joseph, an upright and holy member of the Sanhedrin, or council, who "was awaiting the kingdom of God" (Luke 23:51). Women from Galilee saw the body wrapped in a shroud and placed in the tomb. They returned to their homes to prepare the spices and perfume for his body. But only after they had observed "the Sabbath day of rest, in accordance with the law" (Luke 23:56).

It was a Sunday, the first day of the week after the Sabbath. The women could now return to the tomb to finish the preparation of his body. But the stone in front of the tomb had been rolled back. There was nothing inside. The body was gone. Two men in "dazzling garments" stood near them. "Why do you seek the living one among the dead?" they asked. "He is not here, but he has been raised" (Luke 24:5–6). The women ran back to tell the eleven remaining apostles what they had seen and heard. The apostles refused to believe them. But Peter finally ran to the tomb. He saw that it was empty. "He went home amazed at what had happened" (Luke 24:12).

That same day, two of his followers were walking from Jerusalem to Emmaus, a little village about seven miles from the city. They were talking about all that had happened. A man joined them on the way and he asked them what they were discussing.

Surprised that he had not heard about the events that had the whole city buzzing, they told him of Jesus, "a prophet mighty in deed and word before God and all the people" (Luke 24:19) who had been arrested, put on trial, and crucified. They told the stranger that women from their group "were at the tomb early in the morning and did not find his body; they came back and reported that they had indeed seen a vision of angels who announced that he was alive" (Luke 24:22–23).

The stranger responded that he was surprised at their surprise. He then began to discuss Scripture with them, and the passages referring to the coming of the Messiah. As they drew near the town, they asked him to join them where they were staying as the day was nearly done. He agreed. At dinner, the stranger "took bread, said the blessing, broke it, and gave it to them" (Luke 24:30). In this eucharistic miracle, they recognized him as the risen Jesus, and he was gone. They returned immediately to Jerusalem to report the news to the apostles, telling how they had recognized him when he broke the bread.

As they were talking about the wonderful events of the day, Jesus came to them, and his first words were, "Peace be with you" (Luke 24:36). He was not an apparition, but a real human presence. He ate with them and "opened their minds to understand the scriptures" (Luke 24:45). Then he gave them his final commandment: "Thus it is written that the Messiah would suffer and rise from the dead on the third day and that repentance, for the forgiveness of sins, would be preached in his name to all the nations, beginning from Jerusalem" (Luke 24:46–47). He then took them out to a field where he blessed them, and "was taken up to heaven" (Luke 24:51).

The apostles returned to Jerusalem "with great joy, and they were continually in the temple praising God" (Luke 24:52–53).

The Mystery of Jesus

The New Testament canon is comprised of three other Gospel accounts, as well as the Acts of the Apostles (the story of that new Christian community "speaking the praises of God"), the Letters of St. Paul, the Epistle of James, the two Epistles of Peter, the three Epistles of John, the Epistle of Jude, and the Book of Revelation. None of them give us a life of Jesus, a narrative that answers every question we could have about him. We know virtually nothing of him from after his infancy to his thirtieth year. In the years of his public ministry we have stories, sayings, parables, and even a few personalities. But nothing that we might expect from an annotated biography.

Yet there are certain absolute essentials. All accounts of Jesus are driven by his death and resurrection. All accounts of Jesus make clear the absolute, fundamental belief of the earliest Christians— the very witnesses to the events of his life—that he lived, that he taught and worked miracles, that he was crucified, and that he rose from the dead. Again, Paul sums it up: "If Christ has not been raised, then empty [too] is our preaching; empty, too, your faith" (1 Corinthians 15:14).

Of course, we have all kinds of rational means to sidestep the matter. Yes, we might say, his early followers believed that he rose from the dead. But they believed because they wanted so much to believe. The Gospel accounts, we can say, are colored by the desire of the community to believe so passionately that he was, indeed, the Promised One, the Messiah, the Son of God.

Saying this, of course, means that we can walk away from it. And that's an option that is always there. It allows us the freedom to pick and choose among the teachings of Christ. We like the Beatitudes: "Blessed are you who are poor, for the kingdom of God is yours." But then we can ignore that mystifying story of the Transfiguration and skip entirely all that stuff about the Son of man coming back on a cloud. Most of all, we don't have to believe in the reality of the Resurrection. It is much easier to believe that the Resurrection accounts were the heartfelt inventions of his earliest followers.

It is easier because if we do all that, we don't have to accept certain things about the mystery of Christ. We don't have to accept that in Christ, we have a revelation of God. We don't have to accept that God stepped into history—at a real time, in a real place—and changed history. We don't have to accept that through Christ the redemption of all mankind was accomplished. We don't have to accept that his teachings provide an understanding of how we are meant to live as created beings. We don't have to accept that how we live our lives here will make a difference in our eternal lives. We don't have to accept that his life and teachings are preserved, carried on, and made real today. And we don't have to accept that he lives: "Christ has died. Christ is risen. Christ will come again."

Like the people of Gerasa, there is comfort in a benign agnosticism. But there's not much challenge to it.

Our benign agnosticism creates a nice "white-bread" world for us, like Tom's bland "white-bread" sandwich in the midst of the splendor of Mike's deli. It's a shadow life, a processed creation that doesn't take us any higher. It doesn't demand that we strive to be saints. It makes what little faith we have quaint ritual. Hell, it makes even Christmas boring and Easter nonexistent.

The Gospel accounts are relatively short. Combined, I don't think they equal in size the length of J. B. Phillips' little book, *Your God Is Too Small*, yet they answer that fundamental question. In the Gospel accounts, God is revealed. The message of Scripture is that God is not silent. He has not left us alone in the dark, groping to figure out both who we are and who he is. God is no longer too small—a man-made invention to quiet kids standing in line, or grown-ups who still think of him as a Big Cop. And he is no longer too big—some abstraction of Beauty, Truth, or Love that we can't get a hold of, that our brains can't capture.

We can begin to see God, acting, caring, loving humanity through Christ. We can begin to understand that he is the God of the living, not of the dead. The New Testament is a small series of books. But together they create a living message than can be studied over and over, and deeper and deeper. And, even at that, they are really just a start. "There are also many other things that Jesus did, but if these were to be described individually, I do not think the whole world would contain the books that would be written" (John 21:25).

*   *   *

From the Gospel According to Matthew:
All power in heaven and on earth has been given to me. Go, therefore, and make disciples of all nations, baptizing them in

the name of the Father, and of the Son, and of the holy
Spirit, teaching them to observe all that I have commanded
you. And behold, I am with you always, until the end of the
age. (Matthew 28:18)

CHAPTER 6

Flowers Never Bend
with the Rainfall

**Which are the means instituted by our Lord
to enable men at all times to share in the
fruits of the Redemption?**

The means instituted by our Lord to enable men at
all times to share in the fruits of His Redemption
are the Church and the Sacraments.

Being raised and schooled in and around New York City, I fell
hard for Indiana, particularly the small towns that dot its
flat cornfields. They read like a litany: Corunna, Yoder, Ossian,
Lagro, Bippus, Laud, Roan, Markle, Grable, Shipshewanna,
Dunfee, Luther.

It will happen every so often in Indiana, especially when you are
not a native and get off the interstate: After making a few rights, a
few lefts, then taking a long stretch of road leading to a couple of

unfamiliar choices, you'll cross over a railroad track and find yourself on Main Street of a little town you never meant to get to in the first place. You will take a left off Main Street onto Broadway—which isn't very broad—go down about four hundred yards and the road will stop dead at the edge of a cornfield. You'll do some tight maneuvering to turn around, then pull up by a house where a man of indeterminate age dressed in overalls and a white T-shirt will be trying to get a beat-up lawn mower started. The conversation will go something like this:

"Excuse me, Sir?"

No response.

"Sir?" a little louder.

He will look up, squint at you, and scratch something somewhere on his body. Just hope for the best.

"What you need, young fella?" You will be "young fella" as long as you don't qualify for Social Security benefits.

"Got myself a little turned around, sir. Can you tell me how to get back to the interstate?"

Pause, a little more scratching. Baseball cap removed, forehead scratched. "The interstate, huh. Well, let's see . . ." Pause. Looks up the street. Looks back to the cornfield. Delivers punch line: "Can't get there from here."

Before you can stop him, he'll tell you that he'll step inside, call his nephew that works down at the filling station in Fremont because his nephew knows the roads real well, what with his gadabout ways on a Friday night. You will try to tell him not to bother, but it's too late. He will come back out in ten minutes, tell you that it takes less time to show you than direct you, and he will go around back, get the truck going, and you will follow him for about ten miles, and he'll have you back at the interstate. Make sure to give him a big wave and a thank-you, but don't dare offer him money for his trouble.

That's Indiana: infuriatingly helpful.

Not too far from our house outside Fort Wayne, there is one little town in particular that caught my eye. Take a cutoff from the county line and drive a few miles down a road lined with farmers' fields and it will lead right through the town itself, coming out the other end in about three blinks. There are two back streets running parallel to the country road, connected by three or four blocks of tiny streets that made up just about the entire town. The only retail business in town is a tavern—the Country Inn. But it's no "Inn." It's a bar if I ever saw one. The town used to have a small center, but the few shops have been converted to low-rent apartments. An old fellow's living room has a huge plateglass front that might have displayed fancy hats and ladies' wear a long time ago. Now it just displays a sofa and whatever the gentleman is watching on television every night.

An elementary school still in use sits at one end of the town. At the other end, over the railroad tracks, is a softball field. On a Friday night during the summer every moth, mosquito, and gnat within a hundred miles circles the lights around the field while townsfolk and "people from the country" as they call them watch a game played by the locals against the locals. The Country Inn will do a good business when this one is over. Out in center field, on the home-run side of the fence, is a big statue of a crucifix, with two angels kneeling on each side.

Across the street from the softball field is a Catholic church. Two masses each weekend—one on Saturday evening, one on Sunday morning early. Confessions are by appointment, and the number to call is listed. There is a big old rectory right beside the red brick church, but it is hard to tell if there is a resident pastor living there, though everything looks to be kept up pretty well. The congregation can't be too big. This isn't a city parish and, once outside of Fort Wayne, the Catholic population drops precipitously. But driving by on Sunday morning, they are out there in the parking lot: the men in white shirts; the women in pretty flowered dresses that are whisked gently by the breeze; the kids running around, looking eager to get on with the day.

It's two thousand years since the events described by Luke's Gospel. And this is the church that grew from that Gospel as it is lived in a little town in Indiana where they play ball on sultry Friday nights in the middle of summer.

The Pentecost

One last brief visit with Luke, this time in the Acts of the Apostles, the early history of the Christian community written around 75 A.D. The disciples of Christ were together in the "upstairs room," a short time after the ascension of Jesus. It was the day of Pentecost, a Hebrew feast on the fiftieth day after the Passover. Pentecost was a harvest festival, and many pilgrims had come to Jerusalem. Suddenly, in that upstairs room, "there came from the sky a noise like a strong driving wind, and it filled the entire house in which they were. Then there appeared to them tongues as of fire, which parted and came to rest on each one of them. And they were all filled with the holy Spirit" (Acts 2:2–4). Peter spoke first to the crowds that assembled because of the commotion. His message was simple: "Therefore let the whole house of Israel know for certain that God has made him both Lord and Messiah, this Jesus whom you crucified" (Acts 2:36).

The nuns used to get cute about the feast of Pentecost, fifty days after Easter. In the lower grades at Christ the King school they would have us sing "Happy Birthday" to the church: "Happy birthday dear chuuuuurch, Happy birthday to you!" Even though we were just little kids it made us feel like saps.

Pentecost is seen in the Catholic tradition as the beginning of the church-preaching Jesus. The Holy Spirit promised by Christ was sent by the Father on Pentecost to the disciples in the upper room. As Peter began to speak to the crowd, the church was openly displayed for the first time. With the life of the Holy Spirit, the church began its mission to "make disciples of all nations."

The first question we face is simple, yet it is the only one that really matters in life: Is there a God? A yes, maybe, or no answer will be critical in deciding who we are and how we view ourselves and our universe. If the answer is no, we have opted for a lifelong balancing act to maintain sanity. We need to create a reason for being, a reason for morality, a reason for illness, a reason for death. Frankly, I think its just too much work. Constantly on the precipice of despair in the face of a lifetime of humanity, atheism is a vanity of the young, even though they rarely embrace it themselves. Which why not too many people honestly embrace it at all.

To answer "maybe" is part of the human condition. Even the most devout can slip into the maybe when confronted with life, which can be nasty, brutish, and short. Simply coexisting with humans can create a great maybe in our minds. Yet, it really is no way to live. At least answering no to the existence of God takes us on a journey of sorts as we try to build some kind of humanistic philosophy to replace a spiritual theology of man. To opt for maybe is to not even try. If God doesn't exist, it is not a problem because I haven't thought of it much. If God does exist, I'll be a decent enough Joe or Jane to plug along. It is living as if God doesn't exist, while never taking any kind of plunge. I am fairly well convinced that the people who live their lives under a pallid *maybe* eventually end up old, alone, and with too many cats. It is the consummate unexamined life.

The Adventure

If we answer yes and accept that God exists, the adventure begins, as long as we take that belief seriously. We can still end up being discovered in the middle of a living room full of cats when the neighbor calls because she hasn't seen anyone in two or three months. If we acknowledge that God exists, but then live our lives as if he doesn't, we have effectively answered maybe, because we have committed one of the greatest sins of all: acceptance of the ordinary, in life and in ourselves. But accepting that God exists and setting out to discover what that means, gives purpose to our lives and gives us the opportunity to be great. Because that is what the faith lived is all about: The chance to be great in all that really matters to ourselves, our family, our neighbors, and our world.

When we answer as adults—as big boys and girls—that God exists, then we need to take an inventory of our childhood and our adult rationalizations of what God is. We begin by dismissing the childish images of God created for us when we were children to coerce us to obey the ultimate commandments: that we do not talk in line and that we do not slug our friends and siblings. Out goes God as Cop, God as Unengaged Old Man, God as Nagging Aunt. Out go the esoteric and essentially bloodless abstractions of a God as First Principle or God as Beauty. Out goes God as Drinking Buddy, God as a Little Smarter Me, God as Hippie Buddy. In comes a God that is real, a God who lives, a God who intensely and infinitely knows us, a God who expects that we strive to be great.

Once we accept that God exists, we need to take a few small steps in our thinking. It is a matter of joining reason and faith. If we begin to see God as real, and begin to understand that he is a Creator that would not create life in a senseless cosmic joke, then it all begins to come together. To begin with, all logic, experience, and history of the human race tells us first of an essential flaw in our makeup. How else to explain ceaseless wars, slaughter, death, mayhem, and the idiot kid at the grocery store that bags the can of tomato juice on top of the jumbo carton of eggs? To understand that humanity is flawed requires the simple act of getting up in the morning to take on the day. Staring in the mirror, working up the strength to shave, one essential truth strikes me: Something went awry somewhere. That creation had an essential flaw by its own choosing is perhaps the easiest Christian doctrine to believe because the evidence of it is all around us, including in the mirror.

Scripture tells the story of Adam and Eve as the means to define and locate this original sin in time. Original sin was a choice to disdain our fundamental humanity as created creatures in the ultimate act of hubris and self-loathing: to reject God in the hope of becoming like God. Let's not get caught up in apple eating, the origins of mankind, or silliness concerning evolution. The basics of original sin are cut-and-dried. At some point, humanity made a conscious decision to prefer itself to God and to keep its own company. At a primordial point humanity denied that it was created by God and that it finds its meaning in and through God. Humanity chose to find divinity in itself, rather than through its Creator. Adam's sin was the desire to be like God without God, an impossibility that we are taught just by reading the newspaper in the morning. Scripture's lesson is that the results of this original sin are plain: the serenity of God's creation was broken. Humanity, choosing to live by its own rules, destroyed an essential harmony that existed in creation. Humanity forgot God, and the world—and life—became nasty, brutish, and short. We are told that through this first sin, with creation in schism with its Creator, the world was overcome by evil. So fundamental is this schism that, finally, death makes its entrance on the human stage.

And here we are today.

But the story only begins with that fundamental choice. Any rational understanding of God as Creator also makes it senseless for God to abandon his creation. If God cares at all for his creation, it makes perfect sense that he would want to reveal himself to that creation. This is what has been called "salvation history"—the story of the revelation of God to the people of the covenant, the Jewish nation. To the people of the covenant a Messiah is promised—a New Adam—who will make amends for that primordial sin through the ultimate sacrifice. The heart of Christian belief is that the Messiah, the Son of God, is found in Christ. In Christ, the divinity is discovered; the way, the truth, and the life is revealed. In Christ and through the cross, the redemption of mankind is accomplished.

Revealing Revelation

Okay. In a very few paragraphs I have attempted to summarize two thousand years of Christian theology, philosophy, and reason in explaining the existence of God, our creation and fall, salvation history, divine revelation, and our redemption through the death of Christ on the cross. But there really isn't much reason to go at it again and again. First, because all the words in the world can't do it justice. Second, and oddly enough, I don't really think this is where the problems generally come in. Most of us accept the essential truths of Christendom, even if we can't devise long theological explanations for the core of belief: that we were created by God, that an original sin explains our fallen humanity, that through Jesus God reveals himself ultimately to humanity, and that through the death of Jesus humanity is redeemed. The difficulty comes in what this all means in our lives and in how we are meant to live.

Which raises another question: Does the story end there? Christ ascends into heaven at the end of the Gospels, the Holy Spirit descends on the disciples, they travel around spreading the Gospel message, Paul joins up and we are left with the letters he wrote to the fledgling Christian communities, then all the original witnesses eventually die. And that's the end of that.

In one sense, yes, the story does end there. An additional two thousand years of Christian life adds nothing to that divine revelation through Jesus. Our understanding of that revelation certainly develops. But the revelation itself does not change in time nor have new revelations added to it. But in a vital sense, the story does not end there. Again, let's look at logic and reason. It became very cute a while back when Donovan was lilting out "E-lec-trical Banana" to say that "Christ never intended to begin a church." This was mostly a canned statement meant to shock older Catholics. Perhaps it did. Perhaps it was senseless, too. Clearly, this revelation of God in Christ was not a snapshot meant for one living generation in a small corner of the world two thousand years ago. Again, we would have to believe in God as Cosmic Prankster. Clearly, throughout Luke, we see Christ teaching and prodding his apostles along. The business was meant to continue. Because what came with Christ was not merely a set of wonderful sayings and parables. What came with Christ was grace for mankind. What came at Pentecost was God in the Holy Spirit to invigorate and maintain a faith to last until the end of time. If we see Christ as confined to a few sayings and stories, we are seeing nothing of the Good News. We believe that Christ is risen, is living. We believe that in and through Christ a living faith exists for all generations.

Two thousand years later there's that little church in a small Indiana town carrying on the faith in Jesus. If we take away that church, we take away the living part of that Good News, which is the message of Jesus.

The Brief Sad Story of Mary Margaret

We knew the type in our postcollege days. They were kids who had fried one too many brain synapses when everything went sour with the drugs after Woodstock. At some point the drugs became the point. It all slipped from a flower-child-antiwar-peace-and-love-movement to a stoned pony express. Some never made it out. And a few found a short-term substitute addiction. The "Jesus Freaks" appeared. Kids who had gone way too far down the line grabbed onto sweet Jesus for dear life. Just as they had immersed themselves in drugs, they immersed themselves in a free-floating idea of Jesus. They eventually burned out on the Jesus thing as well.

Mary Margaret O'Connor had been one of the girls all the guys liked when we first started noticing girls during eighth grade at Christ the King. First of all, Mary Margaret was, well, healthy, in a way most of the girls had not yet developed. But just as important back then, she was a really good athlete. If we were one guy short in a pick-up game of softball, nobody had a problem if Mary Margaret volunteered. The girl could hit. And finally, she was just a nice kid. She wasn't the brightest bulb in the chandelier, but she was smart enough to let Ralph know that she wasn't interested. I considered her a real girlfriend, meaning a friend that just so happened to be a girl.

I saw Mary Margaret quite a bit early in high school, when I'd climb off the bus at the End of the Line after a hard day at

Manhattan Prep. The gang from eighth grade stuck together pretty well through the high-school years as we still had the End of the Line as our gathering point. But by senior year, for one reason or another, Mary Margaret had kind of drifted away from the pack. She was not going to college, while most of us would be taking that next step. She began to make other friends, friends that would be doing something else with their lives for the next few years. I'd see her every once in a while going into Mike's deli for a sandwich, or at Baum's after Mass getting the newspaper for her old man. And we'd chat it up a bit. But we were going different places. After high school, I never saw her again.

Sometime shortly after her friends of a lifetime left for college, Mary Margaret began a little recreational drug use—mostly pot, like a lot of kids back then. It was pretty hard to avoid the stuff in those days, and there are not too many people who were young in the 1960s who can say they never inhaled at least one time or another. But like too many kids, Mary Margaret's story went further. The drug use escalated and diversified over time. Pretty soon, the wheels fell off. It was agony for her, agony for her family. She tried various things to straighten out, but it had her by the neck. A few years back, a friend of hers told me that for a little while in the 1970s she "found the Lord." She didn't go back to her Catholic roots but had joined up with a few fellow stoners trying to stay straight reading the Gospels. I'd like to report a miracle. A real warm-fuzzy. But as so often happens with these flirtations without direction, without planting any roots in the reality of the faith, the energy wore off. Screwed-up on Jesus, back to screwed-up on drugs. Exhausted and dissipated from twenty-five years in and out of various rehab programs and from street living, Mary Margaret died in her early forties. Not an uncommon story. There are a lot of occupied cemetery plots from our cavalier attitude toward drug use back in the 1960s.

I wondered for a while why the Jesus thing didn't work for Mary Margaret. But there's no need to get overly theological about it. It didn't work because Mary Margaret hadn't turned her life over to something else. Her brief fling wasn't with faith. It was just a temporary distraction from a preferable embrace. I'd like to think that if the Jesus thing had been really serious, it would have worked and she'd be alive today, complaining about being middle-aged and telling her kids that she could hit a softball so well when she was young that the boys would ask her to play. But the story didn't end up that way. A lot of stories didn't.

The Other Half of the Greatest Story

Things get murky if we try to think of Christ as something separate from the church. Having our own little pet theology of Christ that we will apply to our lives is, to say the very least, a tad presumptuous. I stayed up once until 4:00 A.M. on Christmas Eve trying to put together a play kitchenette for my daughter (I swear, there had to be four hundred screws for that monstrosity). I hate to think what it would mean to try to put together an entire theology of being, an entire Christology, on my own. But it is more than that. Even if I were capable of dedicating a lifetime to theological study, I still could not create a living faith because I am not divine. I could create an opinion. Maybe I could even create a movement within an opinion. But a living faith meant for all people at all time would be an impossibility.

There are numerous scholastic games that are played to liberate Christ from the church. A whole deconstructionist school of thought has attempted to create the image of a church imposed on Jesus in the earliest generations. It sees ancient attempts at understanding the meaning of Christ as simply political battles where the majority imposed their will on the minority. It was just a numbers game, and if things had simply gone another way, our fundamental beliefs in God, the church, and the redemptive mission of Jesus could have been totally different. The church was simply an institution created out of a specific time and history to give organization to a growing number of the followers of Christ. This organization—this church—was a man-made edifice that actually over time dominated and, to a degree, obliterated the "real" message of Jesus. Or so the theory goes.

The difficulty in the theory is essentially that old sin of hubris. If one disagrees with the church as it is lived today in Christ, one simply builds one's own theology of Christ. And it is striking how much these theologies rationalize whatever contemporary mumbo-jumbo or pop psychology passes for a belief system, which doesn't give much sense of permanence over the ages. The logic of it all collapses in on itself. If Christ did not mean for his life and teachings to go beyond his own historical epoch, then his revelation could not have been divine and universal—God-centered and meant for all humanity. And if his revelation was not divine and universal, what's the point? Christ is simply an opinion that became a movement.

But if the teachings of Christ were meant to be both universal and eternal, there had to be a living means to both preserve and pass along that faith and that grace from generation to generation. To argue that Christ "didn't plan to establish a church" is to argue that Christ was irrelevant to mankind. It is to argue with the very evidence of the earliest Christian documents—the letters of St. Paul, the Gospels, and the Acts of the Apostles, which each so clearly portray a community of believers established in the name of Jesus with the infusion of the Holy Spirit. This is what the earliest Christian communities believed of themselves. To deny this is to deny the earliest understanding of Christ's followers virtually days after his death and resurrection.

We base our faith in Jesus essentially on three pillars: the Scriptures that describe revelation; the knowledge that the entire message of Christ as revealed to his apostles is preserved for all generations and spread to all generations; and the teaching authority that is exercised in the name of Jesus and guided by the Holy Spirit. These three things are all interlocking and are as old as the Christian message. We can see them lived in the Acts of the Apostles and the letters of St. Paul. In traditional terms they are referred to as Scripture and Sacred Tradition (which combined are called "the deposit of faith") and the magisterium, or teaching authority that comes in and through Christ. You can't have Scripture that contradicts teaching; you can't have the preserved faith that contradicts Scripture. And where do we find these three pillars?

I think you know where I'm going.

The Cromwell Effect

Dorm life at Fairfield University, like grammar school, was long hours of quintessential boredom punctuated by moments of stark insanity. With no flesh-and-blood young women within at least two square miles, and no cars to get at them, young men were generally reduced to their most common denominator. Four guys sitting in a dorm room in February circa 1968, bored out of their minds. Then someone decides to set up the Sucker. "Did you ever see the Cromwell Effect?" The Sucker responds, "What the hell is that?" And the game is afoot. "It's a simple example of the mental creation of a limited paralysis. You lie on the floor, close your eyes, and I'll place a towel over your face for three minutes. At the same time, I'll hold my hand down on your chest keeping you perfectly flat. Spider will keep the time. The rest of us will maintain complete silence. After three minutes, I will simply give the command 'Freeze,' remove my hand, and as I remove the towel, you will not be able to rise until I counter the command." The Sucker responds, "Get out," to which a third guy in on the action answers, "It's the truth. He did it to me. It's spooky. I'll show you."

He gets on the floor, the towel is placed over the eyes, the hand goes on the chest and three minutes go by. I nod. "Freeze!" He removes his hand and the towel, and the guy struggles to bend from the waist up. But he can't, until freed by the command, "Up!"

Sucker says, "That's a crock! Bet you ten bucks I can do it." And we proceed. Sucker lies down, closes his eyes, towel over his face, hand on chest. Our third man, who has slipped out of the room, returns at precisely two minutes and fifty seconds with an aluminum pie plate filled with shaving cream. Carefully measuring exactly where his face will be when Sucker rises from the waist, he holds the pie plate in perfect position. Ten seconds later, the second young man shouts "Freeze!" and the Sucker zooms straight up and smacks into the pie plate face first before he can stop himself. Voila, a full face of shaving cream. Three people laugh hysterically. Sucker shakes his head, shrugs, and says, "You owe me ten bucks."

Four years of college and more than three decades later I can't even vaguely recall anything of an entire semester of Advanced Calculus. But I remember the demonstration of the "Cromwell Effect" perfectly. A Jesuit education.

It was little demonstrations such as the "Cromwell Effect" that led me to retreat to my room alone as often as possible, particularly in freshman year. My roommate often went home to Long Island for the weekend, allowing me a little time for myself, a rare commodity in dorm life. So I would do what any kid of that time did when depressed and lonely for home. I'd play Simon and Garfunkle albums endlessly. On the *Parsley, Sage, Rosemary and Thyme* album there were any number of songs to exacerbate a late teenage angst. A particular favorite was a little ditty called "Flowers Never Bend with the Rainfall," which was always best for passing a dreary February afternoon when the whole world had simply lost its color. One particular part always lured me to the bottom of the barrel: "I'm blinded by the light of God and truth and right, and I wander in the night without direction. So I'll continue to continue to pretend. That life will never end. And flowers never bend with the rainfall."

At the time, I felt it was a vaguely subversive, antireligious verse, and maybe it was. It would be in keeping with the times.

But hearing it decades later, I give it a different spin. Like any good song, I read into it my own interpretation, just as I did back in the dorm room. Accepting the idea of God can leave us "blinded by the light" if we have no direction. And without direction, we just "continue to continue to pretend," hoping that this life will never end, because we can't see anything after. It was the problem with Mary Margaret's attempt at conversion. She was seeking faith without direction; belief without any knowledge. It was an emotional leap to try to get over the hump. That's a good start sometimes, but it goes nowhere if it is not connected to anything.

It's senseless to think of a divine revelation with nothing to follow. With the last of the witnesses to Jesus dead, the story didn't stop there. Why? Because of another simple progression, the other half of the story. Christ did not reveal God to mankind for one generation. If we miss out—or avoid—the church as the living expression of Christ, we make his revelation nonsensical. And we fall into the trap of enthusiasm—making our faith a brief, enthusiastic response to something appealing in the message of Scripture, but rooting ourselves in nothing. We can become like the parable of the seeds in Luke: "Those on rocky ground are the ones who, when they hear, receive the word with joy, but they have no root; they believe only for a time and fall away in time of trial" (Luke 8:13).

Without the church, without belief in the living presence of Jesus in our own time, and the guidance of the promised Spirit; without belief in something real that we can touch, see, and feel, we are left with nothing. There is just the memory of a pretty story two thousand years old. We'll end up believing anything or nothing. Or that flowers never bend with the rainfall.

*   *   *

O Lord, teach my heart this day where and how to see you, where and how to find you. You have made me and remade me, and you have bestowed on me all the good things I possess, and still I do not know you. I have not yet done that for which I was made. Teach me to seek you, for I cannot seek you unless you teach me, or find you unless you show yourself to me. Let me seek you in my desire; let me desire you in my seeking. Let me find you by loving you; let me love you when I find you.

prayer of Saint Anselm of Canterbury (1033–1109)

CHAPTER 7

Visiting O'Toole's Bar

Why did Christ found the Church?
Christ founded the Church to teach, govern,
sanctify, and save all men.

What are the attributes of the Church?
The attributes of the Church are three: authority,
infallibility, and indefectibility.

Considering we were barely literate at the time, it is hard to believe that we actually memorized things in grammar school that included the word "indefectibility." Like a lot of the Catholic terms from our childhood, it automatically pops up as an error on a computer spell check. (Indefectibility: "By the indefectibility of the church I mean that the church, as Christ founded it, will last till the end of time.")

Married men have to suffer through many things, or at least that's my story. A sunny warm Saturday, and the weather is just perfect for yard work. A rainy cold Saturday, and the weather is just perfect for going shopping. A partly cloudy, lukewarm Saturday, and the weather is just perfect for cleaning out garbage cans. I keep trying to discover when the weather is just perfect for lying on a couch, eating pork rinds, and watching *Bowling for Dollars*. Whatever that weather is, it hasn't happened since college.

So there I was on a rainy, cold Saturday engaged in that strange marital dance of shopping. This particular afternoon, we dipped into an antique shop run by Amish women. It was a Hoosier cornucopia of a rural past: old farm equipment, chairs from a dinner table long forgotten, picture frames with somebody's relatives who had been dead for at least six decades, old oilcans, and unopened boxes of forty-year-old Wheaties.

I wandered off on my own as the salesladies in pale blue dresses with white bonnets focused in on my wife. Glancing around, I suddenly stopped dead in my tracks. I swear on all that is holy that I never thought I would see it again—but there it was, hanging on a wall in a rural shop run by Amish ladies 750 miles from the End of the Line. Among ancient cut-glass crystal vases, handmade doilies, and turn-of-the-century candleholders, there was a slice of my own history looking a little worse for wear, but real as life. I sniffed the air. I swore I could smell a wooden floor soaked with the overflow of a thousand beers. As I closed my eyes, for just a few seconds, the Old Man was there as he was more than four decades ago, leaning against the long wooden bar asking for a cold Schaeffer from the tap. "And Mickey," he was saying, "get a birch beer and a bag of chips for the kid."

A Visit to O'Toole's Tavern

I was the Old Man's excuse when I was a kid. "Hon," he would announce to my mother an hour or so after supper, "I'm taking the kid for a ride." We would hop in the car and head off for about twenty minutes to nowhere. Up and down the hills of Yonkers, the Old Man would smoke a cigar while I prattled on and on about various theories of life I had developed. "Didja know something dad? Didja know you can't die on your birthday?" The Old Man had one hand on the steering wheel, as the other pulled the cigar from his mouth, the blue smoke heading out the partially opened window on the driver's side. "I think Shakespeare died on his birthday," he said. "But maybe not. I'll give it some thought." And on we'd go for a little bit longer until we reached the shrine at the end of this little pilgrimage, O'Toole's Tavern.

The purpose of O'Toole's Tavern was to serve drinks to thirsty men who had to get home to their wives reasonably sober. Women came in, but not too often and not if they were worried about what the End of the Line had to say about them. Most of the men stood at the bar and swapped lies with each other while O'Toole himself worked the taps like a conductor in front of a symphony. Two, three glasses, and a guy would announce that he "better get home to the old ball-and-chain."

No one in the evening crowd stumbled home drunk from O'Toole's. Somebody would give him a ride if he tippled too many. There were never any fights because it was a place you could go where everybody knew your eccentricities as well as your name. The only fight the Old Man remembered wasn't much of one. "Dancing Louie" was a regular. Louie may have been, as they used

to say, a little touched, but he was harmless. He'd put a few nickels
in the jukebox after his third draft and dance around by himself. It
happened just about every night and nobody paid him any mind.
One snowy night, a winter traveler apparently had car trouble and
wandered into O'Toole's to make a call. A stranger in O'Toole's
was not common, and the men at the bar turned to give him a bit
of the once over, which may have made him a little jumpy. Then
Dancing Louie appeared out of nowhere right in front of him,
flailing his arms in one of his less elegant steps. The stranger
thought he was making a move and smacked poor Louie with one
swift shot to the head. The whole bar exploded in laughter and the
stranger, told of Louie's nightly choreography, was mortified. He
picked poor Louie up, set him by the bar, and bought him two cold
ones. Dancing Louie was never happier.

I got the job as the Old Man's companion to O'Toole's because
I kept my mouth shut when we got home. My sister lost her privi-
leges when, after her very first visit with the Old Man to O'Toole's,
she burst through the front door and announced, "Mom, WE were
in a BAR." My sister spoke in capitals back then. The Old Man
would set me up in a booth on the "family side." A few feet of two-
by-four frames covered with paneling and just high enough to satisfy the local law separated the "family side" from the bar. There
were three other booths, but there was never anyone back there
with me. The Old Man would mosey up to the bar, give a few
handshakes and hellos, then turn to the bartender to order a cold
Schaeffer from the tap. "And Mickey," he'd say, "get a birch beer
and a bag of chips for the kid."

Just above the booth where I always sat was this painting recreating the events at Little Big Horn. General George Armstrong Custer stood in the center, sword raised to strike, his last bullets spent. A few soldiers lay dying nearby, managing a final fusillade. In the foreground, one plump, dead cavalryman was having his scalp removed; in the background, Indian reinforcements were pouring to the scene. I would stare at that picture, soaking up every element. To me, this was what art was all about. It had everything you could want: Dead cavalry. Dead Indians. Dead horses. About-to-be-dead Custer. The painting was actually called "Custer's Last Fight" and had apparently been part of a beer promotion sometime way back when. It was the only piece of art hanging in O'Toole's Tavern at the End of the Line in the 1950s. Forget television. I would stare at that picture until the Old Man would give a shout that it was time to go. A good solid belch from the birch beer, one last look at Custer in his final glory, and I was ready to head home.

And there it was, another faded copy staring back at me from the wall of an Amish antique shop in Northern Indiana decades later. I don't haggle well with Amish women. I paid too much. But that Saturday we headed home with a slice of the End of the Line.

Home Where My Music's Playing

It's easy to freeze the church in our memories. A Catholic upbringing in the 1950s, 1960s, and early 1970s leaves an impression, kind of like a dent from a ball bat on the noggin some might say. Our view of what the church is can be stuck in a time warp, like memories of an old neighborhood tavern that effectively disappeared only a short time after *Maverick* went off the air. Ask somebody who hasn't darkened the door of a house of worship since 1972 for a definition of the church. The images burped out have more to do with the things that bowled us over when we were kids than the meaning of the church itself: meatless Fridays, nuns dressed in elaborate habits and Victorian shoes, a parish somewhere in time in a neighborhood that doesn't really exist anymore, and altar boys in flowing red and white robes pounding their chests three times to the tune of "mea culpa, mea culpa, mea maxima culpa." I am of the opinion there was nothing wrong at all with any of that except that it led some of us to define the church by the cultural experience of a slice of history when we were kids, like defining great art by a beer promotion of Custer's Last Fight.

Get behind all the theology, all the razzmatazz from our childhood, and things can be reduced to their essentials. The church exists, simply, as a reflection of Christ in the world. Its purpose is singular: to lead people to Jesus so that they will know God, know how to live, and find salvation through him. Though sometimes they can become distractions when we don't understand them, all the other accoutrements, all the other matters that we attach to the church, are centered on that fundamental purpose.

Let's put the whole theological picture simply: "The Father so loved us that he sent his Son to redeem us. Jesus so loved us that he died and rose again for our salvation. To continue the work of salvation, he selected apostles upon whom he would build his Church, his new body, which would have as its responsibility the task of carrying out and completing the work that he began. The Church, then, shares in the very life of the risen Lord. Its members, those baptized into the Church, form a body with Christ as its head. It is through this Church that women and men are saved by coming to know Jesus Christ and through him are united in grace to the Father through the outpouring of the Holy Spirit" (from *The Catholic Way*, by Bishop Donald W. Wuerl, New York: Doubleday, 2001, p.92).

The word *church* itself reflects three simultaneous realities. It is a word that reflects the community assembled for the Mass, the local Catholic community, and the church universal. No one element of this church exists independent of the other. I admit that I am a sucker for that purely humanistic understanding of *church*. It makes it easier at night when the fears come uninvited. Our lives sometimes seem a random search to get connected to something. That definition of church gives us something to hold onto. It is there in a morning Mass during the week when a few old souls gather together in his name to share in the celebration of the Eucharist. They are part of the church that is that local community in a neighborhood somewhere. That local community is simply part of a church universal, as intimately connected to a Mass celebrated in a Latin-American hamlet as to the liturgy of Easter at St. Peter's Cathedral in Rome.

Spiritually, this universal connectedness is the Body of Christ, the people of God. We are together in the same Holy Spirit that we received at baptism, we are one in the same Eucharist. As believers—and in expressing our belief in the Mass, in the sacraments, and in living the faith—we are never alone, never acting as isolated individuals, but as a part of a glorious whole. Among us mortals in the church there is an invisible union with one another and with Christ.

Of course, that is less comforting when I look back at our experiment with the Cromwell Effect at Fairfield University. It is difficult to think that I was a part of an intimate community of believers when I was laughing hysterically at a guy's head smacking into a pie plate filled with shaving cream on a bored and boring Saturday afternoon in a college dormitory. But while our lives may be mired in a great deal of personal stupidity, that doesn't alter the reality. What we call sin is part of our communal life, and Dancing Louie had his role to play in the mystery of the Body of Christ as much as the next guy. St. Augustine called our lives a pilgrimage, meaning that our lives are a movement toward God, not an arrival at God. The church defines itself as church not just for sinners, but of sinners. This living Body of Christ is perfect through the life of the Spirit and the intimate relationship with Christ. Those who make up the Body of Christ—the people of God—are just we mortals. One of the great lines from Mother Teresa, who cared for the destitute and dying on the streets of Calcutta, described a particularly cantankerous and obnoxious soul demanding their care in his last days. He was, she said, "Christ in his more distressing form." A church that can see Christ in each of us isn't a bad place to be. We stumble along with our imperfections. But we can always stumble toward home because we have the church with us. Like the gang at O'Toole's back in the old days, there's always someone there to give you a ride.

I don't mean this as an unecumenical note, nor to wander into bad theology, but a grace of the church for me is that it would have me, warts and all. I don't trust a theology of the saved, defining the church as a remnant of souls where the acceptance of faith marks you as one of the elect. Certainly, faith is necessary for salvation. As they like to say, we are "justified" by faith in Christ. But it was Groucho Marx who said something like any club that would have him as a member must not be worth belonging to. Not to contradict Groucho, but if the church would have me, it must be a church for everyone.

Fundamental to our belief in the church is that it is not merely a man-made organization. If that's all it is the hell with it. Man-made organizations are structured opinions. I prefer not to pin my hopes on a movement. The church is the accomplishment of Christ. And for what purpose? As the good sisters told us, "To save your miserable little hides."

Of course, if we have a stumbling block, it can come here, and it's a big one. This is where we might want to call the whole discussion to a halt. It's nice to talk about a community of believers picking themselves up. It's picturesque to view life as a pilgrimage and to know that even at our worst, someone can see us as "Christ in his more distressing form." But the idea of the Catholic Church, any church, defining itself as the singular church of Christ seems to smack not only of triumphalism, but of limiting God, of making God so small that his truth would be confined to one wedge of humanity. This is where we begin to want to see the church as a man-made interpretation of the message of Christ. In its best light, we argue that it is a man-made structure evolving over time in history to attempt to pass along its interpretation of the message of Christ. Just don't identify Christ with that one institution, or limit God to one expression of historical faith.

But if we have a very real tendency to tie ourselves up in a view of the church created by the overwhelming American Catholic culture of our childhood, we can also tie ourselves up in adult rationalizations. To see the church as the living Body of Christ is not to limit God to a particular interpretation. It is to accept the idea that Christ came for a reason, and a reason that had to go far beyond the years of his life in real history, and both before and after our lives in real history. To reject the idea of the church is to limit God to a point in time; that Christ somehow exists in this day for us, but did not exist for others before, and others who will come after. There are other points of course: that the faith of the church is found in the faith of the Apostles; that there is a remarkable and clear connection between the beliefs of the early Christian community and the tenets of our faith today; that the history of the church weaves a vital connection through two millennia of time; that the very chaos of that history proves that this church must be something more than man-made—nothing so filled with the fallible could last so infallibly. But the bottom line remains: If we say there is no church, we are saying that God is too small to be a living God meant for all people for all time in the real world.

And if he is that small, then to hell with him too. After all, something around here has to have indefectibility.

Marks, and I Don't Mean Groucho

You might remember this one from the *Baltimore Catechism:*

Has the Church any marks by which it may be known?
The Church has four marks by which it may be known: it is One; it is Holy; it is Catholic; it is Apostolic.

This is actually the formula from the ancient Nicene Creed. These "marks" were meant to describe the church as the church of Christ. These "marks" are, together, the fundamental understanding of the church in its essentials and in its mission of service to spread the gospel. The good sisters in grammar school used these as proof texts to compare our glorious church to the various "Brand X" churches: The church is one while everyone else is divided; the church is holy because only in the church can you find the true path to holiness; the church is universal—it is the same thing wherever you go, anywhere in the world, any time (which always sounded like a threat to any kid considering an escape); the church is apostolic, which means that the church's leadership today can be traced back directly to the apostles. The unspoken idea was "Just try to point to any Protestant church that fits that bill!"

But there is a deeper meaning to these descriptive terms, a meaning that is at the center of just about everything. These "marks" center the understanding of the church in Christ. This is a key to part of our misunderstanding of the church that we inherited from a day when we were more defensive about our

Catholic identity. We defined ourselves as drowning in a sea of Protestantism in a country where, within our childhood, serious people debated seriously whether a Catholic could legitimately hold the office of United States president. Much of that defensive culture rubbed off on our understanding of church. These "marks" of the church were presented as proof texts for the institution of the church, and we would connect them to that. In reality, the ancient church council of Nicea used these terms as a means to define more clearly the centrality of Christ to the church. The church is one, holy, catholic, and apostolic in and through Christ.

The Church Is One

The nuns pounded it into our heads that the church is one because all of its members are in agreement in one faith. Well, yeah. At the heart of it, that is true. But there is more to it. The church is one because of Christ. Christ's death on the cross had an essential purpose: to make us one people, rather than a scattering of individuals. It is through Christ and in Christ that we receive our fundamental unity. It is a unity, of course, that does not erase the individual, but makes the individual a part of a whole. Within this unity of the church, there is an extraordinary diversity that embraces every culture of the world, every ethnicity and every historical era. How we live, what we do, who we are can be universally disparate. Yet, at the same time, in the church we find a fundamental togetherness of an eternal magnitude. It is a unity marked by the profession of the deposit of faith received from the apostles, in our celebration of the same Mass and sacraments, and in the life of our priestly orders inherited from the apostles.

All this, of course, becomes another stumbling block on the reality of history. That essential unity has broken down in the centuries since Christ. The essential affirmation of faith in Christ shattered into a hundred—a thousand—different shades of theological meanings. For close to five hundred years, there has been the single greatest rift in Christendom—the Protestant Reformation. (The Orthodox Schism of the East is primarily a division in the unity of the leadership of the church, as the theological differences that separate so-called Western and Orthodox Christendom are limited. Of course, there are those who could write books about those differences, I suppose. But I'm not one of them.) Yet, even in this great rift of Protestant and Catholic understanding, there are so many essential elements of agreement: belief in the same God, the centrality of faith in Jesus, shared Scripture, the Trinity, the pull of grace in our lives, baptism, the vital necessity of love and charity. There is much that brings us together. The church believes that all "who have been justified by faith in Baptism are incorporated into Christ; they therefore have a right to be called Christians, and with good reason are accepted as brothers in the Lord by the children of the Catholic Church" (Documents of Vatican II, cited in the *Catechism of the Catholic Church*, 818).

At the same time, the church has the deepest reverence for the "children of Israel," the people of the covenant of Abraham. As Pope Pius XI said, spiritually we are all Semites. Unique among the non-Christian religions, the Jewish faithful are our spiritual forebears. We are all descendants of Abraham in faith. Their sacred books are the sacred books of the church. We know that we believe in the same God; we know our faith is rooted in their beliefs.

For other non-Christian religions, the church accepts and understands that God has been perceived differently in different cultures, in different times, and in different ways. With Islam, the church shares belief in the same God who is one. They, too, are children of Abraham. With nontheistic expressions of faith, the church realizes their wisdom and perception and how they can lead people to a positive, enriching life and reflect the eternal truths we share.

Yet, at the same time, it would be attempting a major gloss to argue that the Catholic Church does not acknowledge its firm belief that truth exists, is knowable, and persists in the teaching of the church. Acknowledging the core Christianity of every Protestant denomination, the church still affirms completely that it is the full church of Christ. The church believes that it is the instrument of Christ for the salvation of all.

And there's another rub. First, the lack of Christian unity; and second, in an age of tolerance and uncertainty, the church's claim to have a hold on a universal truth seems awkward if not downright pretentious. In a time when the rules change overnight and a uniform politeness has settled over the land, we feel slightly embarrassed by this singular affirmation of truth. The church believes fully that within it is the path to salvation because through it we most closely encounter the teachings of Christ assured by the guidance of the Holy Spirit. Of course, if the church did not believe that—and if I didn't believe that truth persists within the church—why in God's name would I bother? If I did not believe that the church maintained the greatest affinity to the teaching of Christ, I would look for a church that did. I never viewed the church as feel-good ritualism, though I find grace in the rituals. Without the faith that the rituals are real and that they represent truth, they become mere superstition. We look to the church for salvation, not for a momentary lift of our feelings.

This does not mean that the church demands of us a blind act of faith. That's often the popular image: dumb sheep blindly following dictatorial leadership. The opposite has been my experience in the church. The church relies on the intellect and demands that we use our intellect. It asks us to know the faith and to learn how to apply it in our world—a Catholic definition of conscience. This makes us a people far freer to really think, as opposed to so many today who merely sit and let the propaganda of the times engulf their thinking. The Catholic faith is a faith constantly engaged in the world. It is never a faith that sees itself as outside of the culture, a saved remnant issuing thunderbolts from afar. It is the church, the people of God, engaged in the issues of the day, always studying the faith, always reflecting on the issues and developments of the times. This can be seen throughout the history of the church, and in our own day. Outsiders argue that the church has survived two thousand years because of its institutions. Those within know that it survives because of its divine foundation. But they also know it thrives because it has always been relevant and has never become disengaged from the world.

The Church Is Holy

There was a guy named Chickie at the End of the Line who was rather universally loathed. He went to Christ the King and was about two years ahead of us. Chickie combed his hair with grease and took great delight in smacking around anyone who was smaller than him. There seemed to be one in every neighborhood, and they always had a huge toady who never said much, but lingered in the background ready to impose the master's will if ever challenged. Chickie's toady was an enormous lug named Mulroy. The two things in this world that could frighten Mulroy were a Catholic nun and Chickie's displeasure. Generally, nobody ever challenged the likes of Chickie. He was a lousy athlete who took up cigarettes when most of us were still getting our thrills through Chunky bars. Will Rogers never met Chickie.

I generally passed under the radar of Chickie, though one time he knocked me around a bit. We were playing softball over at the park in seventh grade. Chickie was occupying a bench behind first base with Mulroy, talking about whatever goons talked about when in their own company. I was minding my own business out in centerfield when a guy hit one in the gap to left, and I raced for it. Grabbing it on one hop, I stopped on a dime, turned, and heaved it toward second to try to nail the guy racing for a double. I generally didn't have much of an arm, but this one I actually whizzed over the second baseman. The first baseman missed it, and on the second bounce it hit Chickie in the exact spot from where he hoped one day to inflict more Chickies on the world.

Chickie went into an exaggerated collapse—I didn't throw nearly hard enough to do any real damage—and we all did a little bit of a ha, ha, ha to please his feeble attempt at genital humor. As the inning ended I loped back in from the outfield. Around the pitcher's mound, Chickie caught up with me. "Hey, squirt, what's with hitting me with the ball?" He had an ugly slit of a smirk on his face, the one he usually got when he was about to give a pounding. "Yeah, squirt. What's with hittin' Chickie with the ball?" Mulroy chimed in. Originality was not his strong suit. "Sorry," I explained, knowing that a sincere apology was not going to resolve this matter. Chickie then grabbed me around the neck and bent me over in a headlock. I received, I believe, six quick noogies, a push, and a kick in the pants to send me on my way. I got off easy. At least, thank God, there were no girls around to see the humiliation. Chickie and Mulroy once "pantsed" Ralph in front of God and everyone. For those not of the era, that means they removed his nice pair of bucks and refused to return them. Ralph was left lying on the ground in his BVDs with about eight girls hanging around trying to figure out how good Catholic girls should behave in such a situation.

About two years later, Mike—who had grown to be the biggest, toughest guy around and my very, very best friend—ended Chickie's reign of terror without actually laying a hand on him. He just chased him out of the End of the Line with the simple warning that he was getting on his nerves. Mulroy stood around looking perplexed, which was how he would spend much of his life.

The church of Christ is "holy" because it is the church of Christ. It is holy despite the presence of the Chickies and Mulroys as living members, even if they maintain their essential rottenness these many years later. There is an eternal contrast that we live with in the church. We accept the holiness of the church because its Founder and his teachings are holy, the Spirit that enlivens it is holy, its worship is holy, its sacraments are holy, and its mission is to make mankind holy. "United with Christ, the Church is sanctified by him; through him and with him she becomes sanctifying"

(*Catechism of the Catholic Church,* 823). That does not mean that in the church all members are holy. And that certainly does not mean that its leadership is holy in every individual and throughout history. The grace of the church does not come from its members or its leaders, but from Christ.

That understood, however, a sign of the holiness of the church is the goodness, the charity of the lives of so many of the faithful. The church is the people of God on the path to holiness. For every Chickie and Mulroy, there are many quiet saints who go through their lives with a fundamental decency and a fundamental holiness.

*　*　*

I was sitting in sixth grade, thinking a lot about nothing. It was geography class, after all, one of those midafternoon classes when lunch is long forgotten, but dismissal is distant enough that there's no reason to prevent oneself from sinking even further into a stupor. But then the nun rises quickly from her desk, signaling for us to stand and turn toward the back where a visitor has arrived. From the look on the nun's face—a cross between humility and awe—our visitor has to be the pastor, the principal, or the Blessed Mother.

It's the principal, and she's got company. She is at the door with a man in tow. The guy was a bit disheveled looking, wearing old brown paint-stained work pants and dusty shoes. He also wore a sheepish smile, a little bit embarrassed by what was to come next.

"Children," the principal announced, "this man is here to do work on your church. He is cleaning the statues, oiling the pews, polishing the floors. Now, I want you to look at these hands." And

she had the man show us his hands, palms up, as if we were check-
ing to see whether he had washed before lunch.

"These callused hands," the principal said, "do God's work."
Then she turned and left. The guy gave us a little embarrassed
wave, as if he wasn't sure what all this was about. A few of us
waved back, probably as mystified as he was. The nuns did stuff
like that. They had the impression that most of the denizens of
Christ the King School were rich kids from families that dined,
rather than ate supper. Most of the nuns didn't share that kind of
background. Of course, most of us didn't either. The parish was a
microcosm of the 1950s. Sure, there were kids whose fathers were
doctors, lawyers, and bankers. But there were just as many fathers
who worked in the big carpet mills or in one of the plants down
by the river as there were who took the trains into New York City
for the high-rises. There were milkmen and bartenders, butchers
and shoe salesmen.

We never saw Ralph's dad in anything but work clothes. Even at
church on Sunday he'd manage a white shirt but no tie, his chubby
red neck unwilling to be constrained. Ralph's old man worked
down at the Otis Elevator Company, a big employer in downtown
Yonkers. He brought a lunch bucket to work along with the rest of
the guys, and punched out whatever it was they punched out on
an assembly line. On the weekends, he could always be seen put-
tering around the parish helping out with the endless maintenance
chores or taking care of some minor act of charity that had to be
done—getting an old lady her groceries, driving somebody somewhere they had to be. He even did a shift as president of the Holy
Name Society, though his idea of that lofty post was cooking the

powdered eggs for the monthly communion breakfast the men of the parish celebrated in the school cafeteria.

During the week, when his shift was done at 3:30 P.M., he'd catch the bus for the End of the Line. He'd usually wander over to the park to see what Ralph was up to. As tired as he was, he'd knock us out some fly balls, fetch rebounds for us while we practiced foul shots, or toss a few passes. Around 4:45 P.M. he'd say to Ralph that they better be getting home for supper, and they'd walk together up Corley Street to their little home on the corner. As he got older and we got bigger, he'd just sit on the park bench and watch us play whatever game was in season. When he'd leave for home then, Ralph would say that "he'd catch up," though he never would, having reached an age where taking a walk with the old man was not what you did.

St. Thérèse of Lisieux had called it her "little way." The nuns had turned Thérèse into a plastic saint—the "Little Flower," they called her—and her life seemed pious and unrealistic. I was surprised later in high school to discover that she was named a doctor of the church, along with all the big guns who were great philosophers and theologians. She was honored for her "little way"—her recognition that sanctity could be found in doing all the small moments of life well, motivated by goodness and faith, nurtured in the sacraments. Understanding that most of our lives are small moments, those few big moments will be lived well simply out of the habit of holiness.

There were a lot of people like Ralph's old man around the End of the Line. When their time came, the parish would usher them out with a properly solemn mass, a prayerful internment, and a nice little carry-in parade of casseroles from the ladies of the Rosary

Altar Society at the house they had worked to keep over their kids' heads for most of their lives. They always seemed to pass away about a month after retirement, usually quietly while watching television after supper. Their work was done.

They raised kids, they helped their neighbors, and they tried each day to make the Gospels alive in their own world. In them, charity—divine love—came alive. It was their own "little way."

Sure, there are decent souls who have never darkened the door of a church. But in the church, the battle is never fought alone. We receive strength through the sacraments, particularly through the Eucharist, as we struggle along the daily road to holiness. The church makes the work of holiness easier if we are open to it. Through the church, we have the means to become great.

Even Chickie and Mulroy. Or, as Mother Teresa might have called the two of them together: "Christ in his more distressing form."

The Church Is Catholic

We always thought the statement that the church is "catholic" was the nuns' little redundancy. It was like saying Ralph was Ralph. (Though that did carry a certain logic. Ralph was Ralph. There was no other.) Then she would explain that the word *catholic* meant "universal," which she defined as meaning it was the same everywhere. Then she would get all rhapsodic. "Children, that means that you can go anywhere: Germany, Indonesia, Burma, and you will encounter the church exactly as she is right here in your parish." Actually, that was a very depressing image for most of us. We imagined a group of Indonesian kids stuck in the same desks, dressed in blue pants and white shirts, doing arithmetic. Kids liked to believe that train whistles meant exotic trips to somewhere we had never been before. The nuns painted a picture of a universal trap that we could never escape.

The church universal does mean that the faith is the same in its fundamentals, certainly the same in its worship and the rituals of sacramental life, for all people. It also crosses history. But it is a more complex reality. It means that the centrality of Christ, the teaching of Christ, is not limited to time and space. The church is universal because it is grounded in Christ, and Christ is eternally present in the church. "The Church was, in this fundamental sense, catholic on the day of Pentecost and will always be so until the day of the Parousia" (*Catechism of the Catholic Church*, 830). Parousia, in case you've forgotten, refers to the Second Coming. It's another Catholic word, like indefectability.

The church is also catholic because the mission of the church is to reach everyone with the message of Christ. It is not an exercise in cultural hegemony to state that core belief.

The church is universal because the message of Christ was not meant for one time, one people, one corner of the world. While the faith lives in cultures and is expressed in cultures, it is not confined to any one culture. The faith is a faith of the ages, universally lived and universally expressed. And this universality comes from Christ, whose life cannot be confined to any one people. Again, we make Christ far too small if we accept a definition of him that would limit the Gospels to any single culture.

The Church Is Apostolic

The nun wasn't lying to us. On its simplest level, the church as apostolic does mean that we trace our faith back to the apostles.

But let's look a little deeper. The church defines itself as apostolic in that it is built on the foundation of the apostles. It traces itself in real time and real history to the "apostolic church," the church taught and lived by the apostles. It sees itself as the apostolic mission lived today. It receives its mission from the apostles, the first missionaries, who received their mission from Christ. The core of the apostolic belief of the church is that it is living out the mission of the witnesses to Christ himself.

The church also sees its apostolic nature in Christ by preserving for each generation the essential teaching of the faith as taught by Christ. The church preserves and applies this essential deposit of faith within time. This doesn't mean that the church is a museum piece, safely guarding ancient mysteries. The apostolic mission of the church is vibrant. That mission is to present and apply the teachings of the church to the challenges of every day in each new generation. This is that core understanding of the church incessantly engaged in and with the culture. It is taking the living message of Christ and applying it to the living, breathing world.

The church is apostolic in its mission of evangelizing the faith to each generation. The church both preserves the teaching of Christ and hands on the teaching of Christ. It is not handing on an interpretation; it is not developing a new movement for each new generation. Through the life of the Holy Spirit, the church is making certain that each generation receives Christ in the fullness of his message. The message isn't watered down, changed, or altered for palatability. Yet, it is not a faith frozen in time. In the eucharistic prayer during the Mass, the past, present, and future are brought together: "Christ has died. Christ is risen. Christ will come again." This is the vibrancy of the missionary message of the apostolic church: It is the preservation and presentation of the message of the living Christ to generations past, present, and future.

Finally, the church is apostolic in its leadership. The church "continues to be taught, sanctified, and guided by the apostles until Christ's return, through their successors in pastoral office: the college of bishops, 'assisted by priests, in union with the successor of Peter, the Church's supreme pastor'" (*Catechism of the Catholic Church*, 857).

And there is the final rub. The pope, the bishops, the priests—the whole hierarchical structure of the church. The temptation is to punch the ticket and take the last train for the coast. This is where we see the church once again frozen in a historical gridlock. We can buy the faith, but we don't buy the institution. The faith is believable; the structure is where the faith changes to a man-made movement, a construct. It is especially true because it is easy to paint it black. Flawed priests, flawed bishops, flawed popes. We can take it as a structure. But we don't want that structure sold as faith.

There won't be any gloss here as well. You simply cannot understand the church, or understand the essential teaching of Christ, until that phrase "institutional church" is thrown overboard. There is no church of faith in contrast with a church as institution. The church, through Christ, is divine at its source, divine in its life. The church is also fundamentally human, inextricably tied up in the human condition. It's a bit of a mystery why God chose humanity. We are such screwups. But a mystery is just a truth we cannot understand.

O'Toole's Redux

I went to O'Toole's one summer night after my junior year in college, probably ten years after the last visit there with the Old Man. The bad news is that we grow up. The old panel blockade was gone, along with the booths. O'Toole himself was long dead and the new owners were hoping for a younger crowd. The place smelled like a younger crowd alright, a mixture of Old Spice and urine. A jukebox was blasting out the Stones. George Armstrong Custer was long gone from the scene. A couple of kids were trying to coax a few beers with fake ids. The bartender gave them the bum's rush, then asked me what I'd have. I looked around for a moment and said, "A birch beer and a bag of chips."

"Another long-haired wise guy," he answered and walked away.

*   *   *

Watch, Lord, with those who wake or weep tonight. Give the angels and saints charge over those who sleep. O Lord Jesus Christ, tend your sick ones, rest your weary ones, bless your dying ones, soothe the suffering ones, pity all the afflicted ones, shield the joyful ones, and all for Your love's sake. Amen.

St. Augustine (354–430)

[CHAPTER 8]

Holy Ed and Other Eccentrics

What is the Church?

The Church is the congregation of all those who profess the faith of Christ, partake of the same sacraments, and are governed by their lawful pastors under one visible head.

The pastor of my childhood at Christ the King was Msgr. Edward Betowski. Before coming to Christ the King, Msgr. Betowski had taught at the seminary for approximately 1,970 years. As kids, we believed that if he hadn't met Jesus personally, he had known at least two or three of the apostles on a first name basis. Msgr. Betowski was old and always in bad health, though he would live well into my college years. The nuns were convinced he was a living saint, while the men of the parish, in their less decorous moments, called him "Holy Ed."

We would see Msgr. Betowski about eight times a year at the grammar school when he came over to pass out report cards to each grade. The door would open in back, the nun would rise from her desk as if an apparition had just shown up, wildly signal for us to stand and turn, and then we would all singsong, "Good morning, Mon-SEEN-your Be-tow-ski!" He was okay by us because, as we figured with most saints, he never chewed us out for a bad report card.

Catholic report cards back then listed your grades in front and your character on the back. Numerical grades were given in arithmetic, English, geography, and the like. On the back, you received letter grades for the serious stuff: "Reverent at religious duties" or "Obeys promptly." Msgr. Betowski had a theory that any kid with good grades would have a sterling report on the back of the card. He would be reading off Tom's grades for example—99, 99, 99 (the nuns never gave you a 100 for a final grade as perfection was reserved for the saints). Then he would dramatically turn over the card and announce, "WITH ALL As ON THE BACK!" A kid named Harry would always throw him. Harry was a top student who was rarely if ever reverent at religious duties. Harry had the record for the nun's most humiliating punishment—making him kneel out in the middle of the aisle at church after getting caught snapping the clips on the back of the pew that held men's hats. Msgr. Betowski would read off Harry's string of 99s, turn the card dramatically, and announce, "WITH ALL . . . " and pause for a moment. "Your card, young man," and Harry would come up to

collect his bad character reference. Harry ended up a revolutionary in college in the 1960s.

The other times we would see Msgr. Betowski was at the 9:00
A.M. Sunday Mass, the so-called children's Mass. Msgr. Betowski
routinely said the 9:00 A.M. Mass. The only problem with that was
that Msgr. Betowski always gave long sermons, and they were usually about cancer. He had a thing about cancer. Like a lot of priests
back then, he figured the best way to keep you in line was to scare
the hell out of you. Msgr. Betowski's tales of horror usually
involved tumors. He'd be up there talking about some saint or
some sin, and the conversation would get around to your last days
on this earth. "The tumor on your neck swells until your skin
oozes. The nuns in the hospital will try to help, but the pain will
be unrelenting. It is now that you must draw on the reservoir of
strength from your holy Catholic faith. Will you have the power
to shout as your neck pulsates in agony: 'I offer this up for the poor
souls in purgatory!'?"

And we'd just sit there, scratching our necks.

The Telephone Company

A lot of the priests we remember from the old days had their eccentricities. But being on the dark side of fifty, I'm a little more sym-
pathetic. I've developed a bucket full of eccentricities. Eccentricities
are simply what we were as kids multiplied by the years. Show me a
fifty-year-old guy polishing a red sports car that he doesn't need and
can't afford, and I'll show you a guy who had a new Schwinn bike
when he was twelve . . . that he never let anybody else ride. The

priests of our youth don't seem so eccentric as we look around to see what became of us. Primary lesson: When we were kids we thought all adults were a little nuts. Kids feel the same way today. We were right then, and they are pretty much on target now.

One of the problems we have with the church as we step back and look at it as adults is that we think we are viewing the telephone company. Even when we say, "The church," it comes out sounding like "The Organization." Men in black suits and women in habits run around keeping the operation going smoothly from the parish down the block to the head office in Rome where the chief resides, directing things like a maestro with a finely tuned orchestra watching his every move. The schnooks in the pew are there to provide the prayer, muscle, capital, and kids to keep the operation going. And so it does go, for centuries on end. The view is of a man-made machine, one of the best invented, that percolates along through history watching with a yawn as the rest of the kingdoms rise and fall.

There are two essential fallacies at work here. First, the church doesn't exist in order to exist. It has an essential and singular purpose: to save souls. If anything, it is a bridge in time between the life of Christ and the second coming of Christ. And far from standing idly by in history, the church is an active participant in history. Second, the church is the people of God, not a division among lay, ordained, and vowed, no matter what the nuns told us about our essentially inferior status. Through baptism, all become a part of the Body of Christ, all are called to the mission of evangelizing the good news of Jesus Christ, all exist in a fundamental equality through baptism in the church.

All that the church is comes from and through Christ. The authority that we accept and affirm in the church is the church acting in Christ's name. Christ is the source of all within the church.

It is critical to remember that apostolic nature, which is a fundamental mark of the church. This is central to our self-understanding as Catholics. We believe that the church is built on the foundation of the apostles. It is not merely a message passed down from generation to generation through a man-made apparatus or through oral tradition. Through the guidance of the living Holy Spirit within the church, we understand that the faith we profess and pass on is the faith taught by Jesus and witnessed by his apostles. The deposit of faith is not an evolution in teaching, but the apostolic tradition maintained from century to century within the church. There is certainly a development of doctrine, where truths have become more clearly understood and applied over the centuries, but this is not a movement from error to truth. The fundamental beliefs of the church existed in apostolic times—there has been no additional revelation.

Because of this apostolic understanding, Catholics have never believed in the faith as a matter of private interpretation. That is certainly a sign of contradiction to the culture. There is such a mishmash of belief that there are really no beliefs in contemporary thought. Catholics, however, believe that in this apostolic understanding, the church is "taught, sanctified and guided by the apostles until Christ's return, through their successors in pastoral office: the college of bishops, 'assisted by priests, in union with the successor of Peter, the Church's Supreme Pastor'" (*Catechism of the Catholic Church*, 857).

The Priesthood

Catholics believe in an ordained clergy. We believe that through the bishops in union with the pope the church is led and the deposit of the faith preserved. We do not believe that this is some kind of an institutional historical accretion. The structure of the Catholic Church is not a curious anomaly of an institution somehow grafted onto the faith that became entwined with it. The church is "hierarchial" because the church is intimately connected with the apostles. "The whole Church is apostolic, in that she remains through the successors of St. Peter and the other apostles, in communion of faith and life with her origin: and in that she is 'sent out' into the whole world" (*Catechism of the Catholic Church, 863*).

The hierarchial nature of the church is not some pyramid structure beginning with the great mass of lowly laity and proceeding upward to the very pinnacle of the papacy. There are distinct vocations and roles within the church, roles that differ for the ordained clergy and the laity. But it is not a medieval structure of prince to serf. Again, by definition of our baptisms, there are no distinctions within the Body of Christ. There are, however, distinct roles in how we live out our baptismal vocation.

It is essential Catholic belief that through the sacrament of holy orders, a man is ordained a priest by a bishop. Through ordination, ordinary men become instruments of God's grace. They act in the person of Christ. They are "ministers" of Christ, who is the true priest. Their chief role is in the celebration of the Mass—the eucharistic sacrifice. Priests celebrate the sacraments, witness marriage, preach the gospel, and teach the faithful as best they can how to become saints. Through ordination and through Christ, they forgive sins in the sacrament of reconciliation.

It is sometimes difficult—if not quite nutty—for those outside the church to understand how Catholics view the priesthood. Even at the height—or depth—of scandal, Catholics hold a universal allegiance to the priesthood. The reason is simple: Catholics define both our expression of faith and our daily relationship to God through our sacramental life. The sacraments, instituted by Christ, are at the heart of the faith. We believe that the priesthood is an "icon" of Christ, an image of Christ. It is through the priesthood that we take part in the sacraments. The priesthood is not a vestige of something, or an inherited tradition. We believe the priesthood represents Christ in the sacramental life of the church. The priesthood, like the sacraments, is not a peripheral part of Catholic tradition. It is central to Catholic life.

It has been the constant teaching of the church that ordination in holy orders is reserved to men. It is a sacred tradition that comes from Christ and, therefore, not a teaching that the church has the power to change. In the Western tradition, priests take a vow of celibacy at ordination, an ancient Catholic practice encouraged by St. Paul and first definitively mentioned for priests in the fourth century. It has been mandated by the church in the West for more than one thousand years. Celibacy, though a tradition that can be traced back to the earliest days in the church and one that is certainly modeled after Christ, is a practice and discipline, not revelation.

Ordination, of course, does not make a man perfect by any means. It is an old mistake to think that the priesthood makes saints of men. Very early in the history of the faith, the church had to point out that the validity of the sacraments had nothing to do with the disposition of the priest. Saint or sinner, the grace of the sacrament was through Jesus, not through a fallible man. History has witnessed bad bishops, weak priests, and even cut-throat popes. I daresay the future will witness more unpleasant-ness. It is the human condition. But the Lord loves humanity in all of its sometimes wretched behavior. Ordination doesn't remove the potential for sin, just as confession doesn't mean that we will never have to confess again. But for every fallen one, there have been thousands upon thousands of priests who quietly served God and served man all the days of their lives, despite their eccentricities.

"Let everyone revere the deacons as Jesus Christ, the bishop as the image of the Father, and the presbyters as the senate of God and the assembly of the Apostles. For without them one cannot speak of the Church" (St. Ignatius of Antioch, died circa 117 A.D.). The ordained acting within the church is evident from the very earliest moments in Christian history. In the Acts of the Apostles, there are deacons and presbyters to represent the apostles as leaders—and servants—of the Christian community. Chosen by the community, they "presented these men to the apostles who prayed and laid hands on them" (Acts 6:6). All of us are one in baptism. But through this sacrament of orders, certain men are raised to ministerial service. Through the apos-tolic tradition of the ordained ministry of bishops and priests, we can see in a real, visible way, that Christ is present and leading in the community of believers through all ages.

The Catholic understanding of the priesthood comes from Scripture, particularly the narrative of the Last Supper. When Christ blesses the bread and wine, announcing that this would be his Body and Blood, he instructed the apostles to "do this in memory of me" (Luke 22:14–20). Jesus prayed to his Father for the apostles: "Consecrate them in the truth. Your word is truth. As you sent me into the world, so as I sent them into the world. And I consecrate myself for them, so that they also may be consecrated in truth" (John 17:17–19).

The church has always defined three "orders" within the sacrament of holy orders: bishop, priest, and deacon.

It is central to Scripture and the apostolic understanding of the church that certain men were designated directly by the apostles through prayer and laying on of hands, as leaders of local Christian communities. The earliest tradition of the church defines these bishops as successors of the apostles, continuing in their role to teach, sanctify, and govern within the church. "Christ committed to the Apostles the task of preaching his word in his name—that is, with his authority. He assured them of the assistance of the Spirit, who would guard them in all truth and in speaking (see John 14: 16, 26). He commanded them to teach his word to all nations, binding the hearers to believing their words as the words of God and he promised to be with them in their preaching until the end of time" (*The Catholic Way*, 107).

The basic understanding of the office of the bishop is that Christ did not leave us to fend for ourselves in matters of belief, with each new generation vying to somehow understand what the faith is, what the faith means, and how it can apply to the developments of each day. Each bishop cares for the particular church— the diocese—over which he presides. He is viewed in the Catholic faith as acting as a successor to the apostles. As bishop, he is also integral to the teaching authority of the church universal—the magisterium—in communion with his fellow bishops throughout the world, and in union with the pope.

Papal Bones

It was my only trip to Rome. It was not a pilgrimage—just business. I have never handled traveling well, and this trip was no exception. I spent the evening flying over the Atlantic, watching a movie where all the explosions had been edited out, making it both shorter and pointless. The stewards had wheeled the booze cart into the center of the aisle in business class, allowing us to make our own drinks to pass time, or to pass out. I dozed fitfully until we arrived in Milan. Another flight and a cab ride and I had traveled, in about twenty-two hours, from the cornfields of Indiana to the cradle of civilization, or at least a hotel room just outside the Vatican where I watched "Old Yeller" dubbed into Italian while trying to recover from jet lag.

The old New Yorker in me generally makes for a lousy tourist. Growing up near the City, a New Yorker takes on the affectation of the dutifully unimpressed. Once you have been in the City, your attitude means to suggest that there is nothing much left to see. But enough Hoosier had washed over me that Rome left me staggered. Though caught up in an endless parade of business meetings, there was a little time to see a few—very few—of the sights. Time, a Roman native told me, is an oppressor in the ancient city. In a place where a two-thousand-year-old statue is the new kid on the block, in a Roman culture that the Greeks viewed as a modernist interloper, your view of the individual in history is skewered. As a kid visiting Cape Cod and seeing towns established in the mid seventeenth century, I thought I had encountered an old land. In Rome, I had meetings in offices that were functioning as offices before the Pilgrims passed the turkey and gravy at the first Thanksgiving. It is hard to think of your life as unique in all the universe in a city where they can't put up a parking lot without discovering a cemetery that might be 1,000 or 2,500 years old.

My itinerary left about six hours in total for seeing the sights. My exposure to the Colosseum, for example, was taken care of in a quick peek out a cabby's window as we whizzed past. I managed a total of forty-five minutes within St. Peter's itself, just enough time to stand before Michelangelo's *Pieta* for a few seconds and admire the papal altar that I had only seen on television when the Christmas mass was broadcast back home on tape delay. A friend had arranged, however, for a ticket to the excavations under St. Peter's Basilica. That was something that I made time for.

According to the historical tradition, Peter was killed in Rome, a martyr for the faith. The Christians took his body down from his cross and buried him on the very site where, a few centuries later, the first Christian emperor, Constantine, would raise a church in his honor. Eusebius of Caeserea (260–340) is the "father of church history." His *Historia Ecclesiastica* presents a history of the church from its beginnings to 324 A.D. In it, Eusebius writes of an encounter with a Roman priest who tells him that in that city there were monuments erected over the graves of the apostles Peter and Paul. St. Peter's Basilica is on the traditional site of these graves and that was the belief of the church for many centuries. Excavations began under the old basilica in 1939, revealing an ancient pagan Roman cemetery. The early Christians had also buried their dead there, and it was said that the apostle Peter was among them, his grave marked with a "trophy" or monument. In 1950, Pope Pius XII announced that the grave of Peter had been found, but the bones were soon proven to not be those of the apostle. Later, Pope Paul VI announced that other bones unearthed by archaeologists were those of the apostle. There is no final proof, of course. Just a long tradition and a degree of probability. The bones were the right age. The site has been venerated for nearly two thousand years, but there is no requirement of belief.

We walked through the tiny corridors, a guide pointing out the ancient Roman art and the sarcophagi of the dead. We were told that pictures were not allowed. The art in the necropolis itself was astounding. And then, directly under the cupola of Michelangelo's altar, are the bones that are claimed to be those of St. Peter. They lie where they have been for centuries with no dramatic encasement.

It was one of those stories the nuns loved to tell us:

"It was no time for anyone who called himself a Christian to be in Rome. It was the year 64 A.D., in the time of the Emperor Nero, a madman who was intent on making followers of Jesus the scapegoats for the fire that had devastated the city in July. The warning signals were all up, and some Christians were making their way out of the city. One of them was their leader, Peter, yielding to the pleas of friends to save himself.

"He was barely two miles from Rome, on the old Appian Way, when who should appear before him but the Lord himself. Peter was dumbfounded.

"'Domine, quo vadis?' he stammered. 'Lord, whither goest thou?'

"'I go to Rome,' Jesus replied sadly, 'to be crucified a second time.'

"In an instant, Peter understood the Lord's message. He knew he must quickly return to Rome.

"There he resumed his teaching and his ministry to all, his life in constant danger. The atrocities Roman officials committed against the Christians—on Nero's direct orders—defied belief. Some were sewn inside animal skins to be torn to pieces by dogs. Some were crucified. Still others were covered with tar then set afire—simply to provide torchlight for the emperor's garden. Nero himself drove through this mad scene, disguised as a charioteer.

"Finally Peter was captured, along with Paul, and thrown into the Mamertine Prison. Even there he continued to preach the message of salvation through Jesus—so convincingly that his two guards, as well as many other fellow prisoners, were converted.

"Finally he was sentenced to death by crucifixion in the Circus of Caligula, at the foot of the Vatican. At the last moment, Peter hesitated.

"'I cannot meet death as the Master did,' he told the executioners. 'Place the cross upside down.'

"The guards agreed to this last request, and in that cruel fashion Peter went in glory to rejoin the Lord" (from *Treasury of Catholic Stories,* Our Sunday Visitor).

We loved that stuff. We particularly loved it if we could get the nuns telling stories rather than reviewing arithmetic problems while armed with a red pencil.

The scriptural foundation of the papacy is direct. It was this flawed St. Peter who answered when Christ asked, "But who do you say I am?" Peter answered: "You are the Messiah, the Son of the living God" (Matthew 16:15–16). When Jesus revealed that he was the Bread of Life, and many of his disciples left him after such a hard teaching, he turned to his apostles and asked if they would leave him as well. It was Peter who answered, "Master to whom shall we go? You have the words of eternal life" (John 6:68). It was to Peter, then, whom Jesus promised: "You are Peter, and upon this rock I will build my church, and the gates of the nether-world shall not prevail against it. I will give you the keys to the kingdom of heaven. Whatever you bind on earth shall be bound in heaven; and whatever you loose on earth shall be loosed in heaven" (Matthew 16:18–19).

With Peter's martyrdom in Rome, the bishops of Rome became the successor of the apostle to whom Christ had given singular authority. As the bishops would be inheritors of the apostolic succession, the bishops of Rome would be successors to Peter's unique role. The bishop of Rome as Peter's successor exercises full authority over the whole church. This role of Peter comes from the earliest understanding of the church and is at the very foundation of the church's understanding of itself. We cannot understand the church without understanding this critical apostolic foundation, which takes the church back to the time of Christ.

In Catholic understanding, the primacy of the See of Rome is not simply a position of honor. The church believes that, as successor to Peter, this primacy represents the will of Christ for the church. The jurisdiction of the papacy extends over the bishops. This primacy makes the pope the "first teacher of the faith" with a particular obligation to defend and protect the essential deposit of faith. The papacy is, at its heart, meant to be a conservative primacy as it is also meant to conserve the basic teachings of Christ. That is also why the church believes that the papacy is endowed through the Holy Spirit with infallibility in the teaching of the faith and in defining moral dogma.

This exercise of papal infallibility does not mean that everything a pope might write or say constitutes a statement of truth for all time. Any reading of history would show that this is obviously not true. What it does mean, however, is that the pope as head of the bishops, exercises this infallibility when he formally proclaims by a definitive act a doctrine pertaining to faith and morals. Such an act or declaration of formal infallibility is always done as a confirmation of the faith, not as a "new" revelation of a teaching unknown to the faith.

This "charism" of infallibility exists within the college of bishops when it acts in unity with the pope, particularly acting together in a formal council of the church. This is what is often called the "extraordinary magisterium" of the church—when a doctrine is formally defined *ex cathedra,* or "from the chair" of Peter; or formally defined by the pope in unity with the college of bishops. According to Catholic understanding, this demands the assent of faith from all believers. This is "extraordinary" because it is not an everyday event. The last time such a formal *ex cathedra* definition of doctrine took place was in 1950 when Pope Pius XII defined as Catholic doctrine the ancient belief in the Assumption of Mary—that the Blessed Mother was assumed bodily into heaven. The Second Vatican Council (1962–1965), which actually defined no new or additional doctrine, was the last formal council of the church.

That said, it should also be understood that the church's teachings are not confined to these dramatically formal occasions. Without formally pronouncing a teaching in a definitive manner, the church exercises an "ordinary magisterium" through the pope and bishops, particularly when they speak in one voice concerning a matter of faith and morals, applying the faith to contemporary life. Assent to such expressions of the ordinary magisterium should be a vital part of living faith. The faith is not something kept locked away. It is meant to be lived dynamically in the world and to meet the changing circumstances and challenges of humanity.

What this means is very simple in the lives of the average Catholic. The "teaching authority" of the church comes from Christ and through the guidance of the Holy Spirit. Catholics believe that, as successors of the apostles, the bishops are responsible to teach and preserve the faith. The pope, as the apostolic successor of Peter, has a fundamental primacy in this teaching authority. It all makes perfect sense when we accept that the teachings of Christ were meant for all time, not merely for one era in time. It all makes sense when we accept that the teachings of Christ were meant to be presented authoritatively, not merely as an opinion. It all makes sense when we accept that the teachings of Christ were not meant to be any individual's interpretation of that teaching, but as a preserved deposit of faith. By the teaching authority of the church through the bishops and the papacy, every generation is assured that the faith received is the true faith—the faith that comes from the authority of Christ himself and the guidance of the Holy Spirit.

Got to Get You into My Life

Msgr. Betowski was pretty certain I was cut out to be a priest when I was a little squirt. I had all the right pieces. The fourth of five kids, and the third youngest son, I was a solid throwaway within the Irish Catholic tradition that ruled in our house. First son inherited the estate, second son took care of the parents (and was available for pinch-hitting if something happened to number one son), and third son went to the church. I was also a whiz at the catechism and had consistent As in Reverent at Religious Duties on the back of my report card.

There is a picture in the family album of me around second grade. Big, round crew-cut head with a fittingly pious expression on my face. I am standing next to Msgr. Betowski who has an arm around my shoulder. I'm staring into the camera, he's looking down paternally at me. I'm convinced that he figured that picture would be on my desk down at the chancery when I was the cardinal archbishop of New York, talking to reporters about the priest who inspired my vocation.

Like any Catholic kid of the era, I gave some thought to a vocation to the priesthood. I gave it particularly serious thought after Ralph presented the basics of what we used to call "the facts of life" on the way home from a Cub Scouts meeting. He didn't quite have the story right—I seem to recall that belly buttons and elbows somehow played a prominent role—but it was enough to entrance Tom and me as we absorbed Ralph's gruesome dissertation. We were dutifully horrified. We sat for a long time thereafter, trying to decide whether to become diocesan, religious order, or missionary priests.

By sixth grade, the nuns, who were the chief recruiters, had generally written me off as priestly material. I had made two critical mistakes. First, my astoundingly consistent mediocre grades at the exact middle of the class did not bode well. The nuns generally assumed that God did not grant vocations to dummies. The biggest problem, however, was that I was an altar boy dropout. I had started at it, kicked it around a while, then just stopped going. My primary reason for quitting had nothing to do with the faith, of course. It was just too much work at a time in my life that was dedicated to preserving as much of my free time as possible for cartoons and the *Three Stooges* on television. It was perceived —perhaps correctly— that anyone called to the priesthood would be zealously dedicated to being the very best altar boy imaginable. An altar boy dropout might as well have fallen off the edge of the Catholic universe when it came to consideration for future priestly ministry.

One day in sixth grade we had a contemplative priest visit our class to pitch vocations. He described living with a bunch of guys in a monastery, working in the fields, reading theology, celebrating mass, baking bread, and praying a lot. Looking back on it, my next move made absolutely no sense. I lived with three brothers, and I had no desire to be in the company of men on a daily basis. I wouldn't even mow the front yard, let alone work in the fields. Reading, baking, and incessant prayer had little to do with my three sixth-grade loves: television, baseball, and setting pins at a bowling alley for a quarter a game. And, let's be blunt, I was already starting to develop a rather distinct curiosity about some of the high-school girls who hung around the End of the Line. They were frightening and not a little fascinating, as all girls would be for the next ten years solid. The perception lingers to this day. Anyway, the priest passed out cards at the end of the lecture, and I put down my name and address and handed it back. Tom looked at me as if I had just bit the head off a chicken. "What did you do that for?" he asked incredulously. "I was thinking of what Ralph said," I answered. He looked thoughtful for a moment, then filled out the card and passed it forward. Most of the guys did, actually. I think Ralph had really been spreading the word.

For the next couple of weeks, I dreaded what might happen from passing that card to the priest. I imagined a big, black limo pulling up in front of the house one Saturday and a couple of tough looking monks piling out, walking up the front steps, and knocking on the door. "We're here for the kid, Mrs. Lockwood. We got his card right here." And my mother would look at it and say, "Well, that's that." They'd find me upstairs watching the *Three Stooges*. And just as Moe was poking Larry in the eyes, I would be hauled away, never to see family, friends, or the Stooges again, my last public words being the mournful cry, "Moe, Larry, cheese!!!"

Finally, some mail arrived, literature from the order. It was a nice little brochure. There were some black-and-white photos of the guys weeding gardens, saying Mass in chapel, and even playing basketball. Under a smiling young guy's picture was his story about what his vocation meant to him. He wrote about how he wanted to do something with his life that was not about him, but about the rest of the world, and the next. He wanted to get to know God better. He wanted a life that would mean something more than just making money, or letting everybody else define what it was to be a good man. "It's my way of serving God," he wrote, "and serving my fellow man through prayer." He looked—and sounded—pretty happy with his choice. So did all the guys. There was another card inside to return in the mail if I wanted some additional information. I looked at it for a bit, fingering the end of the card.

"What do you have there?" my mother asked, as she walked by hauling a basket of dirty clothes. I crumpled the card in my hand. She had long passed before I even answered. "Nuttin," I said. I took the pamphlet and the crumpled card and put it all in the garbage, hiding it under newspapers stained with coffee grounds from breakfast. I just didn't want to give her any notions. Then I grabbed my glove and headed out to play ball.

*   *   *

Today no theme of common praise
Forms the sweet burdens of thy lays—
The living, life-dispensing food—
That food which at the sacred board
Unto the brethren twelve of our Lord
His parting legacy bestowed.

Then be the anthem clear and strong,
Thy fullest note, thy sweet song.
The very music of the breast:
For now shines forth the day sublime
That brings remembrance of the time
When Jesus first his table blessed.

Within our new King's banquet-hall
They meet to keep the festival
That closed the ancient paschal rite;
The old is by the new replaced;
The substance hath the shadow chased;
And rising day dispels the night.

Christ willed what he himself had done
Should be renewed while time should run,
In memory of his parting hour:
Thus, tutored in his school divine,
We consecrate the bread and wine;
And lo—a Host of saving power.

Sequence for the Solemnity of Corpus Christi, Lauda Sion,
Thomas Aquinas (1225–1274)

CHAPTER 9

Like a Bridge over Troubled Water

What are the chief effects of the Redemption?

The chief effects of the Redemption are two:
The satisfaction of God's justice by Christ's
sufferings and death, and the gaining of
grace for men.

What do we mean by grace?

By grace I mean a supernatural gift of God
bestowed on us, through the merits of
Jesus Christ, for our salvation.

It was the first break in the Hoosier summer drought. It had rained the night before, and the morning sky, though a bright blue, came with a cool breeze and mild temperatures. I was out in the yard with a shovel and an ax, doing what men do to work off the quiet desperation.

It happens at times. I call it the Curse—but not that one. My wife simply calls it whining. But it seems to happen to every guy at points between graduation from high school and, say, death. The job is going lousy, and, as we seem to define ourselves so much by our jobs, life has generally become simply a pain. That's when we have the bleak breakthrough. We discover the meaning of it all— we work and then we die.

So I'm out in the backyard trying to work through the Curse, which is our usual response, if we can't afford a new car or a bad habit.

"You sweat a lot!" It was the little boy next door, offering an unintended comment on the shape I was in. The kid was about six, staying with his grandmother during the summer, probably to help his single mom save on day-care expenses. That's the way things go now. "What are you digging?" he asked. I started to answer, but before I got too much along he was into a follow-up: "How far down does the dirt go?" Well, I started talking about limestone and sediments, not to mention the whole issue of underground water deposits. He listened for a moment to all that foolishness, his right hand in a small salute as he shaded his eyes to look up at me. He then asked, "What's your favorite color?" And I remembered how this was supposed to go. My kids had reached college age and it had been a long time since I had played the question-and-answer game. The rules were simple. He asked, I listened and started to answer, then we went somewhere else. It was really not important what either of us said. He was just looking for the company of words. And I was happy to supply them.

After a little bit, he wandered away into a small woods near our house, returning every few minutes with a new, spectacular find: an old broken plastic bucket, a cob with all the corn picked off, a rock that looked green. And he asked what it was, where it might have come from, how old it was, and whether I liked hot dogs. I looked up to watch him in the woods as I dug away, a shadow running among the trees, a kid with something to do since the man next door was home on a cool summer day trying to work off the Curse in his backyard.

When I was about four, and the summer days had rolled in, I was on my own most of the time. My two older brothers could wander the world on bikes, my sister could just wander. The old gent who lived next door to us would come out to do work in his yard and I would go over to chatter at him endlessly. My folks were a little worried at first that I might be annoying him, but it became clear that the old gent liked having me around. Maybe he was looking for the company of words. One time, he showed me how he sharpened the blades of his old rotary push mower. He warned me not to touch the blade, but I did it anyway and cut my finger. He carried me home for a mother's attention. That was the only emergency in our relationship, the rest of it being two friends united by a gulf of maybe seventy years, give or take. He had a little toy plastic dog in his kitchen that, I guess, had a magnet in its nose. He would make the head go up and down as he moved a magnet in front of it. I was duly impressed. A few times, if I hadn't been around for a day or two, he would wander over to the back door, knock, and ask my mom if I was sick and, if not, could I come out for a bit. My mom got a big kick out of that.

Well, this lasted two or maybe three summers. It's the usual story. I started making friends my own age around the neighborhood, and we would play ball in the street, or swing on the swings in somebody's backyard, or investigate the empty lot where no one had bothered to build a house. I would see the old gent out pulling weeds in his yard and wave as I was heading out to play with my friends. He would always wave back.

We moved again when I was just past seven, the house getting too small once my baby brother got his walking shoes. I only saw the old gent one more time, when I was a freshman in high school. We had a fund-raising campaign, and I had the bright idea that I could probably pick up an easy donation by surprising the old gent. He'd be so happy to see me that he'd cough up a small fortune to help support the hallowed halls of Manhattan Prep for his old childhood buddy who could also get a day off if his class met its collective goal.

He recognized me right away when he opened the door. He led me in like I was the prodigal son returning, offering me both a seat and an iced tea. He jabbered away about his life—not to complain, but to catch up. He'd lost his wife a few years back. And he didn't see his only son much anymore since he lived on the West Coast. He asked about me and I talked the usual stuff a 13-year-old boy blabs about—school and sports. "Here, I want to show you something," he said, and ushered me into the kitchen. On a corner of the counter sat that yellow plastic toy dog. He made its head go up and down. And he looked at me and laughed. I said, "I can't believe you kept it all these years," not realizing that while the years seemed forever to me, they were just a blink to the old gent. "Reminded me of you," he smiled. "How could I get rid of it?" After we visited a bit more, he asked why I had dropped by. Somehow, I felt like a jerk going into a pitch for money. So I didn't. I said I had a buddy in the neighborhood I was seeing and just decided to stop by and say hello. Every once in a while, you manage to do the right thing. I swear, it's got to be the grace.

One night when I was in college, my mother called to say the old gent had died. Must have been close to ninety, she said, "and he liked you so much." The memory of an old man and a little boy made me smile. Like a bridge over troubled water.

The boy's grandmother shouted that it was time for lunch, and he headed off with a wave. I wished him a good lunch and to drop by any time. He went in, and I put down the shovel. I didn't need to work off the Curse anymore. A kid had stopped by looking for the company of words. That was really all the grace I needed that day.

The Baptism of Vocation

Baptism is our gateway into the life of grace. The rite of baptism is simple. As holy water is poured on the infant's head, the child is baptized "in the name of the Father and of the Son and of the Holy Spirit." The name we receive in baptism is our name for all time. In the afterlife, who you are will live on by the name given in your sacramental baptism. It's a good thought, even if your name is Sylvester. It speaks of the sacredness of the individual, a single life called by one name for eternity.

Culturally, we try to reduce it now to a ritual, like the seventh inning stretch, or a bride wearing something old and something new. But the baptism we received as infants—when we were blessed in the fullness of our names—means something infinitely more than a mere tradition. It was our introduction to the life of Christ. All the sacraments lead to the Eucharist, but baptism is the first of them—our reception into the mystery of faith. God has given the miracle of life; in baptism we were given over to him. The sacrament makes us what the nuns called "adopted children of God," a part of the Body of Christ, incorporated into the church of Christ. In baptism, we take on the "new life" promised by Christ. It is through that sacramental baptism that we find meaning, or vocation, in our lives.

We all know—or think we know—that the earlier we learn the lesson that our lives mean something over and above the time we put in, the less time we waste trying to figure things out. When the nuns talked about vocation back at Christ the King at the End of the Line, we generally thought about riding around on motorbikes in some Far Eastern town as missionaries saving pagan souls. Vocation as it was explained meant the vowed or the ordained life. They might have given a little nod to the vocation of marriage— somebody had to supply the new generation of priests and nuns after all—yet there was a general impression that true vocation was the ordained ministry. But the key to understanding the ordained ministry of holy orders is to see it as a ministry of the sacraments in service to the people of God. What we call the laity—us (face it: If you were baptized in the church you are one of the great "us," even if you haven't darkened the door of a church in years)—is the primary Christian vocation. It is defined as a life lived faithfully in the world and is the essential vocation to which Christ calls mankind. It is the central message of Scripture and the vocation shared by all of us through baptism. Through living that vocation in Christ, we strive to be in that "state of grace"—that connectedness to God—which is the goal of life.

The nuns, of course, talked about "grace" all the time. But they never really explained it very well, or well enough that it made much sense. Most of us get whatever clue we have of the meaning of grace through an old hymn:

> Amazing Grace, how sweet the sound!
> That saved a wretch like me.
> I once was lost, but now I'm found.
> 'Twas blind, but now I see.

Like "Danny Boy," the hymn brings a tear to the eye if you have a soul at all. But what does it really mean? The old catechism delineated two kinds of grace, which really means two ways that we understand this "connectedness" to God in our lives. The first the catechism called "sanctifying grace." "Sanctifying" grace means the action of God that brings us to him, that makes us a part of his life. Sanctifying grace means the habitual grace that comes through baptism. We are all children of God through that enduring gift of baptism. We have God within us.

As the old catechism explained, sanctifying grace "makes the soul holy and pleasing to God." With sanctifying grace come the virtues of faith, hope, and charity, which help us in living this new life of grace in God. Faith is the virtue of knowing God in our lives; hope is our confidence in God that we might believe in a purpose, end, and goal of Christian life; charity, or love, is the most essential virtue of all. Charity is the summation of all the law and the prophets: love of God and love of our neighbor.

Then there is "actual grace," the grace of God in our daily lives to do good and avoid evil. It is what John Henry Newman called a "Kindly Light"—the light of God bringing us closer to him throughout the days and nights of our lives. Actual grace is made up of "the help which God gives us so that we may actually do deeds of love. . . . Every kind of gift by which God moves us toward knowing Him and sharing His life is a grace. Devoted parents, faithful friends, good books, great music—indeed anything at all may be used by God to lead toward life" (*The Teaching of Christ*, 328–29). The feeling of serenity on the beach with an orange sunset bursting across the edge of the ocean; in the forest when we come upon a pristine blue lake where the quiet is so absolute that the only sound you hear is your heartbeat; the first time a father holds his newborn child: these are points of actual grace. But they don't have to be so dramatic. They can be almost anything. Like the philosophers say, perhaps they are points in life when we catch eternity in our hearts for a mere second.

The State of Grace, and Other Rumors

The state of grace is a way of life. The state of grace is not some kind of end point reached—if we are lucky—on our deathbed. It is the way we are meant to live daily. Happy are those who realize that. Damn happy. Most of us rattle around for years trying to figure out exactly why we get out of bed each morning. I was talking with a friend about the end results of a liberal arts education. We could devise intricate mental systems for divining the state of the world, but we couldn't change a tire. There was little that was practical application to our education, except for our ability to dazzle at 1980s cocktail parties with our mastery at Trivial Pursuit. "I know what you mean," he explained. "It's that degree we got in Thinkology."

The simplest truths really are simple: The life of faith with the purpose of attaining greatness, a greatness defined by Christ, is the only goal worth trying for. It will accomplish every other great and good goal in our lives. It is life where we strive to live in the state of grace and where we see, judge, and act in our world through the faith we profess.

Which seems, of course, rigorously pious and stupendously unrealistic. That's probably a defect of our education. The nuns filled us with marvelous tales of the saints that usually involved grotesque suffering and incredible submissiveness to it. But there is more than merely a nun's exaggerated demand of the Catholic life that leaves us dry here. The state of grace implies a perfection unattainable, a dehumanized principle—like making God into an aesthetic principle such as love, perfection, or truth. But the state of grace is decidedly human, a way of living rather than a brief moment in time. It is as comfortable as an old shirt, and more lasting and possible than just a few seconds of spiritual euphoria. The state of grace is the connection to God through a life lived and sustained with the grace of the sacraments. The state of grace is a gift—a sacramental sharing in the life of God in our own lives. Grace, simply, is our sharing in the life of God, a gift we really can't earn. It comes to us in time but through eternity.

A good scriptural story describes it well. Back in our travels with Luke, we encountered the story of Zacchaeus (Luke 19:1–10). Zacchaeus was the diminutive tax collector in Jericho, the shortest man in the crowd. Wanting to see what this Jesus was all about but unable to see over the folks lining the way, he finally scrambled up a sycamore tree to get a better look. As Jesus came to that very spot, he looked up, spotted the tax collector and said, "Zacchaeus, come down quickly, for today I must stay at your house" (Luke 19:5). The people grumbled at Jesus showing such favor to a hated tax collector. But Zacchaeus defended himself, saying he lived honestly, never cheated anyone, and gave half his riches to the poor. Jesus responded: "Today salvation has come to this house because this man too is a descendant of Abraham. For the Son of Man has come to seek and to save what was lost" (Luke 19:9–10).

It is a story of grace. Zacchaeus strives to lead the good life— he gives away part of his wealth to the poor. He treats people fairly. From what he has heard of Jesus, all he hoped for is just a look at the man. Instead, Jesus tells him, "I must stay at your house." That is grace—it is Christ always inviting himself into our lives. It can happen at any moment. And at any moment it is happening. It is the incessant invitation of God to participate in his very life.

The Sacraments in Time

The sacraments are what we do as Catholics. They define us. They are the means through which the church helps us to find salvation in the lives we live. They are our way to sanctity. They are our way to grace.

When we were kids in grammar school at Christ the King, we used to memorize the scriptural proofs of the sacraments.

Baptism. "Are you unaware that we who were baptized into Christ Jesus were baptized into his death? We were indeed buried with him through baptism into death, so that, just as Christ was raised from the dead by the glory of the Father, we too might live in newness of life" (Romans 6:3–4). A reminder that our faith is the faith of the living, not of the dead.

Eucharist. "Then he took the bread, said the blessing, broke it, and gave it to them, saying, 'This is my body, which will be given for you; do this'" (Luke 22:19). And, of course the whole narrative of the Last Supper, as well as so many scriptural quotations: "Whoever eats this bread will live forever; and the bread that I will give is my flesh for the life of the world" (John 6:51). This was called the "hard saying" of Christ, but it is at the sacramental core of our faith.

Confirmation. "You will receive power when the holy Spirit comes upon you, and you will be my witnesses in Jerusalem, throughout Judea and Samaria, and to the ends of the earth" (Acts 1:8). We were told that this sacrament drafted us into the church militant—the nuns loved that expression. And while that is certainly true if you like the militaristic analogy, the sacrament is and represents the life of the Spirit in our lives, intimately connected to the baptismal grace that we might live a life of Christian maturity.

Penance. "Whose sins you forgive are forgiven them, and whose sins you retain are retained" (John 20:23). The sacrament of which a thousand childhood stories can be shared with the boys at the bar, it is where we encounter the forgiveness of God, and the grace to go on.

Matrimony. "So they are no longer two, but one flesh. Therefore, what God has joined together, no human being must separate" (Matthew 19:6). The sacrament where we ourselves are the ministers, the priest representing the witness of the church. It is the sacrament of the Christian family.

Holy Orders. The narratives of the Last Supper in Luke chapter 19, Matthew chapter 26, Mark chapter 14, John chapters 13 and 14. This is our means to the grace of the sacraments.

Anointing of the Sick. "Is anyone among you sick? He should summon the presbyters of the church, and they should pray over him and anoint [him] with oil in the name of the Lord" (James 5:14). I liked it better when we called it extreme unction—it had a great ring to it, one of those Catholic phrases that we loved to bandy about. It is a sacrament that prays for healing of the body and promises healing of the soul.

There is nothing wrong with such a list. The faith is rooted in Scripture and the church surely believes and teaches that the sacraments come from Christ and are rooted in Christ. And their purpose is simple: for us to encounter a life of grace to live in the state of grace. The sacraments are not man-made rituals meant to celebrate points in time. They were made real in Christ's life as a means to fill our lives with sacramental grace. They cover all points: birth, maturity, marriage, sickness, and death. They are there when we fall into sin; they are there to sustain us along the way with the bread of life. Sacramental grace takes us through the pilgrimage. Through the sacraments the daily goal of the life of faith is achieved. We walk with God, in a life ordered to how God wants us to live. It is our fundamental vocation.

Of course, when we say that Christ founded the sacraments—and as we list our scriptural reference points for them—we are not trying to invent a historical fiction. We don't see in Scriptures a definition in matter and form for each of the seven sacraments that looks exactly as the sacraments are celebrated today. We don't have to create a false picture in our minds of the apostles carrying around a sacramental kit filled with the oils for anointing of the sick, or kids in red robes in 125 A.D. preparing for their confirmation at the hands of the bishop and hoping for a scooter as a gift. As we saw before, too often the catechesis of our youth—rooted in *per omnia secula seculorum,* for ever and always—gave us mixed signals. We confused the "how and what" of the ritual with the sacramental nature of the act. The church's understanding of the sacraments, and the rituals to make them visible in our liturgical life, evolved and deepened over the years.

In our own lives, we have seen this evolution. For those who have not popped into a confessional since the old man dragged you over to church when he found the dirty magazines under your bed, you might notice today a substantial change in the form of the sacrament, including face-to-face encounters. Obviously, what we call the "Order" of the Mass has been changed rather dramatically from our youth, if we are old enough to recall the Tridentine Mass in Latin. Most people now receive the Eucharist in the hand and standing; in our youth everyone received it directly on the tongue while kneeling at a communion rail. If such changes in the ritual presentation—the liturgy, if you will—of the sacraments have taken place in our own lifetimes, imagine the changes over two thousand years.

So, no, we don't expect the forms of the sacraments to be the same today as they were 1,500 years ago, or 50 years ago, despite the impression given to us by the good sisters. Similarly, our understanding of each of the sacraments has deepened and grown richer. The church finds, for example, the scriptural basis for the sacrament of confession so clear in the words of Christ in his command to the apostles after the Resurrection (John 20:23). But the understanding of the sacrament evolved over time, with the ancient Christians seeing the sacrament as a onetime sacramental forgiveness for serious faults—such as denial of the faith itself—after a person had been baptized. And this was at a time when most baptisms took place in adulthood. It is said that many would live sympathetically to the teachings of Christ, but would hold off on baptism virtually until their deathbeds. St. Augustine, the great bishop and Christian theologian, wrote in his younger days of his longing for the faith. But the demands of the Christian life once baptism was conferred were simply too much for him. "Give me chastity," he prayed, "but not yet!" A prayer that echoes down to every kid just out of college. Confession of sin after baptism was usually a public, demanding ritual, or undertaken only once and near death. It was unthinkable that the believing, baptized Christian could possibly relapse into serious sin. It was the monks of Ireland who first made the sacramental life of confession both private and frequent. As missionaries in Europe, they raised the understanding of the sacrament as a means of God's continuing mercy and as a way to deepen the life of faith through sacramental grace. Knowing how there aren't many of us who could get by without one good solid rationalization of stupid behavior in any given day, the monks were certainly on to something.

Christ has called us to holiness, to a way of life that is not easy to achieve for a flawed humanity. That way of life demands growth, but it is growth we cannot do alone. We grow with the church, the community of believers. We grow with our effort, but with God's assistance in grace and the sacraments. The grace of God in us is eternal life lived in real time. And that's the state of grace.

Pink Panties and Crazy Frankie

At the End of the Line, we generally kept names simple and descriptive. "Chunky" Malone was named "Chunky" for a reason. "Dirty" Ernie was perhaps the most perfect name I have heard for a human being in my entire life. Then there was "Crazy" Frankie. He received his nickname who knows when. It was passed on from generation to generation of kids.

Crazy Frankie was the End of the Line's head case. His age was indeterminate, somewhere between thirty-five and sixty-five. He wore baggy jeans, an old sweatshirt, and a topcoat with a pair of black high-top sneakers in an age when no one over twelve would be caught dead in sneakers unless on a basketball court. Crazy Frankie had a high-pitched squeal for a voice and a limited vocabulary, except when it came to obscenities, which he liked to yell at passing cars and cats. Rail-thin with a perennial two-day growth on his face, Crazy Frankie's primary occupations were collecting bottles and sweeping the sidewalks in front of Baum's and the bars along the End of the Line for loose change.

Generally, Crazy Frankie got by without the kindness of strangers who would naturally cross the street when they came within a block of him. It was the people of the End of the Line that simply put up with him as one of their own, even if the least likeable of their own. The shopkeepers gently got him out of their stores by handing over his extortion of a little loose change that he was always begging. He'd walk into the stores and just start bellowing: "Some nickels? Some nickels?" And somebody would give him a few nickels and he'd be on his way with a "Thanks, goddammit. Thanks, goddammit."

Crazy Frankie never went hungry; never had to worry that someone would take advantage of him or rough him up. The curious fact in all this is that Crazy Frankie had no redeeming value. He was not pleasant, not someone's idea of blessed innocence because of his mental deficiencies. Generally, Crazy Frankie was just mean. He never said kind things to small children. In fact, most small children were introduced to the more colorful expressions of life through a "Crazy Frankie" harangue as they went in to buy gum at Baum's the first time, an End of the Line baptism under fire. Sometimes he would simply threaten. You'd walk by him, he'd look at you and say something endearing like, "Stick you with a knife when you sleep! Stick you with a knife when you sleep!" Even the dogs that lazed around the neighborhood didn't like him. He was the twist on the old W. C. Fields line: Anybody hated by kids and small dogs can't be much good.

One summer day Crazy Frankie had decided to park himself outside the Chinese laundry. He was actually in a rather good mood that day—for Crazy Frankie—and there shouldn't have been a problem. But somebody—we thought it was Dirty Ernie because it fit the picture—put an idea in Crazy Frankie's head. Every time a lady walked in or out of the laundry, Crazy Frankie would inquire in his loud squeal, "Got pink panties on? Got pink panties on?" Tom and I hung around watching the performance, having nothing else to do with our lives at the time. There is nothing—nothing—that is better in life than a summer day when you are a kid with nothing to do. Of course, you don't know that at the time.

The neighborhood ladies paid no attention. Crazy Frankie didn't bother them, and they had heard worse in their day. Most of them were hardworking women who grew up in the rougher parts of town. A few would even chuckle and say something like, "I haven't seen a pair of pink panties since before the war." A few ladies tsk-tsked a bit, reminding Crazy Frankie that he was being impolite not very far from church, as if by moving a few doors down his insistent inquiry would be more acceptable. But Crazy Frankie would just answer, "Got pink panties on? Got pink panties on?" I think he really just liked the flow and sound of the words. Not that he would have stopped if he realized it was offensive. He would have been downright pleased.

One lady—Tom and I figured later that she must have been Episcopalian or from another neighborhood—did take offense. She walked toward the door and Frankie shouted, "Got pink panties on? Got pink panties on?" She looked at him like he was mold. "Well, I never!" she snapped. That got Tom and I laughing like crazy, which made her all the more steamed.

The lady went in the laundry and obviously said something to the owner. The Chinese guy came out and, like most adults, the first thing he did was to chew us out: "Outta here. Nothing funny. Tell your parents you laugh at dirty stuff. Go! Go! Go!" We sauntered down a block but kept our eyes on the show. The laundry man tried to talk to Crazy Frankie but he was on a roll, getting a kick out of the attention. The laundry man went back in his shop and must have made a phone call. A few minutes later we saw one of the nuns from the convent come down the street. It was Sister Mary Rose, the principal at Christ the King. She walked right by us as if we were invisible. "Have to hear this," Tom said, and we slinked back to the scene.

Crazy Frankie was still shouting about panties as the nun approached. "Franklin," is all she said. We never heard anyone call him "Franklin." Crazy Frankie stopped at once. She just smiled and said, "Franklin, it is such a hot day. Let's get something cool to drink." Crazy Frankie didn't really answer, but there was also no mention of pink panties. "Let's go, Franklin," she said. And he said, "Yes, Sister," sounding like one of us. "You're a good man, Franklin," she answered, and they headed down the street, Sister nodding hello to parishioners who stared at them as they walked by together. Like a bridge over troubled waters.

* * *

Lead Kindly Light, amid the encircling gloom, Lead me Thou on! The night is dark, and I am far from home, Lead Thou me on! Keep Thou my feet; I do not ask to see the distant scene; one step is enough for me. I was not ever thus, nor pray'd that Thou shouldst lead me on; I loved to choose and see my path, but now lead Thou me on! I loved the garish day, and, in spite of fears, pride ruled my will: remember not past years. So long Your power hath blest me, sure it will lead me on, o'er moor and fen, o'er crag and torrent, till the night is gone; and with the morn those angel faces smile with which I have loved long since, and lost awhile.

Cardinal John Henry Newman (1801–1890)

CHAPTER 10

Amazing Grace

How many sacraments are there?

There are seven Sacraments: Baptism, Confirmation, Holy Eucharist, Penance, Extreme Unction, Holy Orders, and Matrimony.

Do the Sacraments always give grace?

The Sacraments always give grace, if we receive them with the right dispositions.

I was home for spring break in my junior year. I had a few bucks in my pocket, courtesy of a little job the Old Man had lined up for me. I went down to O'Toole's early in the evening to see if anyone was around. It would be good to be with a few of the boys at the End of the Line. My life was mostly at college now, and the connections with the old days fewer and fewer. But I was glad to spot Tom taking up a stool at the end of the bar. We managed to see each other a bit during the summer and at Christmas and Easter. He was still in school, racking up very solid grades, but we were going in different directions. Tom was heavily into recreational drug use. I was a bit more of a throwback, overindulging in the booze to drown my common sense. But though the social circles had changed, we always enjoyed our mutual company. Tom was sitting with Eddie Funk. Funk was a heavier druggie who never went to college but managed to avoid the draft, probably through an ever-present smirk. Even the Army loathed him on contact. Funk couldn't stand me. I wasn't that deeply committed. I just thought he was a jerk.

Tom gave me the how-the-hell-are-you and a hug. Funk barely nodded a hello, but without a wise-guy smirk, so I figured he was in a good mood. Tom explained that the funds were low and they were thinking of calling it an early one. I said that there was no need, sat down between them, pulled out a twenty, and slapped it on the bar. The beers would be on me. There was a ball game on the TV, some of the girls from the past might just drop by, and the night was young. It sounded like a good combination.

Tom and I did most of the talking, going back to the days of our childhood like two old men swapping tales on the bench at the park. Funk watched the ball game, chuckled when it was expected, and sucked down each mug of beer when I bought a round. We had enough that the bartender even bumped us one. After a while, the conversation lulled as it often does between two good friends. Nothing uncomfortable about it. I was glancing up at the game when I noticed Funk's classic smirk as he eyed

something on the bar. A Funk smirk was a sure sign that the
world had taken an evil turn. I glanced around and spotted nothing, so I turned back to the television, but kept a little peripheral
vision on Funk. When he started to smirk, I took a quick look
down. Tom had just slipped a dollar out of my change off the bar
and into his pocket. I looked back at the television, embarrassed.
In about another fifteen minutes, he had stolen two more bucks
and both he and Funk were starting to get a good case of the
giggles over it. I got up and went to the men's room, where I
stood for a few minutes staring at myself in the mirror. And I
came up with a question.

The bartender was the usual type back then, a surly guy named
Frank who just wanted your order, not the story of your life.
When I came back from the men's room, I gave him a call. He
noticed I still had half a mug of beer, so he looked at me like I
came into the place with something unpleasant on my shoes.
"What?" he asked.

"C'mere," I said, "I got a question."

He came over slowly, walking like his back heels were stuck on
something. When he finally made the trek, he repeated his first
question: "What?"

"You see over there," I said, turning and pointing to the back wall.
"There used to be a picture of Custer's Last Stand hanging there."

"So?"

"What happened to it?"

"How the hell should I know? Things change."

"Good answer," I said. I picked up a five-dollar bill, the last of
my change on the bar left unstolen. I folded it, reached over the

bar, and put it in his shirt pocket. Then I got up to leave. I wanted to tell Tom that I would have given him every cent I had if he had asked. But I didn't. I just said I had to go. When I looked back from the door, Tom was counting how many bucks he had managed to filch. Funk was looking straight at me. With a smirk.

Sacraments

Despite all the obvious evidence to the contrary in most anything we do, particularly in our callow youth, the church believes that our lives can be great. While most of society opts for the lowest common denominator and is pretty well convinced—and convinces us—that it is the best anybody can do, the church keeps telling us that we can do better. The church believes in humanity, and believes that we can be saints.

That is the odd contradiction between the way the church is portrayed by society and the way the church is. The chattering classes paint the church as the great naysayer, the spoilsport at the orgy. The church, they say, harbors an unrealistic portrait of humanity, denying to its adherents the accepted normalcy of a life lived in these times. They push the idea that we can't really control our darker urges, and that we are at our best when we simply succumb to our common humanity and accept our personal moral failures. It is this culture of mediocrity that invents rationalization, the ability to excuse the inexcusable by finding an excuse. It is a culture that has simply defined deviancy down, arguing that only the most loathsome of sins is worth worrying about. It's a culture that asks to be lead into temptation, and expects little delivery from it.

It's a culture that tells us that sanctity and goodness are ideals to admire in principle, rather than realistic goals to achieve.

Recovering alcoholics in the early stages take great pride in doing things that sober people do regularly—get to work on time, clean up the house, walk the dog, pay the bills. They have failed at these simple human chores for so long that doing them and doing them right is an achievement. While we grant them the right to gloat over these early victories, we know that the path to continued sobriety has to get beyond that. They have achieved only the first level of regaining their souls and must keep growing. Performing the ordinary is just a first step.

When it comes to the way we live our lives, the culture has reduced us to that same level and tells us that we never need grow beyond that. The basic excuse is that the ordinary is good enough. The church just doesn't buy it. The church knows that we can be good and great. It doesn't say that it is easy—Flannery O'Connor's point—but it says it can be done. The church also tells us that we don't have to do it alone. In fact, it tells us that we can't do it alone. The church believes that through the life of the sacraments, we are connected to God in such a way that greatness in this life is right here, right at our fingertips. We don't have to settle for the ordinary, for the good enough. With God, through the grace of the sacraments, anything is possible. And that's a real revolution.

Baptism

If memory serves, it was Bugs Bunny who began his biography, "I was born at a very early age." Most of us were born in faith at a similarly early age. The usual spot was a baptismal font in the back of a church on a Sunday afternoon, with crying baby surrounded by priest, mother and father, Godparents, and assorted friends and family. There's a communal understanding to baptism represented by the loved ones who take part in witnessing the sacrament.

In baptism, we are given over to Christ. It's a done deal. The theology of the sacrament involves original sin and the rejection of Satan: "Almighty and ever-living God, you sent your only Son into the world to cast out the power of Satan, spirit of evil. . . . We pray for these children: set them free from original sin, make them temples of your glory, and send your Holy Spirit to dwell within them" (*Rite of Baptism*). The simplest way to understand what happens to us in baptism is presented by St. Paul: "I have been crucified with Christ; yet I live, no longer I, but Christ lives in me; insofar as I now live in the flesh, I live by faith in the Son of God who has loved me and given himself up for me" (Galatians 2:20). In baptism we have the ultimate answer to ennui, to the great philosophical question of all: Does this life mean anything? The answer is simple. How can a life be meaningless, if Christ lives in that life? As St. Paul concludes, "I do not nullify the grace of God; for if justification comes through the law, then Christ died for nothing" (Galatians 2:21).

We go through it at some point in time. A couple of decades after the work has chewed us up, we begin the "what-the-hells." It's a bad day when we wake up to discover that we got it all and all ain't much of nothing. Men often respond to this great discovery in a fashion as predictable as the ending of a bad mystery novel: a sports car or a lady in a red dress. What we forget or maybe failed to ever understand—as it would have never dawned on the nuns to prepare us for a midlife crisis, which is a luxury they never saw in the world—is that our baptism gave us the means we need for real greatness, a greatness of a life lived as we are meant to live it. It is a life than can be lived in a corporate suite or in a trailer park. It's a life lived in generosity and faith. It is a life lived knowing that in baptism we died to ourselves and were reborn in Christ.

Of course, there is nothing in the theology or the rite of the sacrament of baptism that gives anyone a free pass. There hasn't been a life lived that is a free pass. That's not the human condition. The rite reminds us that we "will have to face the world with its temptations, and fight the devil in all his cunning" (*Rite of Election*). And of that we are absolutely certain as the decades roll by.

The bad news usually comes by e-mail now. There was a time when the death of a friend from the old days came in a hand-addressed letter with a clipped copy of the obit. Now, somebody sends you an e-mail with a link to the newspaper that carried the formularized listing. This time the message—sent along to a cadre of various souls, some of whom you know, other names you don't recognize—was that another one of us was gone, a fellow worker from years back who had slipped away from God-knows-what about a week past. I figured out from the timing in the obit that at the point when he quit this earthly realm, I was two hundred miles away trying to cut the long grass that grew under the rhododendrons. That's the way it goes. One guy is dying while an old buddy is taking care of the yard. The world just keeps on turning.

We hadn't seen each other in a lot of years. But I remembered his story. Pretty wife, a couple of kids just like any kids. Nice house in a nice neighborhood. He was a good guy in his own way. A Yankees fan, from his upbringing just outside the City. And one day around age forty-seven, for no reason other than to add a little zest to a life that was beginning to strike him as boring, he took up with a similarly bored woman. The result was the usual result. A marriage broke down. The kids went on their way, never quite rebuilding a relationship with a father who said by his actions that they were not as important as they had thought. He drove a fancy car for a while, took to the bar scene, then lost interest. Not just in the car, but in everything else. He lived for another eighteen years. But with a simple choice he had become ordinary. When I read the e-mail I offered up a little prayer that he had looked for a graceful beginning even as it was coming to an end.

"I will not treat God's gracious gift as pointless" (Galatians 2:20). Put aside all the good theology and that's the meaning of the sacrament of baptism for each of us personally as we get long in the tooth. Through baptism, we have taken on Christ. We are a part of something infinitely greater than we are. By the sacrament we have touched God. And once we have touched God, we can never allow ourselves to become ordinary.

Confirmation

Confirmation is the sacrament of the Holy Spirit, the "breath of God." It's the sacrament of the earliest moments in the history of the church, a sacramental participation in the miracle of Pentecost when the Holy Spirit, promised by Christ, descended on the apostles in the upper room (Acts 2:1–4). The clearest scriptural presentation of the sacrament is in the mission of Philip in Samaria.

Philip had been preaching the faith, performing miracles, and baptizing. "When the apostles in Jerusalem heard that Samaria had accepted the word of God, they sent them Peter and John, who went down and prayed for them, that they might receive the Holy Spirit, for it had not yet fallen upon any of them; they had only been baptized in the name of the Lord Jesus. Then they laid hands on them and they received the holy Spirit" (Acts 8:14–17).

In the sacrament of confirmation, we receive the Holy Spirit, that same Spirit that enlivened the apostles at Pentecost. It brings the miracle of Pentecost to the whole world, and it is our call to spread the good news of Jesus Christ to all humanity.

Confirmation, at its heart, is about growth in Christ as we mature. In baptism, we were sealed in Christ. In confirmation, we do not have the same singular sacramental moment. Rather, a good way to understand the meaning of confirmation in our lives is to think of it as a part of our graceful growth in faith. We really didn't become the church militant in the third grade with the grace of the sacrament. Rather, we were set on the road to living our lives as adult Christians. It goes back to our vocation of greatness, the refusal to live out our lives in mediocrity. The grace of the sacrament is the "breath of God" in our lives to pull us toward the greatness that each of us can have in the Christian life well lived, by witnessing to Christ in and through our lives. It is the sacrament that recognizes Flannery O'Connor's observation that unbelief is easy, but believing makes for the hard decisions. It promises us the grace to live by those hard decisions when we opt for greatness. It is the sacrament of the vocation to which we were called in baptism. For that reason, though we receive it just once in life, it is a sacrament that means much more to us with every day that goes by.

Penance

By sophomore year in high school, we were officially wise guys. Our personal borders were expanding. Each of us had picked our own high schools from a long list of acceptable Catholic institutions throughout New York City and Westchester County. I went to Manhattan Prep every day down in the Bronx, a forty-five-minute bus trip.

Yet, the End of the Line still remained the focal point of our lives, particularly on weekends and during the summer. The route had changed little—hanging around at Baum's until enough had gathered for some basketball over at the park or the gym at Christ the King. At the park, the boys would play shirts-and-skins while the girls would sit on the wall watching and laughing. We all still went to church, of course, and belonged to the parish teen club.

The four of us were still at it—Tom, Mike, Ralph, and myself. Tom was raking up straight As at a toney Jesuit high school in the city. Mike was an athlete who might be looking to play some serious ball in college. I was surviving—just surviving—under the tutelage of the Christian Brothers at Manhattan Prep. Ralph was taking shop at a local trade school, the only one of us who would be able to use his education practically once school was over. We still had our dreams in sophomore year in high school. Just not all of them.

It was late afternoon on a spring Saturday. We had just finished up a little two-on-two basketball. The girls had already departed to get ready for "the dance." This was a weekly affair at Sacred Heart parish. The priests held a dance every Saturday night during the school year so the high-school kids would have a place to congregate under a loose but real observation. We went because the girls were there. The girls went because the boys were there. It worked because the arithmetic was that simple.

It was Mike who brought it up. "Anybody want to go to confession?"

It was an odd question. We hadn't been to confession regularly on our own since the nuns hauled us over the Saturday before eighth-grade graduation. Maybe during a school retreat; maybe just before Christmas and Easter. While we all still attended Mass, confession had become less a part of our lives. The reason was no great revolution in faith, no grand theological questioning. Simply put, our sins had become a little more embarrassing than "told-a-lie-twice." We knew we should go, but we didn't feel like going because we really didn't want to confess what we had to confess.

"Confession? Jeez, Mike, why do you wanna go and do that?" I whined. I did that a lot.

Ralph said that if he went to confession he'd be putting the jinx on any chances he had of "getting some" at the dance later. Considering that Ralph had been going to Sacred Heart dances for two years and hadn't "gotten some" yet, it wasn't the best of arguments.

"I dunno," Mike answered, ignoring Ralph's fantasies. "I feel like I should get back to some things, you know? All we do is screw around."

He was right, of course. All we did was screw around. He didn't realize that it wouldn't be very long at all before the days of screwing around at the End of the Line would be over forever. In a short five years, Mike would be screwing around in a war in a backwater country in Southeast Asia that none of us had even heard of in our sophomore year in high school. I'd be trying to use just enough revolutionary rhetoric to impress a girl without a bra named Maura at a peace rally in New Haven, Connecticut. Tom had hair down to his waist, a rather serious homegrown pot garden, and straight As at a Midwest Catholic college. Ralph would be married, have a kid, and be starting to get real annoyed at longhairs talking bad about his country. But that was five years from that afternoon.

So we decided to go. We usually did whatever Mike suggested. Not because we were his toadies. But because he usually had pretty good ideas.

Christ the King was no different late on a Saturday afternoon in 1965 than it had been when we were in sixth grade. The lines were still there for confession. People took the far end of the pews to be by themselves—either preparing for the sacrament, or taking care of their penance.

I lined up a pretty straightforward confession in an examination of conscience, though I surrounded the serious business with a few oldies but goodies about lying, slugging, and disobeying. The priest was pretty good—explaining how I shouldn't lie, I shouldn't slug, I shouldn't disobey. And he treated the more serious stuff in between about the same way. What I considered pretty serious may not have been the most serious sins he had dealt with that afternoon. He pronounced absolution—"I absolve you from thy sins in the name of the Father, the Son, and the Holy Spirit"—and sent me out with a decade of the rosary for a penance and a reminder that purity isn't a bad way to live.

The four of us stood outside of Christ the King, comparing penances. Ralph won, explaining that his collection of the "Man from O.R.G.Y." paperbacks he had put together left him with a lot of time on his hands. We made the usual guffaws and arm slugs, then decided to meet at Baum's for egg creams around 7:00 P.M. before we would walk up to Sacred Heart for the dance. As I headed home for dinner, I thought that it would be good to receive communion the next day at Mass. It had been a while. I felt pretty much all right. Pretty good about myself. A clean slate and all that. I started to hum the new Beatles tune as I broke into a trot, heading for home.

It would be about ten years until my next confession.

The good people make confession a routine part of their lives, which seems to be a contradiction. We think of confession as a desperate place for desperate moments. And it can be—a moment of graceful conversion when things have gone terribly wrong. But confession (or penance, or the sacrament of reconciliation—whatever we want to call it) can be a remarkable part of the ordinary. I suppose, as cynics have said, confession really is "cheap grace." I remember reading a book by a Protestant divine written in the 1930s in which his central thesis was that the sacrament of confession in the Catholic Church was the cause of so many Catholics being on death row (not the poverty or the meanness of their lives, of course). Since they sought cheap forgiveness of sin in confession, he argued, they built up a psychological immunity toward sin, believing they could do anything and have it forgiven by a little sacramental hocus-pocus in the confessional. Why worry about sin if it is so easy to get out of it? Of course, his explanation of Catholic belief in confession violates the most basic catechism explanation of the requirements of a good confession—true repentance and a heartfelt pledge to amend one's life. But I'll grant one thing, confession is "cheap grace," in the sense that the sacramental grace is always there and easy to obtain. Sorrow, humility, and the confidence to believe that through the sacrament our sins are forgiven and through the grace of the sacrament we can amend our lives—that's all it takes. Cheap grace. I'll take it.

In its simplest form, in confession we encounter Jesus offering us mercy and forgiveness for our sins. We are reconciled with God, the church, and our neighbors. Through the sacramental absolution given by the priest, we meet Christ in all his mercy. We need this sacrament because of the one unwavering truth of our lives: We sin, and we need to make things right. Through the sacramental encounter with Jesus, we know that our sins are forgiven. There is no need for us to revisit them in a nightly purgatory. Confession allows us to make our past the past and get on with our lives with the firm purpose of changing what had been wrong in our lives.

The theology of God's forgiveness is simple. We believe that as sin entered into the world, sickness, fear, and death came with it. But God is the God of the living. Through Christ, we are brought to a new life and to a fullness of life as mankind never experienced. Through the grace of Jesus Christ—through his death and resurrection—we are restored to the God of the living. It is God alone, of course, who forgives our sins in and through the church.

Our sins are forgiven through the mercy of God and the grace of Christ. The grace of the sacrament may be cheap, but it is real.

Holy Orders and Matrimony

The understanding of the sacrament of holy orders in the church is about as straightforward as you can get. It is a reception into a life where service and ministry to the faithful is primary. The responsibility of the priesthood is clear—celebrate the sacraments, particularly the Eucharist and the forgiveness of sins in confession, preach the word of God, bless the weddings, preside at funerals, save souls. The grace of the sacrament makes one an "icon" of Christ—an image of Christ in the world. The gift of celibacy— where one can live fully and totally in service to God and the faithful—is neither accidental nor incidental to the grace of the sacrament. Its acceptance is a sign of the calling by God to the priesthood, and the means to live out that priesthood of full service.

Holy orders—and matrimony—were traditionally called the sacraments of vocation, until somebody decided that it was wrong not to put the single life under the umbrella of vocation. And that's a point. After all, even the most married of the married (or the priestly of the priests) will live out a chunk of life single. To somehow leave a blank next to the single life when it comes to vocation is to step into that dangerous idea that the demands of the Christian life—the fundamental human vocation of living the way of Jesus—have natural gaps, or that some are called more than others. It doesn't work that way. Rich or poor, married or single, young or old, male or female—the call to the way of Jesus makes no exceptions or gradations. The call is the same no matter what the circumstances.

Priests are ordained in the sacrament of holy orders to serve the faithful. They teach, guide, and, through the sacraments, sanctify. Matrimony is the sacrament that binds together for a lifetime a man and a woman. The grace of the sacrament helps them keep that bond, grow in holiness together, and bring new life into the world. Unlike the other sacraments, the ministers of matrimony are the man and the woman themselves freely exchanging their vows and consenting to be married. The priest is there to receive and honor their consent and to give the blessing of the church.

We live in a culture that downplays matrimony and the sacred nature of both the sacrament and that bond. We can easily look around us and see with our own eyes the results of matrimony not understood sacramentally. But we still want to argue that the flaw is in marriage itself, rather than the failed human condition. We have this collective human desire to rationalize our screwups, to point the finger at the good and decide that the very existence of the good is the cause of the problem—things wouldn't be bad if we didn't have the good making us feel guilty. But the argument is not really with matrimony. The argument is what we do with it.

There is a whole wealth of sacramental theology and imagery within the Catholic understanding of matrimony. Matrimony is a reflection of the union of Christ with his church. As the union of Christ with the church makes the church holy, so too the marital union sanctifies both spouses. The very mystery of Christ in his death and resurrection—giving himself completely for the sanctification of the church—reflects the mystery of the unity of matrimony, a total giving of oneself for the other. The unselfish love of Christ for his church reflects the unselfish love of the marital bond.

And all that is true, a rich theology of marriage that is the foundation of so much that the church teaches concerning the marital bond. As it reflects Christ and his church, marriage lives out that sacramental mystery. It is centered in the same eternal realities of that divine relationship: constancy, fidelity, sanctification, permanency, and a deep and rich openness to life. All that the church holds sacred in marriage reflects what is held foundational to Catholic belief: Christ lives intimately today in his church that brings his good news and grace of salvation to each new generation.

Matrimony is a sacrament instituted by Christ, its foundation traced to his very first public miracle. The story is a favorite, a picture worth considering. Jesus was in Cana in Galilee with his disciples attending a wedding. We can't help but think of the laughter, the music, the dancing, the celebration that was as much a part of a wedding in Galilee two thousand years ago as it is today. It is what we forget to think of when we meditate on the living Jesus— a man among friends, among his people, enjoying the witness of two lives joined together, and what it means for them, their families, their community, and their world. Marriage is saying an all-embracing yes to the future of mankind, and Jesus was there to celebrate it.

The mother of Jesus, who was also at the wedding, notices something. The wine has run out. This is not just a case of the party coming to an abrupt end. It is an embarrassment, a source of shame for both the parents and the newlyweds. She decides to do something about it. She approaches the table where her son sits with his friends. "They have no wine," (John 2:3) she says to him, no doubt quietly, so as not to make too much of it. The response of Jesus is interesting. He tells her, simply, "Woman, how does your concern affect me? My hour has not yet come" (John 2:4). That's an answer that could lead to an hour's conversation. What did Jesus mean, exactly? By his saying that his hour had "not yet come," we can understand that he is essentially telling her that it was not yet the time for him to make known that he was the Messiah. His public ministry—his announcement to all Israel—was to be at some point soon, but not yet. It is the first part of the answer that seems almost callous, a bit dismissive if you will—"So they ran out of wine! You seem upset, but it's not any of my business." Of course, the answer was in his response—a response understood completely by his mother. She knows that he will not let this be, even though it is a simple thing, really. A moment of embarrassment at a wedding, like Uncle Fred falling into the cake. "No wine left, folks. Sorry about that, but the party's over. Thanks for the presents!" Yet, it is at that moment when Jesus will begin the public life that changes everything, done in a moment of time at a wedding in a little town to save a newlywed couple from beginning their lives together with the smallest of shadows. Marriage will be forever graced because of it.

His mother understands. She tells the servers to do whatever he tells them. There are large stone water jars standing empty nearby. Jesus tells the servers to fill them to the brim with water—each holding fifteen to twenty-five gallons—and bring them to the headwaiter. They do so. The headwaiter tastes them, then wonders what exactly is going on. This violates the normal custom. So he asks the groom: "Everyone serves good wine first, and then when people have drunk freely, an inferior one; but you have kept the good wine until now" (John 2:10). We are not told the groom's response, but it must have been something like, "Huh?" John concludes the story: "Jesus did this as the beginning of his signs in Cana in Galilee and so revealed his glory, and his disciples began to believe in him" (John 2:11).

The grace of the sacrament of matrimony is to help us down the road. The sacraments are meant for this life—to establish and nurture that "connectedness" with God that can take us through anything. The grace of the sacrament of matrimony is the special grace of mutual friendship leading a couple together to holiness, to sanctification. Because that is what marriage is, of course: our most intimate human friendship. "For friendship, in its most authentic form, is an unselfish and mutual love persons have for each other, as each knows he or she is loved by the other. In sincere friendship the tie of love is enduring, for it is not based on the hope of gratification from personal traits that can fade with time, but on the free and firm commitment of each to pursue the good of the other, for the other's sake. To speak of married friendship is to recognize the fundamental equality of the husband and wife, and, therefore, the possibility of intimate sharing of life not only on the physical level but also on the level of mind and spirit" (*The Teaching of Christ*, 446).

The point is reached with every parent of a child. That intense and complete love of a child never ends. But there comes a recognition that a time of parting has come, just as we parted from our own parents. The boy becomes the man, the daughter becomes the woman. The love will never change, but we separate as they build their own lives and their own families. And it is perhaps at that point that we turn to the spouse, smile, and know we are sharing the same pain. We will go along in love together, waiting for the next chapter in the pilgrimage together. A spouse is the most intimate friend a human being can ever have in this life.

My wife was heading out of town for a few days. One of those rare times in our lives when we wouldn't be together at least for a few hours in a day. She left a note for me on the table for when I came home. "Bob," it read, "Dishes in the dishwasher are clean. Underwear in dryer. Love ya!" That's marriage.

Up until she was nearly in high school, my daughter thought that I had met her mother when I was coming home from church choir practice. "I was walking down the street when this girl pulls up in a red sports car. She slows down alongside me, whistles, and says, 'Hey, cutie! Need a ride?'" I had made up that story as a way to tease her mother. My daughter believed it. What was there not to believe?

Actually, I met my future wife on a blind date arranged by a married friend who didn't like her husband hanging out with a bachelor. We dated for nearly two years, then married on a July evening. The first full day of our marriage we had made it to Pennsylvania from Indiana. Our destination was a honeymoon on Cape Cod. We were just kids then, on the sunny side of twenty-five. I was still routinely asked for identification when I tried to buy a six-pack. I shaved every day, but didn't have to. And there I was, driving down the road in my wife's red sports car, married less than twenty-four hours.

We were getting low on gas, and I told her that I would take the next exit and stop at the first station. She said, "Make sure they check the oil and the water level." That's something you had to do in those days. Cars would overheat if you looked at them the wrong way, particularly on a day so bright that you couldn't imagine that rain ever existed. So we pulled into a gas station, one of those places just outside a little town that everybody hoped to escape then spent the rest of their lives trying to recapture somewhere else. A kid sauntered out, walking like a middle-aged guy though he couldn't have been more than sixteen. He strolled right in front of the car as we pulled in, and I nearly ran him over. He looked up as if we would have done him a favor. She said, "I don't think he's the brightest bulb in the chandelier."

The kid leaned in as I rolled down the window. "Hep yinz?" he asked.

I couldn't have translated that on a bet, but some conversations are always the same. "Filler up," I responded, like a man of the world, and glanced over to see if my bride noticed.

"Water and oil," she whispered to me, so I said to him, "And check the oil and the water!" like I was used to giving orders.

"Yassir," he said, as I popped the hood.

After pumping the gas he proceeded to take about ten minutes to find exactly where to check the oil and how to check the oil. He did the procedure three or four times, finally walking over to the boss who sat by the front door wondering exactly what he was going to do with that kid. He came back, leaned in, and said the oil was fine and gave us the price for the gas. The hood was still wide open.

"The water?" she asked.

He looked past me at her for a second or two, blinked, then said, "Wadder, I yal check it."

He walked in front of the car, looked in, spotted the water valve, and gave it a twist like he expected it to fight back. The valve exploded off the radiator, hot as it was from running straight through Ohio to Pennsylvania on a summer day. Water and coolant erupted out like a geyser. Thank God the kid jumped back far enough to avoid being scalded. The boss stood straight up, and the kid just marveled that one small radiator could hold so much fluid that now roiled and boiled along the pavement, into the street, and threatened to overflow a sewer.

Finally, when Vesuvius had calmed to a simmer, the kid nodded a couple of times to himself, walked over to my side of the car, leaned on the window once again, and looked me straight in the eye.

"It's low," he said.

"What?" I asked, still trying to understand exactly what had happened.

"Wadder's low," he said.

My bride started to laugh; I looked over at her and started to laugh—until we were both virtually in tears from laughing.

From that day on for a few decades now, no eruption can be big enough that one of us won't finally say, "Wadder's low." Then we'll both laugh and get on with it. That's marriage.

Anointing of the Sick

My mother was comfortable with death. We considered it part of her Irish heritage. Death was something you did, and if you did it well, it provided an interesting story for those left behind, which is simply good form.

"Your Great Uncle Harry was a marvelous man," she would explain, "and we all felt just terrible when he died."

"How did he die?" I asked, my curiosity betraying my Irish inheritance as well.

In a lowered voice, as if Death might overhear her, she said, "It was all of a sudden." That was her favorite kind of death. Somebody just going along minding his own business and the end comes in a blink of an eye—that made the best tale.

I was sitting at home at about age eleven, bored as only an eleven-year-old could be on an early August afternoon. Summer had stretched on long enough that all the luster was gone, yet there was enough of it left that there was no sense of urgency to accomplish great things before the return of school. My mother walked in the door with a package.

"You might find this interesting. I just bought it," she said. She opened the bag and inside was a wooden box in the shape of an oversized crucifix. I wondered what was the catch. We had any number of crucifixes here and there around the house, which was another reason why faith was like breathing out and breathing in.

"It's not a crucifix itself. Watch this." She slid off the top and another crucifix was inside. That crucifix could be stuck at the top of the felt-lined box so that it stood straight up. There were also two wax candles inside that could be put in the "arms" of the original crucifix box.

"Now do you see," she said. I didn't see.

"This is a deathbed crucifix. You can set it out on the nightstand and light the candles for when the priest comes to give extreme unction." She was very proud of this. I was glad that I didn't feel sick. We never got to use her deathbed-in-a-box, but it was good to know that we were prepared.

We call the sacrament the anointing of the sick, and the emphasis, though not the meaning of the sacrament, is different today. It was generally called extreme unction when we were young, and was associated with the final moments. The priest was called when death's door had already swung wide open. But our God is a God of the living. The grace of the sacrament is not about death, but healing and preparation for the journey, wherever it might take us. The Scripture on it reflects that meaning. As old as the church itself, we read in the Epistle of St. James: "Is anyone among you suffering? He should pray. Is anyone in good spirits? He should sing praise. Is anyone among you sick? He should summon the presbyters of the church, and they should pray over him and anoint [him] with oil in the name of the Lord, and the prayer of faith will save the sick person, and the Lord will raise him up. If he has committed any sins, he will be forgiven" (James 5:13–15).

So, at the very infancy of the church, it was understood that God was the God of the living. Through the grace of the sacrament of anointing of the sick, we pray for healing: physical healing if that is part of the divine plan, but certainly spiritual healing. In the end, it is the forgiveness of sins—sins we all have—that is our hope for eternal life: "The prayer of faith will save the sick person, and the Lord will raise him up" (James 5:15). It is reclamation and restoration of a soul.

Rather than the lonely deathbed scene we enjoyed in the pictures and the television shows of our ill-spent youth, the church envisions that wherever possible the rite of anointing of the sick is done during the context of a Mass. The sacrament is meant for the seriously sick, those in danger of death, and the frail elderly, with the special grace of the sacrament meant to give healing, comfort, and strength. Often, the sacrament is accompanied by confession for the forgiveness of sins.

Anointing of the sick offers not only the possibility of healing, and the promise of healing of the spirit, but also an understanding of sickness, aging, and death in the life of the Christian. As St. Paul explained to the infant church: "We are not discouraged; rather, although our outer self is wasting away, our inner self is being renewed day by day. For this momentary light affliction is producing for us an eternal weight of glory beyond all comparison, as we look not to what is seen but to what is unseen; for what is seen is transitory, but what is unseen is eternal" (2 Corinthians 4:16–18).

The sacrament of anointing of the sick is closely connected with the reception of the Eucharist. The Eucharist received by the dying is called viaticum, "food for the journey," which is the kind of eucharistic poetry that just makes you want to weep.

*   *   *

And all this being so, it seemed to me that it was impossible that every kind of thing should be well, as our Lord revealed at this time. And to this I had no other answer as a revelation from our Lord except this: What is impossible to you is not impossible to me. I shall preserve my word in everything, and I shall make everything well. And in this I was taught by the grace of God that I ought to keep myself steadfastly in faith, as I had understood before, and that at the same time I should stand firm and believe firmly that every kind of thing will be well, as our Lord revealed at the time. For this is the great deed which our Lord will do, and in this deed he will preserve his word in everything. And he will make well all which is not well.

Julian of Norwich (1342–c. 1423)

CHAPTER 11

A Song for the Asking

What is the Mass?
The Mass is the unbloody sacrifice
of the body and blood of Christ.

How should we assist at Mass?
We should assist at Mass with great interior
recollection and piety and with every outward
sign of respect and devotion.

You want to know scary? I'll tell you scary.

Outside, it's a rainy Thursday morning. Inside, I am standing in front of about one hundred Catholic high-school kids in an auditorium. I am about to give a speech to them. I realize that there is nothing I will say that will entertain these kids. That's scary.

But I'm a game old rooster so I launched into my talk on "What Is News" to kids allegedly interested in writing. I went for a few cheap laughs early and got nowhere. Nothing ugly happened—nobody made funny noises with their armpits to set them giggling, as I would have done when I was in high school. No one-liners at my expense, as I would have done when I was in high school. They just stared back at me like I was a wall drying a fresh coat of paint—as I did most of the time when I was in high school. I dribbled on and on about "news" and the task of writing the news. I strung together sentences with a lot of "ands," talked faster, the old New York accent got heavier and heavier. All sure signs that I was desperate. My ringing conclusion: "And an important part of what we are looking for in the news is truth. And anyone who wants to write news better have a commitment to truth." The end. Polite applause. No questions. Exit stage left.

The next speaker was kind enough to pick up on my last sentence, noting the importance of truth. He spoke about truth in different forms of writing—the truth of fiction or poetry, for example, as one would compare it to the truth of news reporting. It all sounded very interesting, though he wasn't getting anywhere with the crowd either. But I had to admire him. You can always tell a Catholic get-together. Somehow truth always ends up central to the discussion. We've been like that since Pilate shrugged and asked Jesus, "What is truth?" (John 18:38). As he went on, I started to survey my surroundings. It was a classic Catholic school multi-purpose arena—gym, stage for the school play, lunchroom facilities. It had seen untold performances of *Billy Budd*, more cheese toasties than could be calculated, and St. Peter wiping the floor with St. John the Baptist, in a basketball game of course.

And then there were the dances. It looked like a gym that would hold the high-school dances. There was the girls' room tucked over to the side, with enough room for at least forty of them to pile in and review which boy asked which girl—and which boy didn't ask which girl—to slow dance. There were the two doors at the entrance of the gym that swung open where a girl on each side would sit by a card table. They would check your ticket and high-school ID to make certain you were from one of the invited Catholic boys' schools. By 9:30 P.M. you would be back outside with a few of your buddies sitting on the handrails shooting the breeze about nothing and everything. Your hand would be stamped so that you could get back in. A few of the braver guys would take a bender around the corner of the school and try to sneak a smoke before a nun caught them.

Jack Frateli was in our class at Manhattan Prep. He joined our gang early, even though he wasn't from the End of the Line and was neither a schnook nor a loser. He was an almost-basketball-star: good enough to be about the best player in our junior class, but not good enough that it would make a difference against any other team. Frateli was also a good student and a self-proclaimed "ladies' man." There was going to be a Saturday night dance at Our Lady of Sorrows Academy, a girls' school up in Westchester. It was their first dance of the year, and those were always the best. Summer romances were done and everybody was looking to meet someone they'd never met before. New school year, fresh beginnings. A few of the girls from the End of the Line went to Our Lady of Sorrows, and Frateli asked me if I could hook him up with someone if he went. I said I could, thinking immediately of Madeline Blisky, a good friend of mine because she was so stunningly beautiful that I talked to her like a real person, not a girl, since there wasn't a chance that it would go any further. All the pressure was off. I described her to Frateli and he was impressed. We decided that he would come up to the End of the Line from the City on Saturday. We'd do a little hoops, maybe a little football. Then we'd go to the dance and he would bunk at my place after, heading home Sunday afternoon.

"I'll help you out," Frateli said. "I know a girl who goes to Our Lady of Sorrows. Nice kid. She's short like you. You guys will get along. I'll check if she's going to the dance and introduce you."

"What's her name?" I asked.

"Uhh, we call her 'Rat,'" Frateli said slowly, then added, "but don't take that the wrong way."

"Why would I?" I said and spent the rest of the week imagining what a girl nicknamed "Rat" might be like. I didn't come up with a lot of positives.

The Old Man drove Jack, a few other guys, and myself to the dance that night. He'd pick us up at 11:00 P.M. sharp when the dance was over. Our Lady of Sorrows was buried off the beaten path up county. Like most Catholic girls' schools, it was modeled after the motherhouse of the religious order running the joint— hidden from prying eyes. We hung around out front of the building for a half hour or so. This allowed time to eyeball the girls going in, and slug the shoulders of various guys that you knew as they showed up.

"There's Madeline," I said, as she walked by with a few friends. She was her normal stunning.

"Hi, Bobby," she said and flashed me a smile to die for, though she had an eye on Jack at the same time. I had told her in advance that I was going to hook them up. Jack was impressed with her and, after a few more minutes, announced that we should head in. We paid fifty cents and got our hands stamped. It said on the back of our wrists in red ink: "BMPFU." I stared at it, wondering what it meant. Jack interrupted my meditation: "Hey, there she is. Introduce us." Madeline was over by the corner of the stage with a few other girls I didn't know. The records were already started—45s spun by a couple of volunteer girls with the player set up in the center of the stage— and the nuns were already beginning to patrol the dance floor. The baskets on each side of the gym had been raised and lunch tables set up with Cokes and punch available in Styrofoam cups for ten cents each. We walked over to Madeline's group. Madeline hung around with her own kind. They were all tall and gorgeous. Jack, right away, got the look from a couple of the girls. I was ignored like I was someone's little brother. For the five thousandth time in high school I asked God why he couldn't make me just four crummy inches taller.

Jack asked if Madeline would like some punch or something. She said yes, gave me a quick good-bye, and headed off with him. I stood there for a minute with her friends, who were nice enough not to say anything rude. Then I slowly backed away, announcing that I could use a little punch myself.

About forty-five minutes later, Jack walked up to me and asked if I wanted to meet Rat. "Sure," I answered, which was a lie. I was scared to meet any new girl. Particularly one named Rat.

We walked up to the usual gaggle of five girls standing around chattering away. Jack tapped the shoulder of the shortest girl in the group. She had on a tan skirt with a matching vest over a white blouse, brown knee-high socks, and penny loafers—sharp for the fall of 1965. She turned around and gave Jack a big hello. She was pretty.

"This is the guy I mentioned," Jack said. "Sally Houlihan, meet Bobby Lockwood."

She smiled, stuck out her hand, and I shook it. I asked her if she wanted some punch. She said yes and we walked over to the table.

"Rat" turned out to be very nice. And we did hit it off. We'd end up going to our respective senior proms together and stay good friends throughout college, writing letters back and forth pretty regularly, which was amazing for those crazy times. Jack and Madeline were less successful. They didn't even make it together to the end of the dance. Madeline understood that he had only one thing in mind. So did Jack. Not the stuff of lasting relationships.

The rest of the dance went the way most went back then. A couple of guys got busted for sneaking cigarettes. A few girls had to go to the ladies room and lower their hemlines by order of the nuns. One girl got sick. And by 9:30 P.M. at least fifteen guys were hanging around outside shooting the bull. But I wasn't with them. I was inside with Rat. We were slow dancing to Skeeter Davis singing about the end of the world when I thought to ask her: "Hey, what do those letters stand for on the rubber stamp?"

She looked at her hand, then said: "Blessed Mother Pray for Us."

Of course.

When Jack and I got in the car that night after the dance, the Old Man asked what Mass we wanted to get up for in the morning. "I go to the 8:00 A.M. The 9:00 A.M. is the kids' Mass from the school. Then there's a 10:30." "Let's shoot for 9:00 A.M., Mr. Lockwood," Jack answered. And I agreed. After leaving grammar school I had begun to enjoy watching the little kids at the 9:00 A.M. Mass, even though it meant a cancer sermon from Msgr. Betowski. The next morning, the Old Man rousted us just before he left. As we were walking over to church I told Jack that the Old Man had spotted me a buck and we could get a couple of egg creams and hard rolls at Baum's after Mass.

"Why wait?" Jack asked. "Let's go now."

"We won't have enough time before Mass starts," I said.

Frateli looked at me like I just put something disgusting in my mouth. "You're kidding me, right? We're not going to Mass. Let's wait it out over at Baum's. Somebody will be able to tell us what the Gospel and sermon were after Mass."

He wasn't kidding. Frateli was talking about cutting Mass, something I had never done purposefully—Sunday or Holy Day. I was no saint, by any stretch, but Mass was something you just did—like breathing out and breathing in. I couldn't imagine not doing it. But on the other hand, I didn't want to look like some kind of eight ball to Frateli. It was a moral dilemma. I wasn't good at moral dilemmas. As we got closer to Christ the King, Frateli said, "Are you going or not? If you're going, let me have your Old Man's buck so I can get something to eat. You can tell me about the Gospel and the sermon." He wasn't really saying I couldn't go, or that he'd think less—or more—of me if I went. He was simply a neutral tempter and that made it worse. He was leaving it up to me. I've always hated it when my moral failings cannot be laid on outside sources. Five minutes later we were at Baum's shooting the bull and having breakfast.

It was no problem. Nobody at home asked about the Gospel or the sermon, though I had made elaborate preparations just in case. I wasn't run over by a bus and doomed for all eternity. But I felt wrong all week. My conscience itched like a bug bite until the next Sunday found me at the 8:00 A.M. Mass with the Old Man, pretty well convinced I'd never make that mistake again. And it was weeks before I purposely skipped Mass again. By freshman year in college it had vanished from my life.

First confession, then Mass, then nothing. The nuns were right after all.

We often see the faith, if we look at it at all, by the roles we have in our lives. Men in particular succumb to this. The faith, such as it is, might be seen as a handy guide to be a better husband, a better father, a better member of the community. Of course, there is nothing wrong with the faith lived in these roles. The faith is meant to be integral to every part of us. But often we root the faith in those roles, rather than grounding those parts of our lives in the faith. We rarely see the faith nakedly for ourselves, for who we really are and in the deepest meaning of our lives.

We see that in our approach to the Mass itself. Many who regularly practice the faith—particularly as they practice it for support in their "roles"—never really enter into the Mass. As kids, the Mass was often something we just did—it was a part of our lives like the air we breathed. We didn't really see what it meant, understand it, feel it. Hell, we were just kids. That was why, in our salad days, we could dismiss it by saying that we found God better in nature and found sunrise a better prayer, which was really a lot of squash as we soon discovered that we didn't pay much attention to God in nature and we were never up—unless we never went to bed—in time for the sunrise. Once the Mass was out of our lives, the faith went by the wayside, no matter how many walks we took in the woods. Without the Mass and the Eucharist, the intensity of Christ's presence in our lives dimmed.

The nuns told us, "Act as if you have faith and faith you will have." But faith has to be understood to be believed. When it seemed an act of rituals barely understood, lost in words we didn't understand, we left it all behind. Without understanding our beliefs as adults, we brushed it off as meaningless pious ritual imposed on us. Yet, at the same time, the nuns were right. Once we ceased to practice the faith, we had no faith, or we let a thousand other bits of nonsense take the place of faith. That's how we ended up worshipping Jerry Garcia or a day at the track. If we don't practice the faith, we will not have it; if we don't lead a life of faith, we can't be faithful. Belief without the Mass is not likely despite the puffery of our youthful rhetoric about nature and sunrises. In fact, it is pretty much impossible. Too often, the real choice is between the Mass or nothing at all, and the questions that haunt us at the shank of the evening.

The Joy of My Youth

Introibo ad altare Dei. / Ad Deum qui laetificat juventutum meam.
I will go to the altar of God. / To God who gives joy to my youth.

The Eucharist—from the Greek, meaning "thanksgiving"—is at the center of Catholic life, as Christ himself. It is the Mass that defines who we are and what we believe. Our eucharistic faith is simple: We believe that the Mass is the sacrifice of Jesus on the cross made present, "its memory preserved to the end of the world" (so said the Council of Trent). We believe that in the Eucharist, Christ himself is real and present. That about sums it all up. To accept what Scripture teaches on these basic truths is, so to speak, nonnegotiable. A million things might attract people to the Catholic faith: the profound beauty of the liturgy, the goodness of its saints, the warmth of its imagery, the strength of its history. But all that, while certainly rich and important, pales in the light of the central paschal mystery. It is the eucharistic belief in the absolute and real presence of Christ in the church that is the foundation of our faith.

The scripture of the Last Supper describes it: the establishment of the sacrament of holy orders to make the miracle of the Mass real, and that key moment in the New Testament where the Eucharist became our life:

> While they were eating, Jesus took bread, said the blessing, broke it, and giving it to his disciples said, "Take and eat; this is my body." Then he took a cup, gave thanks, and gave it to them, saying, "Drink from it, all of you, for this is my blood of the covenant, which will be shed on behalf of many for the forgiveness of sins." (Matthew 26:26–28)

The Eucharist instituted by Christ as the Last Supper was fore-shadowed earlier when he told the crowds: "I am the bread of life, whoever comes to me will never hunger. . . . Amen, amen, I say to you, whoever believes has eternal life. I am the bread of life. Your ancestors ate the manna in the desert, but they died; this is the bread that comes down from heaven so that one may eat it and not die" (John 6:35, 47–51). John tells us that this was a "hard saying," even among his disciples. "As a result of this, many [of] his disciples returned to their former way of life and no longer accompanied him" (John 6:66). But Jesus didn't run after them saying that he didn't mean it. Or that they shouldn't take him too literally. He just turned to the Twelve and asked, "Do you also want to leave?" (John 6:67). And it was Peter who answered for them: "Master, to whom shall we go? You have the words of eternal life. We have come to believe and are convinced that you are the Holy One of God" (John 6:68–69).

So here we are, returning to our very first question. Do we believe there is a God? If we believe, do we believe that he would reveal himself in time and history? Do we believe that in Jesus Christ we have that revelation of God? Do we believe that Christ, made present in time and history, lives truly real and truly present in our own lives? And if so, then we must believe what he said: "I am the bread of life . . . whoever eats this bread will live forever" (John 6:48, 58). At some point, there is no backing away any longer. No escaping the faith taught by Jesus in Scripture. No excuses of lousy explanations passed along in our childhood, or looking at the faith only through the understanding of our childhood. At some point we have to grasp the call of faith as adults, seek it out, and understand it to the best of our ability. The time comes when we have to grow up, when we have to accept or reject the heart of the Catholic faith: that Christ has died, Christ is risen, and Christ will come again; that Jesus is truly present in the Eucharist; that through him our sins are forgiven; and through the bread of life we will have eternal life. For our God is the God of the living: "I am the resurrection and the life; whoever believes in me, even if he dies, will live, and everyone who lives and believes in me will never die" (John 11:25–26). And then we make it real, living and present.

> "What God's son has told me, take for truth I do;
> Truth himself speaks truly or there's nothing true."
> *Thomas Aquinas, translated by Gerard Manley Hopkins,*
> *cited in the* Catechism of the Catholic Church

The Mass in Time

The earliest Christians did not call it "the Mass." They had many names for it, often depending on where they came from. In Rome it was often called simply "the sacrament"; the Greeks referred to the "mysteries." The "Lord's Supper," "giving thanks," and "the presence" were other names for the eucharistic liturgy of the earliest Christians. Our term comes from Old English and was drawn from the dismissal at the end of the Mass in the Latin rite: *Ite missa est*—"Go, it is ended." In Scripture, we see the earliest references to the Mass after the Last Supper in Paul's letter to the Corinthians:

Therefore, my beloved, avoid idolatry. I am speaking as to sensible people; judge for yourselves what I am saying. The cup of blessing that we bless, is it not a participation in the blood of Christ? The bread that we break, is it not a participation in the body of Christ? Because the loaf of bread is one, we, though many, are one body, for we all partake of the one loaf. You cannot drink the cup of the Lord and also the cup of demons. You cannot partake of the table of the Lord and of the table of demons. For I received from the Lord what I also handed on to you, that the Lord Jesus, on the night he was handed over, took bread, and, after he had given thanks, broke it and said, "This is my body that is for you. Do this in remembrance of me." In the same way also the cup, after supper, saying, "This cup is the new covenant in my blood. Do this, as often as you drink it, in remembrance of me." For as often as you eat this bread and drink the cup, you proclaim the death of the Lord until he comes. (1 Corinthians 10:14–17, 21; 11:23–26)

In the Acts of the Apostles, Luke's virtual eyewitness account of the earliest history of the church, the centrality of the Eucharist is summed up in the description of the first generation of converts to Christ: "They devoted themselves to the teaching of the apostles and to the communal life, to the breaking of the bread and to the prayers. Awe came upon everyone, and many wonders and signs were done through the apostles. All who believed were together and had all things in common; they would sell their property and possessions and divide them among all according to each one's need. Every day they devoted themselves to meeting together in the temple area and to breaking bread in their homes. They ate their meals with exultation and sincerity of heart, praising God and enjoying favor with all the people. And every day the Lord added to their number those who were being saved" (Acts 2:42–47).

There are numerous references to the most sacred act of the early Christian community from both Christian and pagan sources. St. Ignatius of Antioch, who died for his faith in the year A.D. 107—just one lifetime after the death and resurrection of Christ— refers to the bishop of the churches and reminds Christians, "See that you follow the bishop, even as Christ follows the Father. . . . Let that be deemed a proper Eucharist which is administered by the bishop or by one to whom he has entrusted it." The first complete description of how the Eucharist was conducted is in St. Justin Martyr's account in the First Apology of 150 A.D.:

> On the day which is called after the sun, all who are in the towns and in the country gather together for a communal celebration. And then the memoirs of the Apostles or the writings of the Prophets are read, as long as time permits. After the reader has finished his task, the one presiding gives an address, urgently admonishing his hearers to practice these beautiful teachings in their lives. Then together all stand and recite prayers . . . the bread and wine mixed with water are brought, and the president offers up

prayers and thanksgivings, as much as in him lies. The people chime in with an Amen. (And this food itself is known amongst us as the Eucharist and no one may take part in it unless he believes that what we teach is true, has received baptism for the forgiveness of sins and new birth, and lives in keeping with what Christ taught.) Then takes place the distribution, to all attending, of the things over which the thanksgiving had been spoken, and the deacons bring a portion to the absent. Besides, those who are well to do give whatever they will. Which is gathered and deposited with the one presiding, who therewith helps widows and orphans.

Justin Martyr was explaining the Mass in a document for the Roman emperor Antoninus Pius. The Christian community believed in keeping silent concerning the actions of the Mass, a silence born of awe and reverence. As a result, accusations and gossip spread about what happened behind closed doors in the Christian community. Justin was breaking the silence to explain that the Christians were not harmful or subversive. (He was wrong, of course. They were fundamentally subversive.) A philosopher and wandering apologist for the faith, Justin was beheaded by the Romans around 165 A.D. for his persistent Christian beliefs.

In Justin's description of the Mass—a combination of two Masses celebrated at that time in Rome, which he recounted for the Emperor—we find a concise outline of the Mass as celebrated today.

The Mass is the summation of the divine blessings in our own day, the paschal mystery in the age of the church. The Mass is Christ glorified from the time of the church of the apostles to our own day. The Mass is the memorial of Christ's sacrificial death. In the Mass "we offer to the Father what he has given us: the gifts of his creation, bread and wine which, by the power of the Holy Spirit and by the words of Christ, have become the Body and Blood of Christ. Christ is thus really and truly made present" (*Catechism of the Catholic Church*, 1357). The Mass, the Eucharist, is thanksgiving and praise to God the Father, the memorial sacrifice of Christ, and the presence of Christ through the power of the Holy Spirit. "Where two or three are gathered together in my name, there am I in the midst of them" (Matthew 18:20). Beats the hell out of a walk in the park.

The Mass

The Mass is not a blessed ritual, a collection of ancient and beautiful readings and prayers, or a gathering of the people of God to acknowledge a shared faith together. It is these things, of course, but collectively much more—infinitely more. From the simplest morning weekday Mass in a little church just outside Fort Wayne to a shack in Indonesia, the Mass is the work of God.

Introductory Rites

Entrance. We assemble for Mass as the people of God, united in two thousand years of faithful belief and sacred tradition, "with great interior recollection and piety," usually kneeling in personal prayer before we begin. The Mass—the Sunday Mass—begins with an entrance procession with the priest, altar servers, and the reader for the Liturgy of the Word holding aloft the Sacramentary, the formal book of prayers and ritual used by the priest in offering the Mass. A separate book, called a Lectionary, includes the readings from Scripture for the Mass. This procession is greeted with a hymn in spirit with the liturgical season or the theme of the readings of that Sunday's Mass. At the altar, when the opening hymn is concluded, the priest leads the congregation in invoking the Trinity with the sign of the cross and a prayer: "The grace of Our Lord Jesus Christ and the love of God and the fellowship of the Holy Spirit be with you all."

Confiteor. We then acknowledge the one cold, hard fact of our lives—that we are sinners. In the Mass, we are in the sacramental presence of Christ. To properly prepare for Mass, we have to recall our sins and seek pardon. This is not sacramental confession, but the proper realization of what we are and the forgiveness we seek. We recite together with the priest the Confiteor, with its humbling admission: "I confess to almighty God, and to you, my brothers and sisters, that I have sinned through my own fault . . . " For all of us, the priest responds: "May almighty God have mercy on us, forgive us our sins, and bring us to everlasting life."

We follow with the Kyrie eleison. A prayer in praise of the mercy of God, it is a response that dates from at least the seventh century. The threefold prayer—"Lord have mercy, Christ have mercy, Lord have mercy"—is really more of a response of praise than of supplication. Perhaps a better understanding of the words *Kyrie eleison* is "Lord, you are ever merciful."

Gloria. Except during the penitential seasons of Lent and Advent, we move from acknowledgment of our sins to a song of praise and glory to God. We use the words of the angels after greeting the shepherds in the fields with the astounding news of the Incarnation: "Glory to God in the highest, and peace to his people on earth." This prayer, which dates from the Christmas Day Mass of the popes in the sixth century, is a song of glory to the greatness of God and the "Lord Jesus Christ, Son of the Father."

Opening Prayer. With this song of praise, the priest concludes the introductory rites with an opening prayer that establishes in a prayer of petition the theme of the Scripture readings we are about to hear. Our prayer is that our minds and hearts will be open to the Scriptures—the word of God—that will be proclaimed in the Mass.

The Liturgy of the Word

Readings. After acknowledging our sins and asking forgiveness and singing a song of praise to God, we are ready to hear Scripture—"the memoirs of the Apostles or the writings of the Prophets" as Justin Martyr described it in the first century after Christ. In daily Mass during the week, there are two readings from Scripture. At Sunday Mass, the first reading is from the Old Testament. The second reading is from the Psalms, the "prayer book of the church," traditionally attributed to David. The third reading is from the Acts of the Apostles, the Epistles, or Revelations. There is always a theme that links these readings and will find its definitive statement in one of the four Gospels, the stories of the life and teachings of Christ.

The Gospel. The word *alleluia* is from the Hebrew, meaning "God be praised." Before the Gospel—where the words and life of Christ will instruct us—we pause with an "alleluia" verse to give praise and thanksgiving to God. The Gospel is a selected reading from the evangelists. It is read by the priest (or deacon) and is related to the aspect of the life of Christ celebrated in the liturgical season. It presents his teachings and words of life to us. When the priest announces the reading, we make the sign of the cross on our foreheads, lips, and heart. This means that we will know the teachings of the gospel, we will evangelize or "speak" the teachings of the gospel, and we will make them a living part of us in our hearts. It is our assent in faith to the gospel of Jesus. Out of respect, awe, and gratitude, we stand to listen to the gospel of Jesus Christ.

Homily. The priest, for whom the homily is always reserved, will then connect these readings together and apply the teachings to our lives. As Justin Martyr explained, "The one presiding gives an address, urgently admonishing his hearers to practice these beautiful teachings in their lives." The homily is as old as the Mass itself, the period of instruction and inspiration in the word of God before we express and acknowledge together the great summary of our faith.

Creed. Having meditated on the word of God in the homily, we make a profession of faith. The creed—a statement of our basic beliefs shared uniformly throughout Christendom and throughout the centuries—comes to us from two councils of the church in the fourth century. The faith we affirm is: belief in God who created all things, including us; belief in the incarnation of the one Lord, Jesus

Christ, who "for our salvation . . . came down from heaven"; belief
in his passion, death, resurrection as real events in real history and
real time, and his return in glory; belief in the Trinity, and the Holy
Spirit as the inspiration of the Scripture read at Mass; belief in the
church of Christ and its authority to speak for Christ—"one holy
catholic and apostolic"—and the grace of the sacraments; and
belief in life eternal, that our God is the God of the living:

> We believe in one God, the Father, the Almighty,
> maker of heaven and earth, of all that is seen and
> unseen.
>
> We believe in one Lord, Jesus Christ, the only
> Son of God, eternally begotten of the Father,
> God from God, Light from Light, true God
> from true God, begotten, not made, one in Being
> with the Father. Through him all things were
> made. For us men and for our salvation he came
> down from heaven: by the power of the Holy
> Spirit he was born of the Virgin Mary, and
> became man.
>
> For our sake he was crucified under Pontius
> Pilate; he suffered, died, and was buried. On the
> third day he rose again in fulfillment of the
> Scriptures; he ascended into heaven and is seated
> at the right hand of the Father. He will come
> again in glory to judge the living and the dead,
> and his kingdom will have no end.
>
> We believe in the Holy Spirit, the Lord, the
> giver of life, who proceeds from the Father and

the Son. With the Father and the Son he is wor-
shipped and glorified. He has spoken through
the Prophets. We believe in one holy catholic and
apostolic Church. We acknowledge one baptism
for the forgiveness of sins. We look for the resurrection of the dead, and the life of the world to
come. Amen.

So be it.

Prayer of the Faithful. After affirming our faith, we can then turn
to God in confidence. Before we begin the Liturgy of the
Eucharist, we ask God to hear our prayers of petition. We pray for
the needs of our world, the needs of the church, the needs of our
parish and our neighbors. After we petition for all this, we can then
in our silence pray for our own needs.

The Liturgy of the Eucharist

Having asked pardon for sins, offered praise and thanksgiving to
God, been instructed in Scripture, affirmed our one, holy, catholic,
apostolic faith, and offered our prayers of petition, we are now ready
for the great paschal mystery of the Last Supper, which makes the
sacrifice of the cross present in our lives. We take up the collection,
echoing again the description of Justin Martyr that those "who are
well to do give whatever they will." The eucharistic gifts of bread
and wine are brought forward and will be made into the body and
blood of Christ. We are now ready for the central act of our faith.
The eucharistic prayer begins with a prayer of joy, acclaiming the
greatness of God, echoing the angels in the Old Testament and the

crowds that lined the streets of Jerusalem to welcome Jesus: "Holy, holy, holy Lord, God of power and might. Heaven and earth are full of your glory. Hosanna in the highest. Blessed is he who comes in the name of the Lord. Hosanna in the highest."

Eucharistic Prayer. There are seven alternative eucharistic prayers used by the church, all ancient and all with the same essential elements. Four of these are generally used at Sunday Mass. They share common elements. Beginning with the preface of the great hosanna we offer prayers of thanksgiving to God for his eternal blessings—for life, for grace and sanctification, for our salvation. We ask blessings on the church that it might carry forward the message of salvation in Jesus to all generations. We offer the gifts of bread and wine and ask that the Father send the Holy Spirit to bless them "so that by his power they become the body and blood of Jesus Christ and so that those who take part in the Eucharist may be one body and one spirit" (*Catechism of the Catholic Church,* 1353).

We then have the most solemn moment of the liturgy: the narrative of the Eucharist at the Last Supper. It is through the words and actions of Christ, the power of the Holy Spirit, that in recitation of this narrative by the priest and "under the species of bread and wine" Christ's body and blood are sacramentally present. The church has honored the great command of Christ to "do this in memory of me."

We then "proclaim the mystery" of our eucharistic faith: Christ has died, Christ is risen, Christ will come again. Or: "Dying you destroyed our death, rising you restored our life, Lord Jesus, come in glory"; "When we eat this bread and drink this cup, we proclaim your death, Lord Jesus, until you come in glory"; "Lord, by your cross and resurrection, you have set us free. You are the savior of the world."

The offering of Christ, body and blood, has been prepared. Intercessions are then offered, prayers by which "the Church indicates that the Eucharist is celebrated in communion with the whole Church in heaven and on earth, the living and the dead, and in communion with the pastors of the Church, the Pope, the diocesan bishop, his presbyterium and his deacons, and all the bishops of the world together with their Churches"*(Catechism of the Catholic Church, 1354).*

The eucharistic prayer concludes: "Through him, with him, in him, in the unity of the Holy Spirit, all glory and honor are yours almighty Father, for ever and ever."

To which we respond with: "Amen."

Communion Rite. In the presence of the body and blood of Christ, we "pray with confidence to the Father in the words our Savior gave us." We then recite the prayer Jesus taught to the apostles when they asked, "Lord, teach us to pray"—the Our Father. The priest sums up this petition with a prayer each of us can make our own, especially in the shank of the evening when the fears come: "Deliver us, Lord, from every evil, and grant us peace in our day. In your mercy keep us free from sin and protect us from all anxiety as we wait in joyful hope for the coming of our Savior, Jesus Christ." We exchange a sign of the peace of Christ with those around us, then offer a prayer that the Lamb of God have mercy on us and grant us peace. The priest then breaks the host and prays that "the body and blood of our Lord Jesus Christ bring eternal life to us who receive it."

Holding the host in front of him, the priest announces: "This is the Lamb of God who takes away the sins of the world. Happy are those who are called to his supper." Priest and people then acknowledge the most obvious of truths: "Lord, I am not worthy to receive you, but only say the word and I shall be healed." These are the words echoed down through the centuries of the Roman centurion who begged a cure for his servant from Jesus. When Jesus offered to come to his home, he explained that he was a pagan, not worthy of such a guest. He said that as one who commanded men he expected to issue orders that would be followed. So he knew that Christ need only say the word and his servant would be healed. Jesus praised him for his great faith. We hope to emulate that faith, knowing that if Christ but say the words, we will be healed.

We then process to receive communion. "The body of Christ," we are told, and we respond, "Amen." If the cup is offered, we are told, "The blood of Christ," and respond, "Amen." We receive the body and blood of Christ—the Eucharist. "I am the bread of life . . . whoever eats this bread will live forever" (John 6:48, 58). Our God is the God of the living.

Concluding Rite. With Christ received in the Eucharist, we are ready to return to our lives. The priest offers us a blessing in the name of the Trinity and we are told to "go in peace to love and serve the Lord."

And we respond: "Thanks be to God."

The God who gives joy to my youth.

*   *   *

Let us pray with confidence to the Father in the words our Savior gave us.

> Our Father,
> who art in heaven, hallowed be thy name;
> thy kingdom come, thy will be done
> on earth as it is in heaven.
> Give us this day our daily bread;
> and forgive us our trespasses
> as we forgive those who trespass against us;
> and lead us not into temptation,
> but deliver us from evil.

CHAPTER 12

The Great Life

Is it enough to belong to God's Church in order to be saved?

It is not enough to belong to the Church in order to be saved, but we must also keep the Commandments of God and of the Church.

Which are the Commandments that contain the whole law of God?

The Commandments which contain the whole law of God are these two:

1. Thou shalt love the Lord thy God with thy whole heart, with thy whole soul, with thy whole strength, and with thy whole mind;

2. Thou shalt love thy neighbor as thyself.

My old buddy Tom's pilgrimage through a prestigious college had finished with graduation and grades at the very top of his class. But he had bought into the 1960s and hadn't yet graduated from that epoch. As he explained, it was all "drugs and rock 'n' roll," omitting the third element of that trio—"sex"—as that was one part of the career that hadn't changed much from high school.

I had been out in Indiana and away from the End of the Line for more than a year after finishing college. I was taking on all the signs of a failed revolutionary: shorter hair, a full-time job that required a tie and pressed pants, a place that I rented with utilities in my own name, a car loan, a voter registration card, and an extra ten pounds that showed up almost as soon as I took to working at a desk. Then I got the call from Tom. He was in Yonkers, but looking for a little working vacation. "Could I crash with you if I came out? I'm gonna look for a little work—in a factory or something—to build up the cash reserves. Sort of lie low." I told him that would be great. And I meant it. I had always liked Tom. I had almost forgotten that disturbing night in O'Toole's bar, when Tom and his creepy buddy, Funk, stole my change off the bar. With the job and all I couldn't go home again. But a little bit of home could come to me, I thought, imagining how the End of the Line would shake down in a small Hoosier town.

He showed up a week later, looking like a throwback to my junior year in college. Long hair, unkempt beard, bell-bottom jeans, and the mystique of marijuana about him. Everything he did was just a little vague. But, damn, it was good to see him. Tom settled in easy for a few days. He slept on a secondhand couch in my living room, and he would try to shake himself awake as I got ready for work in the morning. He'd roll over as I entered the room, pull his legs onto the floor, then reach for the joint he had left on the end table. He'd light it, suck in as much illegal substance as hard as he could, then proceed to cough for about a minute. Rheumy-eyed, he'd look at me, shake his head, and announce: "Those first few minutes of reality can kill you."

Tom would spend the next few days studiously avoiding that reality. While I trudged off to work every morning, he existed on making bread from scratch, watching the little black-and-white television that pulled in three stations, reading old paperbacks, and walking the neighborhood where he became good friends with a retired railroad worker and an old lady who would read your palm for a buck. On the weekend, we sat around drinking cheap beer by the case while discussing philosophy and theology.

By that time in my life, I was coming back to the faith after the college hiatus. Don't get me wrong. I was like the fellow in the old joke, sitting in the stands at the Colosseum, watching the Christians being torn apart by the lions. "Aren't you a Christian, too?" the guy next to him asks. And he replies, "Yeah . . . but I'm not a fanatic about it." I was barely practicing, barely involved, barely living it. But I was heading in some kind of direction unclear to me at best. Tom was footloose and fancy-free. And a lot smarter than me. We spent a lot of time discussing the moral life. Tom was of the view that the moral life no longer needed God "as the Big Prop." His belief was that morality had naturally evolved from essentially a cultural carrot-and-stick over the ages. We recognized collective good as the best for the individual good, that's all. The idea of objective good from a grander scheme of things was an invention to keep religion in business, he declared. It was kind of a vague combination of Jean Jacques Rousseau and Jim Morrison theology.

I mumbled along in response. I discussed natural law—a remnant of my Jesuit education before it imploded—and with it the idea that man as a created being had a natural, if flawed, understanding of morality that couldn't come from an evolutionary stew. I argued that God was not a prop, but a source, and that man's attempt to invent a morality separate from God was doomed to fail on the rocks of our own infallibility and self-justification. Morality was based not on self-protection, but on our understanding of the respect due to another human being, a respect that can only come from our understanding that each being is a created life from God. Tom scoffed. God, if he did exist, could not be reduced to the level that man could understand. It would be a self-contradiction. If God is God, humanity can't understand him. The finite cannot know the infinite. And if we could not understand God, we could not understand his morality. I tried to counter with the idea of revelation—of God injecting himself in human history—but Tom rejected that out of hand as "children's tales and myths." His was a God that took the last train for the coast long before the music died.

In other words, we were two young guys with too many beers subtracting from the sum of human knowledge.

I kept reminding myself not to interject into the discussion what I had never mentioned to him—his theft of the beer money just a few short years back. But as Tom prattled on about mankind's self-perfecting capabilities and that the idea of objective morality "dictated by some God" was the small concept of small minds, I could feel myself starting to lose it. It was the smugness of the beer—his and mine—that finally did it. We have a lot of good ideas after six beers. The mistake is that we follow up on them.

"Well let me pose something," I said, "an example from life."

I paraphrased the tale of a friend stealing money from a friend at a bar, a virtual retelling of that night at O'Toole's with the names changed to protect the guilty. I explained the moral of the little tale: That relying on our own devices in creating a personal morality is a tricky business when dealing with human beings who will generally put their own short-term interests ahead of everything, including lifelong friendships.

As I finished the story, Tom just looked at me for a moment quizzically. "The rhetoric of experience isn't much for establishing broad principles," he said with a shrug. Then he went back to repeating himself that self-justification shouldn't be dismissed out of hand as a source for morality.

As he babbled along it hit me that he had long ago dismissed the details of that night at O'Toole's. It had meant so little to him that it was simply gone from his conscience, forgotten as a moment so meaningless that the brain never even considered retaining it, which made me feel that I had made my point completely. But it also made me feel a lot worse.

Just a few days later, Tom announced that he was heading back to the End of the Line. His pilgrimage had lasted a little more than a week. "This place can grow on you," he explained, "and that's not necessarily a good thing." That final morning he got up and joined me on the way to work, fighting reality all the way. My office building was right on the main drag heading back east. He crammed his stuff in a duffel bag and threw it in my back seat. We drove the short trip to my parking lot where we shook hands and made all kinds of promises for the future. From the office window I watched him as he stood by the road, thumb out, hitching a ride. A guy from work was standing by me, sipping coffee, as a car stopped to pick up Tom. He opened the back door, threw in his bag, then turned and flashed me the old "V" peace sign. The 1960s would never leave him. I waved back. The guy next to me said, "You look like you just lost your best friend." And I said, "I probably do."

I never saw him again.

Finding the Life

We were made to lead a great life. Except for the occasional Eddie Funks of the world who make a concerted effort to be creeps, most of us decide that we are pretty much decent sorts just trying to get by. The trouble we run into with this self-image the older we get is twofold. The first is my understanding of the true cause of original sin. Theologians have argued over the sin of Adam and Eve from the day Scripture dawned. Some state it was the sin of hubris, the desire to be godlike; others the sin of envy, where man was successfully tempted because he was envious of the omniscience of God. Still others have argued that it was greed—man had everything that could make him happy but wanted still more. Me, I believe it was simpler than that. It was the sin of rationalization. The great sin that chases us down through the ages is the desire— and the ability as sentient beings—to rationalize what we want to do as good, particularly if it isn't. "The woman saw that the tree was good for food, pleasing to the eyes, and desirable for gaining wisdom. So she took some of its fruit and ate it; and she also gave some to her husband, who was with her, and he ate it" (Genesis 3:6). Since then, we have decided that we are generally the decent sort just trying to get by so that nothing we do or fail to do is of any great moral consequence. It's just not that big of a deal. If I am generally a good guy by my own definition, what I want to do, even if not so good, becomes good since I am good enough. With such reasoning, we have learned to rationalize away all faults under the grand cloak of decency.

With this comes the bedfellow of rationalization, the other trouble we run into—the acceptance of moral mediocrity. It takes some decades worth of living to beat out of ourselves the idea that we can be saints. Mankind's lot is that we usually manage to do it, settling into a comfortable routine of the ordinary. We have learned Flannery O'Connor's warning and taken it to heart: The faith takes work. It's nonbelief that is easy, or living our lives as if we don't believe. We paint the demands of the new covenant in glowing terms, and even get a little misty when reading them. But we decide that they are for better souls, for the saints. They become unattainable ideals, not real in our lives. It's time to settle for being good enough, though we are never quite certain how much good is enough and can never quite understand why we look around in middle age—or late middle age—and wonder what the hell the last few decades have been all about.

The time comes when we have to grasp that God is the God of the living—that the Lord calls every person to a great and noble life. That great life holds all one can possibly hope for and expect in this world, even if this world is not altogether a happy place. In this great life, purpose, meaning, and fulfillment are found. We don't have to search for it in cultural fads and material baubles. If we spend our lives trying to be great rather than settling for mediocrity—or the shiny little nothings up for grabs in the cultural lottery—the moral decisions become easier, the choices of conscience clearer, the will to do good stronger and stronger. The pilgrimage gets easier, and the grace-filled connectedness to God more and more natural.

At least that's the plan. That's the plan most of us have for ourselves, or would like to have. The difficulty that we run into is that it is so damn hard to do it on our own. Trying to discover the great life on our own and living it on our own is perhaps the greatest hubris of all.

"For man it is impossible but not for God. With God all things are possible" (Matthew 19:26).

One of the best descriptions of the church came from Hilaire Belloc. He described the church as "Here comes everybody!" The church is made up of everybody with all their faults and foibles. Everybody understands it is the church of sinners struggling to be saints. What roots the whole thing together is grace—the grace of God found in the sacraments instituted by Christ. This is what gives everybody the possibility of sanctity, not relying for a moment on everybody. But relying on a new birth in baptism, the strength of the Holy Spirit in confirmation, the forgiveness of God in confession, the living bread of the Eucharist, the sacraments to bless our vocations, and the healing touch of God's love—that is where everybody finds hope. That is where everybody finds the great life.

And how does a person manage to lose all that? In a thousand ways, but with a common tale at the bottom of it all. Worship, practice, prayer, and Christian living—they are a delicately woven pattern. Take out any of the threads and the whole pattern unravels. Simple truth: Most of us stop believing when we stop acting like we believe. We lose the great life because we no longer practice the faith in which it is grounded. Then we find we can't pray because we do not live life in a way that is open to prayer. We do not live that life because we abandoned worship of God and the practice of the faith. All the parts create the whole. The key to the thing is this: You can't lead the great life without believing the great life is possible. And without the grace of faith, practice, prayer, and worship, there is no foundation to lead one to believe the great life is possible. It ends up like the 1960s revolution, all gone to seed in a world of wishful thinking.

Knowing the Life

The great life is summed up simply:

"There was a scholar of the law who stood up to test him and said, 'Teacher, what must I do to inherit eternal life?' Jesus said to him, 'What is written in the law? How do you read it?' He said in reply, 'You shall love the Lord, your God, with all your heart, with all your being, with all your strength, with all your mind, and your neighbor as yourself.' He replied to him, 'You have answered correctly; do this and you will live'" (Luke 10:25–28).

Love the Lord our God; love mankind that surrounds us. And live like we mean both. The great life isn't terribly complicated.

It is a summary of the Ten Commandments, of course, which were not given solely to keep kids from chewing gum in line, smart-mouthing their parents or other legitimate authority (i.e., the good sisters), and using foul language. Unfortunately, our main exposure to the Ten Commandments was in grammar school and by the movie of the same name. We think of them as rather childish, because they were presented to us as children so that we might have a vague notion of what they mean. And to keep us from chewing gum in school. But the great life is grounded in the Ten Commandments, that original theophany from God to Moses—a direct experience of the Lord—that spelled out the hope of human existence. In a few millennia plus, mankind has failed to come up with anything better.

The problem is that we haven't reexamined them as adults. We think of them as another set of rules imposed on us when we were kids because that was how they were explained to us. They were used to enforce a code based on where and when to ride a bike, or not spitting in your little brother's cereal. The examples by which we define the Commandments are still stuck in a world where *Maverick* was new. But like every aspect of the faith, we need to look at them now through adult eyes, and begin to discover the myriad depths of meaning.

The first two commandments—"You shall worship the Lord your God and him only shall you serve" and "The name of the Lord is holy"—seem simple but have many layers, like a peeled onion. The first requirement of the great life is that we root it in faith and love of God. In a properly ordered life God must be the first and elementary reality. The practical aspect of the great life in these commandments is that we do not substitute all the other gods—particularly the big three of Money, Power, and Sex—for God. The most popular sin against these commandments, as one grows tired of sex, has little money, and less power, is that in the end we substitute worship of self for worship of God. At heart, however, these first two commandments tell us that we must take the existence of God seriously and that our greatest failure is in living our daily lives as if there is no God. The great life has as its premise the understanding that God is real and personal. God is not an abstraction; God is not a prime mover that set the wheels in motion and took the last train for the coast. God is close and we lead our lives to reflect his closeness. We acknowledge, particularly in prayer, that closeness and intimacy.

And so it goes with the other commandments. "Remember the Sabbath day, to keep it holy." "This is the day the LORD has made; let us rejoice in it and be glad" (Psalm 118:24). The danger is abandoning faith in the greatness of God and the natural adoration mankind should have for God. We begin to put the premium on ourselves, rather than God. Keeping the Sabbath holy is the means by which we offer worship to God and keep ourselves humble. When we acknowledge the greatness of God it is hard to take ourselves too seriously—an absolute requirement for the great life. The celebration of the Lord's Day in the Eucharist is at the very heart and center of the life of the Church. The great life cannot exist without its graces.

"Honor your father and your mother, that your days may be long in the land which the Lord your God gives you." The goal of the great life is to pull away from self-centeredness, beginning with the recognition that it is God that must be adored, not ourselves. With that foundation, we can move to our relationship with mankind, beginning at the beginning, with those closest to us. *Honor* is the operative word here. This commandment places the family at the center of honor in the great life. In the family, the community from which the universal community derives its existence, the great life is first learned.

"You shall not kill." This commandment is the foundation for the teaching of the church on the issues of life and death that contemporary culture has so complicated. The essential belief is this: Human life is sacred. Life is sacred because each life is uniquely created by God. God brings each human life into existence. Every life remains for eternity in a special relationship with its Creator and that leads to a basic understanding: "God alone is the Lord of life from its beginning until its end: no one can under any circumstances claim for himself the right directly to destroy an innocent human being" (see *Catechism of the Catholic Church*, 2268).

"You shall not commit adultery." Yeah, well, obviously. We're old enough to know that this commandment holds a world of truth. But it is more than a commandment not to cheat on your spouse. It is the foundation of Catholic sexual morality, of our understanding of the meaning and richness of Christian marriage and human sexuality. This human sexuality "in which man's belonging to the bodily and biological world is expressed, becomes personal and truly human when it is integrated into the relationship of one person to another, in the complete and lifelong mutual gift of a man and a woman" (*Catechism of the Catholic Church*, 2337). The great life is lived with the understanding that the truly sexual is not found in porno, premarital sleepovers, postmarital affairs, or a hundred other sexual temptations the world offers us on a platter. If we know anything by now, it is that the promise offered by erotic titillation is nothing, a mere candle in the wind. The true gift of sexuality, sexuality in expression that is always open to life, is found in the married love of a man and a woman. Living it and embracing it is the greatest of human blessings.

"You shall not steal." Again, simple on the surface. But this commandment takes on far greater meaning than just warning against ripping off a candy bar when we are seven years old. In its essence, this commandment provides the foundation of Catholic social justice. This commandment demands respect of the rights and property of others, that we cannot unjustly take and keep that which belongs to another. But that means not just their tool set or their lawn mower. You cannot steal by paying unjust wages, business fraud, taking advantage of another's ignorance, using the power of money to hold others down. And more, much more. It implies a whole system of how we relate together in an economic culture: "The development of economic activity and growth in production are meant to provide for the needs of human beings. Economic life is not meant solely to multiply goods produced and increase profit or power; it is ordered first of all to the service of persons, of the whole man, and of the entire human community. Economic activity, conducted according to its own proper methods, is to be exercised within the limits of the moral order, in keeping with social justice so as to correspond with God's plan for man" (*Catechism of the Catholic Church*, 2426).

In its most positive way, this commandment demands love of the poor and leads naturally to what we called the corporal works of mercy, which are the Beatitudes of the Sermon on the Mount practically applied: feeding the hungry, sheltering the homeless, clothing the naked, visiting the sick and imprisoned, burying the dead. It demands that we do not generate economic systems that create and exploit or extend these inequities. These corporal works of mercy are an integral part of the great life, both personally in our daily lives and in how we view the world in which we live. And we mirror them in the spiritual works of mercy: instructing, advising, consoling, comforting, forgiving wrongs, and bearing them patiently.

"You shall not bear false witness against your neighbor." The simple goal of the great life is that we live in truth. The most important command of the great life is that we accept that truth is real, and we reflect the truth in every word and deed.

The last two commandments are usually summed up as, "You shall not covet your neighbor's wife" and "You shall not covet your neighbor's goods." The layers of the onion are peeled back: "You shall not covet anything that is your neighbor's. . . . For where your treasure is, there also will your heart be" (Matthew 6:21). There is a focus in these last two commandments—and rightly so—on what they say about a life lived in chastity. Chastity is the misunderstood virtue, often confused with celibacy and virginity. It is neither. Chastity "lets us love with upright and undivided heart" (*Catechism of the Catholic Church*, 2520). Chastity roots our sexuality in respect for ourselves and others. It is a way of living that refuses to see others as sexual objects to be used. At its heart, a chaste life is a life that is grounded in respect for the dignity of others and the dignity of humanity as a whole. Recognizing human sexuality for the blessing that it is, for its centrality in the true dignity of each human being, chastity is the opposite of the sullen, spread-eagle world that confuses erotic with sexual.

The older we get the more we come to understand all that, and not just because we are threatened with diminished libido. (To the contrary, the chaste life is the divine aphrodisiac—by understanding our sexuality for what it truly is, we never tire of it, as we do the merely erotic that always gets boring as we proceed down the various levels of broken taboos.) But what holds our imagination in the great life is the final part of that final commandment: "For where your treasure is, there also will your heart be" (Matthew 6:21). Dickens explained it in *A Christmas Carol*: "We wear the chains we forged in life." We become what we have lived. What we desire, what we aim for, where we expend our energy and determination, is what we become for good or bad. If what we want is money, sex, and power, our lives will be defined by that, no matter how much we protest to the contrary. If that is where our heart is, that is what we will become. If our heart wants the great life—if that is what we really treasure, what we really search for in ourselves and others— that is what we will become. The old line is that the face we have at twenty is the face we were born with; the face we have at forty is the face we have sculpted with our lives. The person we are at forty, fifty, sixty and beyond, is what we have sculpted with our life. The difference is that we are stuck with that face we've sculpted. With God's grace, we can change the person we created any day at any age. We just have to find—or redefine—what we treasure. Because there also will be our heart.

Virtue

Exploring how the great life is lived can be easy or hard, like everything in the church I suppose. By that, the wise guy in me means
that there are always different levels, different understandings,
more to learn and more to explore. After all, they can fill books
with the intricacies of moral theology. The commandments themselves can be explored until the heart is content or confused. As
mentioned, contained within one commandment are the seeds of a
century of Catholic social teaching, wherein we can explore everything from the Catholic principle of subsidiarity (the concept that
the most effective agent of social action is that which is closest to
the level of the intended agent of change) to the debate over fundamental option (whether mortal sin exists in a single act or is representative of a life inclined toward evil by a series of life choices
over time). Or something like that.

It is all great fun, but at this point in my life on earth, I am moving from the complex to the simple. We want to find a way of living different that makes a difference. At some point, we boomers
get tired of making a college course out of everything. In looking
for a guide to living the great life—something that I can aim for
and achieve—I reach for the old compilations familiar from a lifetime of memory. The grace of the sacraments—baptism, confirmation, confession, and the Eucharist—promises us that we can live
the simple virtues if we try to live them. And in living them, the
key to the happiness we can expect in this life is found. There
is nothing complicated in discovering them for they are what we
naturally admire in others. The nuns called them the cardinal
virtues: prudence, justice, fortitude, and temperance.

Living the great life then becomes a rather simple task. It's not dreaming an impossible dream, nor is it settling for mediocrity and the ordinary. Nor is it some mystical quest for spiritual bromides that pass for insight in circles that make me nervous. It's not caught up in fanciful imagery, emotional wimpiness or self-confirming feelings shared over hot cocoa. It's not a lot of fluff and stuff where we take any remaining sense of masculinity and hide it outside the church door. The faith lived is here for the everyday Joe, a spirituality and lifestyle for the boys at the bar.

Though they aren't meant that way, the commandments can give a sense of the negative to the great life by warning us to avoid the common errors of mankind. If lived, they are the key to sanctity. But the cardinal virtues are the positive witness to the active pursuit of the commandments. They are what we grow to be, particularly as the years go by. We come to understand pretty quickly, for example, that pornography is not only degrading but boring. So we avoid it, and rightly so. But where we give positive witness is when we begin to understand Christian sexuality as a life dedicated to the joy of the loving expression of our sexuality with our spouses. Virtue is the great life lived.

Prudence. Prudence is using our reason to look for the true good in every circumstance and to choose the right means of achieving it. Essentially, prudence is the mirror of its evil twin, rationalization. To live prudently is to let our big head do the thinking for our little head, for example. But more than that, it is the virtue of disassociating our desires from judging what is right and wrong in a given situation. It allows us to see what is right and good by reasoned discernment, making that discernment in kindness and truth, and following through on that discernment. Prudence defies selfishness and is summed up in the old motto of Catholic action: See, judge, act. See the choice that exists, judge the good that must be chosen, and act on it without letting our own prejudices muck it all up.

Justice. Our goal is to live in and with justice toward God and justice toward neighbor. Justice means to respect the rights of everyone, and to seek harmony and the common good in all our judgments and actions. It means that we respect the word of God and struggle to make it fundamental to our lives. That sounds terribly self-righteous—the "God-fearing soul" hurling thunderbolts in a blind devotion to truth as he sees it. But it is not. It is putting on the Lord, acting each day as if we believe that God is and that living that belief should not be put off to the fringes. It is defining ourselves by our core beliefs, then acting in concert with those beliefs. It also means that we accept our neighbor as a created creature of God demanding justice and true respect from us. It means that we live positively, seeking out the good for all based on the goodness of God who created all things. It means that we want to create harmony and peace in our world, but not through compromising in our own lives the only truths that can lead to peace.

Fortitude. Perhaps the one virtue taught in old movies. This is the virtue that helps us through the night when the miseries come. It is the virtue of living the faith not only in the good times, but also in the lousy times. It is the key to what we hanker for most as we get a bit long in the tooth—serenity. Serenity, of course, is not the meek acceptance of life's pitfalls. To the contrary, serenity is fortitude lived. And fortitude means firmness in times of difficulty and constancy in the pursuit of the good. This virtue allows us to conquer fear when we face that which is fearsome, and to live with hope in hopeless times. It is true Christian courage.

Temperance. Got a lot of nerve pointing to temperance. After all, most of us dedicated a few decades of our lives—if not more—to the pursuit of both legal and illegal substances. Temperance, of course, does not equate with abstinence, and its application solely to booze is a fundamentalist twist rather than a Catholic understanding. But a bit of the Carrie Nation standard definition does hold. Many of us, and it should be abundantly clear that I'm a standard-bearer here, spent a lot of our lives seeking a touch of oblivion. We had in mind avoiding a lot of things—such as day-to-day life—through various playful substances. We insulted creation—and the Creator—by trying to avoid its tender gifts and challenges, living the gift of life in a haze. Some of us kept it up a long time, and temperance narrowly defined is not something we should summarily dismiss. Of course, temperance in the Catholic sense implies moderation in all things. It is the virtue of keeping our desires and wishes within honorable limits. Temperance is to live sober, upright, and godly. It's not teetotaling; but it's also not making an excuse for foolishness.

Simple, really. Remember the Golden Rule. Know the commandments. Live the virtues. The great life ain't rocket science.

Spider and Mad Dog

The phone rang in the office, and, as always, I looked at it. Sometimes you can stare it down. But this time it went to the third ring and, like death and taxes, I knew it had to be answered. "Lockwood."

"Is that you, Spider?" the caller asked. "It's me—Mad Dog." A bad day suddenly turned very bright.

It had been twenty-five years since the whole world—or at least the entire Fairfield University community—had known me as "Spider." It was a name I had picked up early in freshman year. We were playing a two-hand touch-football game, and I was picking off passes on defense like a star. I was always pretty good at touch football since I could catch, run, and my 125-pound physique wasn't quite the handicap that it was in tackle football. I was absolutely fearless between the lines in touch football. If tackle was the game, I was a better-than-average referee. We were all fans of the New York Giants, who were particularly lousy in those days. One of the few bona fide stars was a defensive back named "Spider" Lockhart. The last name being close enough, I was quickly anointed "Spider." There are guys today—good friends from college—who I goofed around with during four years of my life, who couldn't tell you my real first name on a bet. I was Spider and that's all they knew.

"Mad Dog," on the other hand, was the rather privileged nickname of a fellow named Jerry McHugh. Only a few people called him by that moniker. It happened during sophomore year. He found himself in desperate straights. It was a Wednesday night, a mere forty-eight hours before Friday night and a planned road trip to Marymount College, where the good Catholic girls were known to be able to drink anyone under the table and swear with the best of them. McHugh was dead broke. The thought of a Friday night on an all-male campus was more than he could bear. He needed $10 and he needed it fast. But having already used up a great deal of credit with the boys in the dorm—he had this nasty habit of playing cards badly—he couldn't scare up a loan. Then one of the guys—it was Kilty, a tall glass of water from Long Island—offered him a deal. "I miss my dog. Pretend you're my dog for forty-eight hours and I'll loan you ten bucks." McHugh agreed without a second thought. He then curled up at the foot of Kilty's bed and went to sleep. He got the "mad" added to it the next morning when he brushed his teeth. (Kilty was no slouch himself. I walked into his room once and noticed he had a sweet potato on his dresser. "What's up with the sweet potato?" I asked. "Quiet," he said. "He thinks he's a rutabaga.")

"Spider Lockwood, how the hell are you?" Mad Dog said over the phone decades later. And you know the rest. Lies, braggadocio, tales from the good old days, and whatever-happened-to for five or ten minutes. Eventually he got around to talking about the upcoming twenty-fifth reunion of our class. "We ought to round up the old gang for an underground reunion. None of us have been to any of them, I think. If we all go, we'll have some folks to hang around with." *Or go to jail with,* I thought. It was true. I had not gone to a reunion since I graduated. I had moved to Indiana just a few months later, and it was a long trip back just for two solid days of drinking beer. But with Mad Dog on the phone, it seemed like a good idea. "It would be good to drink with you guys in person," I said. "I'm getting tired of having a taste alone every December." He

paused a second, then said, "You still do that every Christmas?"
"Sure I do," I lied. "Me too," he lied.

It was a week before Christmas in my sophomore year at
Fairfield. A small group of us had been left on campus, just five
guys knocking around in a dormitory that slept hundreds—Mad
Dog, McNicholson, Harrison (we called him "The Lacker," but I
don't member why), myself, and a guy named Murphy who was
always referred to as "The Great Murphy." As I recall, Murphy's
claim to fame was drinking sixty shots of beer in an hour. Someone
had read somewhere that it would get you deliriously drunk and
Murphy took him up on the bet. He was a short, kind of pudgy guy
who sat there, drank his sixty shots in sixty minutes, and was none
the worse for wear. He did nothing else in four years other than
graduate but was thereafter known as "The Great Murphy."

Classes were done for the holidays, but the five of us, for one
reason or another, were still on campus for a few days. My reason
was simple enough. The Old Man was my transportation and he
was on a business trip. I would spend two more days knocking
around a virtually empty campus before he came to get me. We all
had family and girlfriends back home, as well as buddies planning
some big Christmas parties. We were itching for liberation.

The five of us sat in one of the television rooms one night, listening to Christmas carols on an old radio and generally feeling
sorry for ourselves. We were sampling some ill-gotten wine that
was called, I swear, "Screamin' Lucy." I think it cost about sixty
cents a gallon and is the likely explanation for the gastrointestinal
problems suffered decades later by a whole generation of Fairfield

alumni. Actually, booze wasn't allowed on campus yet, but there wasn't anyone around to enforce the blue laws that night. So we sat, sulked, and drank bad wine.

It was The Lacker who came up with it. We needed a toast, a bleak Christmas toast of "Screamin' Lucy." And then he called for an oath: "From now on, every year on the evening of December 18th, we'll take a sip and remember this night. We'll remember friendship, and Christmas away from home." Two years later we graduated, and I never saw any of them again. I never seem to remember to have a taste when the evening of December 18th rolls around.

We never got together for our underground reunion. Mad Dog and I made some phone calls and caught up on old times with a few of the boys. But mostly, we struck out on the reunion idea, particularly with the other guys from our Christmas pledge. The Lacker was polite but uninterested. Messages were left for The Great Murphy, but he never called back. I got hold of McNicholson's number, the last of us. When I called, it was his business phone. The message on the phone said that he would be delighted to get back with me if I would leave my name and phone number, and that he looked forward to meeting my household appliance needs.

The last time I saw McNicholson was at college graduation. He was talking about getting home, grabbing his dog, jumping in his old car, and just taking off. McNicholson and his dog would be "seeing America." I don't know if he made it or not. He also mentioned something about a summer job.

Some guys prefer that the past remains the past and have long since decided to let it all go, which sometimes isn't all that bad.

I decided not to leave a message.

*   *   *

I asked for strength that I might achieve; I was made weak that I might learn to humbly obey. I asked for health that I might do greater things; I was given infirmity that I might do better things. I asked for riches that I might be happy; I was given poverty that I might be wise. I asked for power that I might have the great praise of men; I was given weakness that I might feel the need of God. I asked for all things that I might enjoy life; I was given life that I might enjoy all things. I got nothing I had asked for, but everything that I had hoped for. Almost despite myself my unspoken prayers were answered; I am, among all men, richly blessed.

"A Prayer for Right Living," by an unknown Confederate soldier.

CHAPTER 13

The Only Living Boy
in New York

What is prayer?

Prayer is the lifting up of our minds and hearts
to God to adore him, to thank him for his benefits,
to ask his forgiveness, and to beg of him all the
graces we need whether for soul or body.

Is prayer necessary to salvation?

Prayer is necessary to salvation, and without it
no one having the use of reason can be saved.

My last day at the End of the Line was on a late October
Tuesday in 1971. I had accepted a job in Indiana with a
publishing company. The Old Man had strongly suggested that I
take it. He had seemed less than enthused with my original career

path after graduating from Fairfield the previous June. A guy had offered me a job teaching tennis beginning that fall at a local Catholic girls' school, and I had lined up a nighttime gig bartending as well. The Old Man considered that a rather unformed plan for the use of my college degree in history. Looking back from the perspective of decades, it is one of the few times that the Old Man was dead wrong.

The night before my departure I had packed up the classic vehicle—vintage 1962 with a good 125,000 miles on the odometer—that I had purchased for the princely sum of $250 from Ralph. We had been spending time together that summer, the first really since high school. Ralph, married and with a kid, had felt out-of-the-loop when the old gang had gone off to college and he had gone off to the factory and marriage. But that summer we had hooked up again. Though I didn't know what was down the road for me, Ralph seemed to have a clearer idea of my future now that the nonsense of higher education was out of the way. "Almost time to grow up, buckaroo!" he would give as an opening toast at O'Toole's on the summer Friday nights when, in his own words, he was "allowed out to play." I loved the guy, but his life, and his prediction for mine, gave me the shivers.

The last night at the End of the Line I spent at O'Toole's watching *Monday Night Football*. None of the old gang was around, my only company being the more serious football fans and the even more serious drinkers. I was starting to worry about where I fit in there. Most of the old friends had left the End of the Line by then, refugees from the college years heading down roads not traveled. By then I was pretty well convinced I was the only living boy in

New York. "Half of the time you're gone and you don't know where," I thought, which meant I was starting to get maudlin. I decided to go home, not having to bother to say my good-byes to anyone at the bar.

When I got home, the Old Man was just about ready for bed. He shook my hand, slipped me $20 for the road, and said goodnight. The next morning he had left for work when I got up, and my mother was about to leave. With my little brother away at college and no one left in the roost, she had taken a job to keep herself busy. She told me to be good and drive safely. It was like I was going on a date, rather than seven hundred-odd miles across four states and out of her life. "Why you bought that bucket of bolts from Ralphie, I'll never know!" She still called all the old friends by their diminutives. As she got to the door, she turned and said, "And that reminds me, Ralphie called last night."

"Did he want me to call back?"

"No, he just left a message."

"What was it?"

"It's time, buckaroo!" She shrugged over the meaning of that one, kissed me on the cheek, and then she was gone. It was 1971, for God's sake, and you wouldn't expect much more than that from a guy's parents. If we had understood how little we would really see each other from that day on, things might have been different. But maybe not.

I poured myself into the bucket of bolts and decided to take a quick last spin through the End of the Line. I stopped once. I walked down the aisle of Christ the King church, knelt, whiffed a quick sign of the cross, and sat in the pew. On the boys' side of course. The old days might be dead, but not the old habits. Over a door that led out from the pews to the far side of the altar was that artwork of a hand descending from the clouds. I must have stared at that about eight thousand times when I was a kid at Christ the King, wondering when this or that service was going to end. I never understood what it meant. I looked at it and realized it represented the hand of God. I should have been able to figure that out even when I was a dumb kid, I thought. I sat there for about ten minutes. Finally, I said to the artwork over the door in the empty church of my childhood: "God, what the hell am I supposed to do now?"

Then I got up and left the End of the Line for Indiana. It was my first real prayer in a long time.

A Prayer in Time

Prayer is an odd thing. It has as its basic assumption that a person can speak to God; more improbably, that God will listen; and most improbably, that God might somehow speak in return. Of course, if we have abstracted God out of existence—so infinitely removed from the life of mankind that he or she, it or what, becomes a vague universal Cosmos—then prayer is ridiculous. We cannot speak to a Great Something so far removed from humanity that our prayers are merely lost words in the wind, finding nothing and meaning nothing. Generally, if we cannot believe in prayer it is because we have succumbed to an unbelievable concept of God.

It goes back to our old friend J. B. Philips, who we met in freshman year at Fairfield University. We make three mistakes when it comes to prayer and the God of our own invention.

First, and usually based on a carryover from childhood, we invent a God that is too small—a God as cop, a God as nag, a God as avuncular buddy. The older we get, the more that childhood image of God resembles ourselves and our own outlook. The trouble comes when we can't find the answer anymore. We are looking for God, and the only image we really have is a slightly improved self. Often, when we think God has no answers, the real discovery is that we don't have any answers.

Second, of course, in reaction to the God of our childhood we have imagined this hugely abstract God, a God of Great Intellectual Pretense. We have created a God that has nothing to do with us. We can't pray to him because we can't know him in the least. We can't approach this God when the terrors of the night have arrived, or the chest has tightened like a knot, or the kid's life is going to hell, or the job is leading to a very loud desperation, or, simply, it all just can't be tolerated anymore. What would Beauty know of the daily grind? How exactly do we speak to Beauty when our problem is that the mole has changed color, the job is vanishing when the kid's tuition is due, and our best friend collapsed in a heap and he's never getting up this side of heaven? If the God we have created in our adult minds is too big, too relentlessly abstract and cerebral, then prayer is as pointless as spitting in the ocean.

Third, prayer makes little sense if we have not tried to find God in the way we lead our lives. Prayer that is not rooted in faith lived, faith believed, and faith practiced is attempting to do the near impossible. It is trying to speak to God when everything we do in our lives is a conscious act of nonbelief. We cannot expect to be what we do not live. If faith is meaningless, prayer is meaningless; if God is irrelevant to our daily lives, prayer is irrelevant to our daily lives. We cannot pray to what we do not believe, we cannot believe when we live without belief, and we cannot hear what God has to say to us if we cannot pray. It's a nasty little circle. It's not that we don't believe in prayer; it's that we have chosen to live life as if there is no God to hear our prayers.

Prayer makes sense, however, if it is rooted in an understanding that God is consciously real. Prayer makes sense if we try to make God a real part of our lives. Our understanding of God comes from Christ, and the God revealed in the teachings of Christ is "Our Father," not an abstraction. It is all really a wondrous thing that can only be believed in and through prayer—that God stepped into history, took on our humanity, and offered the sacrifice of his son that we might be saved. It is God who walked the earth to teach us how to live. It is God to whom Christ prays relentlessly in Scripture, and to whom he invites our prayers. It is the God whose Spirit we received in baptism that gave us new life. The God to whom we can pray is the God who knows us intimately, as he is the source of our very existence. It is God who is "Our Father." Through and in Christ, we have an understanding that God intensely loves his creation—not in general, but in particular. And that is why prayer is both natural and miraculous to our lives. It comes with the territory of our fundamental belief in God. If God is real, if God is the source of our creation, if God stepped into history in Jesus Christ, then prayer makes perfectly wonderful sense. If God is none of this, then prayer is not worth the breath it takes to bring it into existence.

This is why we cannot divorce prayer from faith. A free-floating idea, common to every age, is that there is a mystical spirituality out there, distinct from a spirituality grounded in religious faith, that presents some kind of work-free contact with an Almighty Something, like a diet without the exercise. Usually, it is found in an attempt to glom onto a spirituality from another religious expression—whether Judaism, Buddhism, or a Native American spirituality—without bothering with the religious grounding from which the spirituality developed. Practically speaking, except for the momentary high of pursuing the momentarily fashionable, it just doesn't work. Spirituality grows naturally in the religious faith from which it is formed. Prayer without grounding in belief—and a belief expressed in a life well lived—is just a collection of empty words. Like an agnostic donning ashes at the beginning of Lent, it is empty ritualism.

What we begin to discover as we revisit our faith through the eyes of an adult is that it has been there all along. The spirituality we seek, the prayer life we hope to have, that way of living our lives daily as if we are touching the infinite, has been there waiting for us. Waiting for us to explore, waiting for us to look back, waiting for us to look forward, waiting for us to come home.

Beginning at the Beginning

For a Catholic, finding a life of prayer begins with the Mass. The Mass is essentially the perfect prayer, making up all the great components of prayer—adoration, meditation on Scripture, profession of belief, petition, sacrifice, grace for the body, and grace for the soul. It is the "lifting up of our hearts and minds to God." Many of us began to lose our sense of prayer when the Mass became less important to us, less a part of our lives. The first way to recapture prayer in our lives, to recapture a sense of spirituality, can be found in the Mass. The first step in returning to a real practice of the faith as an adult, even before confession, is to return to the Mass.

Fundamental first suggestion for building a life of prayer: Attend Mass alone one time. Don't go with your spouse, with the kids, or as a part of any organization. In fact, go to Mass where nobody knows you. The point is to go to Mass with yourself, for yourself. Listen. Hear the connections among the readings, listen to what is being said in the creed, try to absorb the miracle of the Liturgy of the Eucharist.

Forget about attending Mass when you were a kid, when every fiber of your being wanted to be somewhere else. Forget about attending Mass when you were a teen and you kept scanning the church for a certain hot number in a very short skirt. Forget all the silliness about finding God in the woods or in something you might have smoked or otherwise ingested. Forget about a lifetime of looking everywhere else you have looked for a hint of how to get by. Look, see, know, and feel the Mass as an adult searching for prayer. Because we are those restless pilgrims who will never find true peace until we rest in God.

Think of the Mass as the perfect prayer, particularly in the Eucharist, a litany of prayer: "Blessed are you, Lord, God of all creation. Through your goodness we have this bread to offer, which earth has given and human hands have made. It will become for us the bread of life." A prayer of thanksgiving for what the earth gives and mankind creates—all blessings that come from God. From these gifts of God and works of human hands, a miracle will come among us.

"May the Lord accept the sacrifice at your hands for the praise and glory of his name, for our good, and the good of all his Church." It is a prayer said in unity with the priesthood of Christ, in understanding, thanks, and praise of the sacrifice of the cross.

The eucharistic prayer is a prayer of thanksgiving and praise, of calling on the Holy Spirit, of the great words of consecration where the Last Supper is re-presented, and of the bread and wine sacramentally transformed into the body and blood of Christ. The passion, death, and resurrection of Christ is made present, and we are united in the faith of two thousand years in the living Christ. The dead are remembered, as we pray with the living. The eucharistic prayer concludes with the great doxology, a final hymn of prayer for the miracle that has taken place. "Through him, with him, in him, / in the unity of the Holy Spirit, / all glory and honor is yours, almighty Father, / for ever and ever." And it is affirmed with a great "Amen."

To find prayer, to find the richest spirituality we can ever know, we need look no further than the Mass.

A Season in Time

Time, that old bastard. "Of all life's mysteries," Ben Stein wrote, "the strangest is this: That time, which seems so permanent at the moment, passes and is gone forever." Like a barge on the river, time moves along ever so slowly, and then you look up and it is long gone. We all mark time in our own way. The Old Man always said that he was never bothered much by counting his own years, but his kids reaching middle age scared the bejeezus out of him. I thought of his philosophy of time when, talking to my daughter, I realized that when I was her age she was already born.

Time, of course, is sacred, which is why I should not take it so personally that I call it names. It is sacred because it is the seconds and moments of our lives hurrying by. Our lives are lived in time and with time. One of those great discussions in sophomore year of college over a few beers: Does the present exist, or is all reality simply past and future? All that exists, we argued, has already existed once we sense it, hear it, or smell it. The present is just the past recognized. We convinced ourselves that there was no present—only the past sensed, and the future in potential. It's the kind of thing you think when you are nineteen and the world is your oyster. We never thought to consider the timelessness at the center of time. As St. Teresa of Ávila prayed in the sixteenth century: "Let nothing disturb you. Let nothing frighten you. All things pass. God does not change."

The church has a cycle of prayer in time. The old monastic ways broke the day down into cycles of prayer based on the Old Testament Psalms, a way to consecrate a day to God and to make it holy. The day of prayer begins with Matins, prayer anticipating a new life from the darkness of our old life: "Come, let us sing joyfully to the LORD; / cry out to the rock of our salvation. / Let us greet him with a song of praise, / joyfully sing out our psalms" (Psalm 95:1–2). Lauds is the prayer of that joyful hour when the night gives way to the morning light. It is a Resurrection song: "All you peoples, clap your hands; / shout to God with joyful cries, / For the LORD, the Most High, inspires awe, the great king over all the earth" (Psalm 47:2–3). Prime is the morning prayer as the day has begun. Its themes are penance and preparation for the work of the day that will be dedicated to God: "Who may go up the mountain of the LORD? / Who can stand in his holy place? / "The clean of hand and pure of heart, / who are not devoted to idols, / who have not sworn falsely" (Psalm 24:3–4).

Terce is the prayer of the ninth hour of the day, a short pause in the morning's busy pilgrimage to remember the source of our strength: "The LORD is my light and my salvation; / whom do I fear? / The LORD is my life's refuge; / of whom am I afraid" (Psalm 27:1). Sext marks the prayers at noon, and the theme is a powerful reminder of our salvation: "Thus should all your faithful pray / in times of distress. / Though flood waters threaten, / they will never reach them. / You are my shelter; from distress you keep me; / with safety you ring me round" (Psalm 32:6–7). None marked the hours of the late afternoon, when "the day the Lord has made" is nearly done. The reflection is on our own beginnings, and our own end. "Our soul waits for the LORD, / who is our help and shield. / For in God our hearts rejoice; / in his holy name we trust. / May your kindness, LORD, be upon us; / we have put our hope in you" (Psalm 33:20–22).

Vespers is the evening prayer, looking back in thanksgiving for the graces of the day just passed: "The LORD is your guardian; / the LORD is your shade / at your right hand. / By day the sun cannot harm you, / nor the moon by night. / The LORD will guard you from all evil, / will always guard your life" (Psalm 121:5–7). Compline is the final prayer of the night before sleep, a moment to make our peace and contrition with God, and an understanding that our God is the God of the living: "Turn, LORD, save my life; / in your mercy rescue me. / For who among the dead remembers you? / Who praises you in Sheol?" (Psalm 6:5–6).

Seasons in Time

The prayer of the church in a year marks the ebb and flow of the faith through the seasons. It is the faith lived and celebrated in points of time, rooted in the day-to-day of humanity. The faith is always expressed in creation, like the bread and wine that are made Eucharist. It is that mix of the human and divine that is the mystery of the Incarnation, and our understanding of sacrament as a meeting of earth and heaven.

A year is a year. We might break it down simply by the seasons: spring, summer, fall, and winter. The more intense among us might break it down from board meeting to board meeting, sales season to sales season. Perhaps others look at spring training through the World Series, the college season to the bowls, the pro game through the Super Bowl, and the NCAA tournament, which finishes just shy of baseball's April opening day game. In any case, we mark the calendar, the procession of days through the year, which brings us from the start, to the finish, to the beginning by whatever reckoning we chose to take.

The seasons of the church year are a reckoning in prayer, bringing us through a cycle in the mystery of the life, death, and resurrection of Christ. It's a living year, not a series of memorials, where the presence of Christ among us is not recalled, but experienced. The church year of prayer begins on the first of four Sundays in Advent, the last Sunday of November or the first Sunday of December depending on the calendar. Advent is the season of anticipation, reflecting the days when the world waited for the coming of the Messiah. It is the season of John the Baptist—a lone voice crying in the wilderness—demanding reform and conversion to "make ready the way of the Lord." It is the season of Mary, the Mother of Jesus, learning that she would be the *Theotokos*—the God-bearer—who would pray in joy: "My soul proclaims the greatness of the Lord; / my spirit rejoices in God my savior, / For he has looked upon his handmaid's lowliness; / behold, from now on will all ages call me blessed" (Luke 1:46–48).

The season of waiting is finished, and Christmas comes. At Midnight Mass the church welcomes in joy the Word made flesh. The "Gloria" returns to the Mass after the Advent season, reflecting the joy of the angels that a Savior has been born to the world. In the church, the celebration of the nativity of the Lord lasts long after the trees have come down, the toys broken, the lights put away. It begins with the vigil Mass of Christmas, and ends the first Sunday after January 6. A season or Ordinary Time follows, leading up to the Lenten season.

Lent begins on Ash Wednesday, forty days before Easter. The priest administers ashes to our foreheads, in a reminder that now is the time to turn away from sin to prepare for the dreadful majesty of Holy Week and the glory of the Resurrection: "Remember, man, you are dust and to dust you will return" (Genesis 3:19). It is the beginning of a traditional penitential season made up of prayer, fasting, and works of mercy. There are six Sundays in Lent, with the last being Passion Sunday, where the crucifixion of Christ is recalled, and Holy Week begins. "From noon onward, darkness came over the whole land until three in the afternoon. And about three o'clock Jesus cried out in a loud voice: *'Eli, Eli, lema sabachthani?'* which means, 'My God, my God, why have you forsaken me?' Some of the bystanders who heard it said, 'This one is calling for Elijah!' Immediately one of them ran off to get a sponge; he soaked it in wine, and putting it on a reed, gave it to him to drink. But the rest said, 'Wait, let us see if Elijah comes to save him.' But Jesus cried out again in a loud voice, and gave up his spirit" (Matthew 27:45–50).

Holy Week begins with Passion Sunday and contains the Easter Triduum (Latin for "three days") from the Mass of the Lord's Supper on Holy Thursday, through Good Friday, and ends with the evening prayer on Easter Sunday. It is the sacred center of the liturgical year. Holy Thursday begins the Triduum and commemorates the institution by Christ of the sacraments of the Eucharist and holy orders. Most dioceses celebrate a Chrism Mass at the cathedral on Holy Thursday morning. Priests of the diocese celebrate the Mass with the bishop. Ordination vows are renewed during the Mass, and the oils that will be used throughout the year (for the sacraments of baptism, holy orders, and anointing of the sick) are blessed. In the evening of Holy Thursday, the Mass of the Lord's Supper is celebrated, memorializing the institution of the Eucharist at the Last Supper. The second reading of the Mass of the Lord's Supper is from St. Paul, writing just a few years after the death and resurrection of Christ: "I received from the Lord what I also handed on to you, that the Lord Jesus, on the night he was handed over, took bread, and, after he had given thanks, broke it and said, 'This is my body that is for you. Do this in remembrance of me.' In the same way also the cup, after supper, saying, 'This cup is the new covenant in my blood. Do this, as often as you drink it, in remembrance of me.' For as often as you eat this bread and drink the cup, you proclaim the death of the Lord until he comes" (1 Corinthians 11:23–26). There are no Masses celebrated on Good Friday and Holy Saturday.

On Good Friday, the crucifixion of Jesus is recalled. A day of strict fast and abstinence, the liturgy evokes all the drama and mystery of the faith. There are readings from Isaiah of the lamb led to slaughter, from Hebrews where Christ's suffering becomes "the source of eternal salvation," and from the Gospel of John, and his last words: "It is finished" (John 19:30). Prayers follow, and extended series of petitions that remind us that Jesus died for all. A ceremony of veneration of the cross follows, then distribution of the hosts consecrated on Holy Thursday.

There is no Mass on Holy Saturday, and the movement from the somber memory of Good Friday to the glorious celebration of the Resurrection begins on the Easter Vigil at sunset. A lit candle—the paschal candle—is brought into the darkened church, and the light is passed from one candle to the next, symbolizing Christ, the Light of the world. At the Easter Vigil, "catechumens"—those who are preparing to enter the church as adults—are baptized, and, with them, the entire congregation will renew their baptismal vows. The masses of Easter day continue the celebration, and the Easter season will last fifty days, from Easter to Pentecost. It includes the celebration of the feast of the Ascension, and the themes of the church's life in prayer are the resurrection, and our resurrection from a life of sin through the power of the Holy Spirit.

The season of Ordinary Time begins again on the Monday after Pentecost and will end on the Saturday before the First Sunday of

Advent. The last Sunday in Ordinary Time is the feast of Christ the King.

The liturgical calendar is fixed on the fifty-two Sundays of the year, as Sunday is the day of commemoration of the Resurrection. Throughout the year there are also feasts and celebrations to focus our prayer on special aspects of the faith. Solemnities are the great feasts of the year—Christmas, Easter, Pentecost, and the Ascension. They include the feast of Mary, Mother of God on January 1, the Assumption of the Blessed Virgin Mary on August 15, All Saints' Day on November 1, and the Immaculate Conception on December 8. There are also the solemnities of the Epiphany on January 6, St. Joseph on March 19, Corpus Christi and St. Peter and St. Paul on June 29. There are also feasts, such as the Transfiguration, the Presentation, or All Souls Day on November 2. There are memorials for the saints or optional memorial days important in different countries or cultures.

It is faith celebrated in time, alive as well with numerous private and liturgical devotions that enliven the life of prayer. Of course, some of them might be the stuff of bad memories, like Friday Lenten stations of the cross where the only relief for a Catholic grammar school kid was to see if one of the altar boys would manage to set his hair on fire with one of the candles; or Benediction when somebody might pass out if the priest got carried away with the incense. It is surprising when, as adults, these devotions are revisited, and we discover just how powerful and moving they are as prayer.

The liturgical year is the faith carried through the seasons of the year, and the seasons of our lives. It is our prayer rooted in time and creation.

A Life in Prayer

Prayer can be a howl, a scream, a cry, a whimper, or a whisper. It can be poetry and song; it can be a stammered wish or a simple sentence. The means of prayer are less necessary than the meaning—lifting our hearts and minds to God. The forms of prayer and spiritual expression within Catholic life are numerous. Pick a card, any card. They are all worth exploring, particularly as one's life and one's needs change.

Myself, I have kept it simple. There is no reason to make prayer complicated. The best prayer I have found is theft. Of course, in Catholic tradition it is called *divina lectio*—spiritual reading. Dipping into the thoughts and prayers of the great spiritual writers leads me in better ways than I can create myself.

> Steer the ship of my life, Lord, to your quiet harbor, where I can be safe from the storms of sin and conflict. Show me the course I should take. Renew in me the gift of discernment, so that I can see the right direction in which I should go. And give me the strength and courage to choose the right course, even when the sea is rough and the waves are high, knowing that through enduring hardship

and danger in your name we shall find comfort
and peace.

St. Basil (329–379)

If you can't find prayer on your own, simply make the Prayer of
St. Francis of Assisi your prayer. It is the model of personal prayer
created by the mind and heart of humanity:

> Lord, make me an instrument of your peace:
> where there is hatred, let me sow love;
> where there is injury, pardon; where there is
>   doubt, faith;
> where there is despair, hope;
> where there is darkness, light;
> where there is sadness, joy.
>
> O Divine Master, grant that I may not so
>   much seek
> to be consoled as to console,
> to be understood as to understand,
> to be loved as to love.
> For it is in giving that we receive,
> it is in pardoning that we are pardoned,
> it is in dying that we are born to eternal life.

It is a prayer that appeals to all that is good in us. We pray, not
for ourselves except only that we can be better—an instrument of
the Lord's peace. We want to be great, not just good enough. Then

we ask that we might lead the good life so that we can be to others what we hope for ourselves, but without any bargaining in return: love, pardon, faith, hope, light, and joy. If we can give those great gifts to others, we bring to an end in some small way those effects of original sin that generate mankind's loneliness: hatred, injury, doubt, despair, darkness, and sadness. Then, we acknowledge the Lord, our divine Master, and we ask that we be given the grace to console, the grace to love, the grace to give, the grace to pardon. So, at the end of our time, we know that our death will mean a birth to eternal life.

I didn't know it when I left O'Toole's on an October evening in 1971, but just about every friend of my youth had already been frozen in the mind's eye and would never age from that moment on. There would be no great *American Graffiti* finish to it where we find out what happens to all the characters when the deal is done. I would hear hints and allegations over time through my mother. So-and-so had married; she was divorced. But most have remained forever kids in my mind's eye. I never saw Mike or Ralph again. Tom and I had that one visit and then he was gone for good. We all went on to our own lives, wherever that was and whatever it has meant. All I can do is pray and hope that the pilgrimage is going well.

Cardinal Joseph Bernardin of Chicago was dying of cancer. In his book, *The Gift of Peace: Personal Reflections*, he wrote:

> Many people have asked me to tell them about heaven and the afterlife. I sometimes smile at the request because I don't know any more than they

do. Yet, when one young man asked if I looked forward to being united with God and all those who have gone before me, I made a connection to something. . . . The first time I traveled with my mother and sister to my parents' homeland of Tonadico di Primiero, in northern Italy, I felt as if I had been there before. After years of looking through my mother's photo albums, I knew the mountains, the land, the houses, the people. As soon as we entered the valley, I said, 'My God, I know this place. I am home.' Somehow I think crossing from this life into eternal life will be similar. I will be home.

*   *   *

May he support you all day long, till the shades lengthen and the evening comes, and the busy world is hushed, and the fever of life is over, and our work is done. Then in His mercy may He give us a safe lodging, and a holy rest and peace at last.

Cardinal John Henry Newman

CHAPTER 14

The Tavern at the End of the World

What is heaven?
Heaven is the state of everlasting life in which
we see God face to face, are made like unto Him
in glory, and enjoy eternal happiness.

The Old Man helped me to avoid the 9:00 A.M. Sunday Children's Mass and Msgr. Betowski's cancer sermons as often as possible. He was an early riser on the weekends and hated to waste any part of a Sunday morning on something as unproductive as sleep. When I was seven, eight, nine, and ten—before I was of an age where meeting the guys at Baum's was the preferred method of liturgical preparation—I would let him haul me out of bed early for the 8:00 A.M. Sunday Mass at Christ the King. After I managed to pull on my Sunday clothes we headed out the door without any breakfast because of the eucharistic fast. We would get to Christ the King early, and he would plop me down in a back pew, then make for the church vestibule.

The Old Man always ushered those Masses. I watched him get people to shove over in the pews to make room for late arrivals. Then he went from row to row with the collection basket at the end of a long pole. The whole thing looked like a pretty sharp job to me. After Mass, I would meet him in the vestibule. When everyone had left, the collection would be bagged and labeled, then dropped off at the rectory. Two guys would carry the bags over, and I asked the Old Man why two guys did what one guy could have accomplished. "Just in case somebody wants to try something," he said, which made me think that in addition to everything else, the Old Man was like a cop for the church. Pretty sharp job, indeed.

One Sunday, when I was around seven or so, I was sitting in my usual spot in back of the church as the collection began. I was horrified to discover that my children's offertory envelope with its twenty-five-cent donation inside had vanished. The Old Man was working the other side of the aisle and there was nothing I could do. I had another quarter in my pocket, my weekly allowance that had actually survived unspent since the Old Man had doled it out on Saturday morning. I had no choice. I put the quarter in the passing basket, silently saying good-bye to a soda and a couple of candy bars.

After Mass, as we walked over to Baum's to pick up the Sunday morning paper, I told the Old Man what had happened. He smiled, said, "You did a good thing," then reached in his pocket, pulled out a quarter, and gave it to me. I truly believed—and believed for at least a couple of years—that the Old Man had spotted my very own quarter amid all the lose change from the collection, plucked it out, and returned it to me after Mass. I don't know why I thought that. But as God is my witness, it seemed perfectly natural that the Old Man could routinely perform little miracles just like that. After all, this was my Old Man—a guy who could work as a cop for the church.

About four decades go on fast forward, like all the decades go now, and the call came just before I got home from work. It wasn't unexpected, as much as we ever expect that call. My daughter was hanging up the phone just as I walked in the door. "I don't know how to say this dad, so I'll just say it. He died a few minutes ago." We buried the Old Man on All Saints' Day. The Mass was actually part of the regular Holy Day schedule of Masses, so they took up a collection. I put in a few bills. Then I added a quarter. I figured the Old Man and I owed it to them.

The Last Things

The nuns, of course, laid it on thick. Heaven was described in glowing terms: lying in the arms of Jesus, the beatific vision and the sheer eternal joy of seeing God face-to-face, a front-row seat in the celestial choir, singing the praises of the Lord for all eternity. All things that defined a nun's heaven. It sounded like a crashing bore to us. As Dante, we could focus better on the everlasting torment of doomed sinners. With hell, they had a point, and we could see it all readily, taking some comfort that at least two or three of the older kids at the End of the Line that made our lives miserable would have their own damned corner for ever and always. Then there was the Hail-Mary pass of purgatory, a thin victory by the skin of our teeth. One of the nuns in fourth grade handed out a holy card portraying the poor souls in purgatory. Four or five people, dressed rather nattily as I recall, were standing amid the flames, hands folded in prayer, with rather goofy smiles on their faces. The nun explained that though they suffered indescribable torment—an indescribable torment that she did her level best to describe—for their sins, they were at peace knowing that the beatific vision was just a rung up the ladder. We liked purgatory, a reasonable theology for kids who spent their days in torment but knowing that at 3:00 P.M. it would be over and done with.

Of course, the whole thing is pointless if there is no afterlife. Christ came to teach us how to live. And fundamental to what he taught is that God—Our Father—is the God of the living, not the dead. Over and over again, Jesus describes his mission in terms of life, a new life, meant for all. The fundamental truth taught by Jesus is that death is not annihilation. Life is not meaningless, genetic happenstance that created animated meat. Jesus came that we may have life, and have it abundantly.

Like our childhood view of God, our view of the afterlife is similarly too small. We try to fit the infinite and eternal into limited and mortal understanding. We carry a lot of dull imagery, or pictures from a holy card, and dismiss the reality. Of course, if it made an old nun happy to use terms like celestial choir and beatific vision, that's not so unforgivable. What it means to each of us is that heaven is real; that God is real and life is a pilgrimage to God. The human search for the love of God ends when we find that love in life after death in what we call in our incapable language, heaven. We perceive heaven's existence because we perceive God's existence. We understand with every fiber of our being that life means more than just a whisper in time. We can feel the presence of God in more moments than we dare to admit. They are glimpses of an eternal presence—an eternal life—for which we were created. Heaven is to love infinitely, and to be loved by Infinite Love.

Purgatory is a word we use for our encounter after death with that divine love, and our own painful realization of how much our lives fell short of that divine love. Perhaps Dickens described purgatory when he thought he was defining hell in the *Christmas Carol*: Purgatory is God revealing all of our opportunities to intercede for good in human affairs when we have lost the ability to do so. Purgatory is our reflection in God's presence—a God aware of all our secrets, all our private thoughts—on how much our lives fell short of greatness when we had every chance to be great. Purgatory is our lives reviewed without benefit of rationalization.

And what of hell? Church history tells us that belief waxes and wanes over the eternal damnation of souls. At one time, it was commonly believed that far and away, the majority of mankind was slouching toward perdition. Contemporary man chooses to believe that there is no hell, or if there is, it is for no one. Another comforting rationalization. Jesus spoke of hell, of course, so we know it exists. Even an old atheist like the French existentialist Jean-Paul Sartre could agree, finding hell to be other people. But perhaps hell is the opposite, an eternity chosen to be alone. It is the result of choices and acts in life—singularly or collectively—where we rejected divine love and that which divine love created, our fellow human beings. It is arguing over angels fitting on the head of a pin to say how many choose by their lives to spend eternity separated from divine love. I can barely figure out my own methods and motives without trying to figure out those of anyone else. But we know that the potential is there, the ability and the will to live a life that consciously rejects God.

Our belief is simple: God is revealed in Christ, and he is the God of the living. Death does not hold us. If that is not truth, then there is no truth at all.

One more time: "For if the dead are not raised, neither has Christ been raised; and if Christ has not been raised, your faith is vain, you are still in your sins. Then those who have fallen asleep in Christ have perished. If for this life only we have hoped in Christ, we are the most pitiable people of all" (1 Corinthians 15:16–19).

There's an old book by Myles Connolly called *Mr. Blue.* The lead character is a will-o'-the-wisp kind of guy, a bit of a modern day St. Francis. Connolly has him describing his idea of heaven, long after this old world has come to an end.

> When the day comes that the sky is emptied of stars, and the sun is black, and the distraught winds have only the void for their lament, I am sure that somewhere men will be merry together, somewhere good hearts will greet good hearts, and somewhere our dreams of unbroken love and good talk and laughter will come true. This is a glorious Somewhere, and it is far nearer to us than the stars. . . . It is a good place, this Somewhere. It

has been called Paradise. It has been called the Tavern at the End of the World. And it has been called Home.

And that's where I figure the Old Man is waiting.

And in the End

For many boomers born into the faith, raised in Catholic homes and Catholic grammar schools from an era now dead and gone, the faith might be only something dimly practiced, a habit dragged out of childhood like the way we brush our teeth.Or maybe we drifted away entirely for our own reasons, if for any real reason at all. I had no real reason for leaving the faith for a while except to say it was the 1960s. For many of us, we never really left the faith so much as we signed up for the mediocrity of the general culture, fell away from the practice of the faith, then somewhere along the line fell away altogether. There was no great apostasy, no great moment of fission to take away faith. It was simply an apostasy of apathy, built on nothing more or less. Even if we still slouch along tied to the church in some way, it hasn't really made much of a difference in our lives since we were kids. Once there was a way to get back home, it seems, but there's no one around anymore to sing a lullaby.

There's no story to tell about my coming back to the faith. It was a pilgrimage taken over the years. It began, I suppose, when my brother dragged me to an uninteresting Christmas Mass late in the season of my college years. Many of us have come back to the faith along a similar path. And the reasons for coming back are as many,

I suppose, as there were for leaving. But the unifying bottom line is
that there was more—infinitely more—to the faith once we began
to view it, see it, touch it, and study it as adults than we ever saw,
or understood, as kids. We began to look at the faith again through
adult eyes, and realized that there was so much more truth and
trust than all the little truths we had toyed with for too long and
never really trusted.

For some of us, maybe it was an intellectual attraction that first
got us to take a look back. We discovered Augustine and Aquinas,
or Dorothy Day and Thomas Merton. A dramatic intellectual heritage rooted in faith opened up to us that was beyond any of the
formulas of childhood. Maybe we were drawn back to the richness
of the devotional practices where, through new eyes, we could see
what we never understood as children. Or we were caught up like
nineteenth-century Oxford dons in the discovery of the true apostolic nature of the church and couldn't avoid the reasoned understanding that the church was the only source back to the apostles,
the original witnesses of Christ. There was the appeal of stability,
the miracle of an institution of faith two thousand years old, a faith
that had built Western civilization.

Of course, for some the story is more personal, a pilgrimage that
began with the loss of a loved one or with a crisis that simply told
us it was time to come back.

But whatever the original spark, we stayed because we fell in
love with Christ and found him in the church. We began to not
only acknowledge that God exists, we also discovered a God no
longer too small from our childhood or too abstract from our adult

intellectual games. We found that the God revealed in Christ is "Our Father."

We began to see that a response in faith to the whole mystery of Jesus was demanded of us. We began to realize that assenting to belief in God and belief in Jesus has to demand some changes in the way we think and the way we go about the business of our lives. We learned the wisdom in Flannery O'Connor's observation: "What people don't realize is how much faith costs. They think faith is a big electric blanket, when of course it is the cross. It is much harder to believe than not to believe. . . . Don't expect faith to clear things up for you. It is trust, not certainty."

We realized that the New Testament is not a story that will respect indifference. Jesus either meant what he said, or he is meaningless, and the dead are simply dead. But we saw, through his own words, that he came for our salvation, to reconcile humanity with God. He came to save us from death, and to assure us that we can know God's love for us. He came that we might know how to live; and that we might have life, because God is the God of the living. He came to show us that we don't need to struggle through the insufferable benign agnosticism of the ordinary. There are miracles, in other words, and miracles mean we have work to do.

We began to understand faith as the virtue of knowing God in our lives; hope as our confidence in God that we might believe in a purpose, goal, and end in Christian life; and that charity—love—is the summation of all: love of God and love of neighbor. To live charity is to live the great life. We began to recognize that with God, anything is possible.

We saw that the sacraments are not man-made rituals meant to celebrate points in time. Rather, they were made real in Christ's life and are the means by which the divine and the human connect. They are the continued presence of Christ in the world. We found that the key to understanding sanctity is the realization that it is impossible on our own. Relying on a new birth in baptism, the strength of the Holy Spirit in confirmation, the forgiveness of God in confession, the Living Bread of the Eucharist, the sacraments to bless our vocations, and the healing touch of God's love—that is where we find hope.

We could find nothing on this good earth that could bring us to Christ better than the church of our childhood when seen and experienced through adult eyes. That is where we find the great life.

In the old movie *City Slickers*—required viewing for any guy over the age of forty—the old cowboy explains that there is only one important thing in life. And you've got to find out what that is. We began to see that there is only one important thing: we don't have to settle for the ordinary, the good enough. With God, through the grace of the sacraments, anything is possible, and nothing, particularly life, is meaningless. How can life be meaningless if Christ lives in that life? Again, my old Bible says, "I will not treat God's gracious gift as pointless" (Galatians 2:20).

At some point, there was simply no backing away any longer. No more excuses of lousy explanations of the faith when we were kids. No more stories—exaggerated a hundred times in the telling—of battle-ax nuns and boring liturgies, no more looking at the faith only through the eyes and understanding of a child. At some point, we decided to listen to the call of faith as adults, seek it out, and understand it to the best of our ability. The time came to grow up and to accept or reject the heart of the Catholic faith: Christ has died, Christ is risen, Christ will come again.

The nuns told us, "Act as if you have faith and faith you will have." In one sense, they were dead wrong. Faith was never really faith if it was never understood. It became a force-fed act to many of us that was lost in a maze of symbols and wooden words that we never really grasped. Without interiorizing the faith as we entered adulthood, we left it behind. Without understanding our beliefs as adult Catholics we dismissed the action of faith as pious ritual imposed by nuns, priests, and parents on little children and unthinking adults. But the nuns were also dead on target. Once we ceased to practice the faith, we had no faith. Or let a thousand other bits of nonsense take the place of faith. We began to see that faith is not something we can have in halves. If we don't practice the faith, we will not have it; if we don't lead a life of faith, we can't be faithful.

If there was that final point of conversion—or reversion—to the faith, most of us had it when we rediscovered the Mass as adults. The Mass is not a blessed ritual, a collection of readings and prayers, a gathering of the faithful. It is these things, of course, but infinitely more: "All the good works in the world are not equal to the holy sacrifice of the Mass because they are the works of men; but the Mass is the work of God" (Cure of Ars).

Worship, practice, prayer, and Christian living are a delicately woven pattern. Take out any of the threads and the whole pattern unravels. Most of us stop believing when we stop acting like we believe. We lose the great life because we no longer practice the faith in which it is grounded. Then we find we can't pray because we do not live life in a way that is very open to prayer. We do not live that life because we abandoned worship of God and the practice of the faith. All the parts create the whole.

We found that the simple goal of the great life is that we live in truth. The most important command of the great life is that we accept that truth is real, and we struggle to reflect the truth in every word and deed. "For where your treasure is, there will your heart be also" (Matthew 6:21). What we desire, what we aim for, where we expend our energy and determination is what we become for good or bad. If our heart wants the great life—if that is what we really treasure, what we really search for in ourselves and others—that is what we will become. With God's grace, we can change the person we created any day at any age. We just have to find—or redefine—what we treasure.

What we began to discover, finally, as we revisited our faith through the eyes of an adult, was that it has been there all along. The spirituality we seek, the prayer life we hope to have, that way of living our lives daily as if we are touching the infinite, has been there waiting for us. We found that there is a way to get back home.

Anyway, that's my story.

*   *   *

God has created me to do him some definite service. He has committed some work to me which He has not committed to another, I have my mission. I may never know it in this life, but I shall be told it in the next. I am a link in a chain, a bond of connection between persons. He has not created me for naught. I shall do good; I shall do his work. I shall be an angel of peace, a preacher of truth in my own place, while not intending it if I do but keep his commandments. Therefore, I will trust in Him, whatever I am, I can never be thrown away. If I am in sickness, my sickness may serve Him, in perplexity, my perplexity may serve Him. If I am in sorrow, my sorrow may serve Him. He does nothing in vain. He knows what He is about. He may take away my friends. He may throw me among strangers. He may make me feel desolate, make my spirits sink, hide my future from me. Still, he knows what He is about.

Cardinal John Henry Newman (1801–1890)

Acknowledgments

There is a stable of literature referred to as "fictional memoirs"—stories rooted in time and experience remembered, but conveyed in the fashion of fiction. This isn't a fictional memoir. The End of the Line is there and ready for a visit, though it hasn't been the actual end of the bus line for decades. Christ the King is a living, breathing parish, while Fairfield University remains a living, breathing college. Manhattan Prep is neither living nor breathing, but was both when I attended. Despite rumors to the contrary, Indiana also exists. In most of my stories, however, the names have been changed to protect the guilty and confound the innocent. Identities have also been meshed together or pulled apart. But all the stories are true, or at least as true as memory can have them. In any case, they are my memories and I'm sticking with them.

How do you thank a lifetime—or at least a middle-aged lifetime—of relationships that have gone into the creation of a book? I can't, so I simply thank them all, with special gratitude to the living and the dead from the End of the Line and classmates from sixteen years of Catholic education.

But just a few must be specifically identified. There is Jim Manney at Loyola Press, who believed in this from the start and encouraged me in every step of the process, along with his entire publishing team. Jim and I first discussed this book over breakfast at a Holiday Inn in Ann Arbor, Michigan. I bought.

I may be the only author to credit another publisher in a book, but I also have to thank all my old and dear friends at Our Sunday Visitor. I once told them that in my particular case, never was there a greater sinner, and never was God kinder to one. That still holds.

At the same time, I have to thank a book. The prayers you find in this work are all from the Catholic tradition. You can repeat them anytime without having to seek permission from anyone. But they are marvelously collected in a *Manual of Prayers,* published by the Midwest Theological Forum and also available from Our Sunday Visitor. It is the prayer book of the Pontifical North American College in Rome. I could not recommend a prayer book more highly.

Then there is my mentor, the late Maryknoll priest, Father Albert Nevins. He got me started. And the late Father Ronald Lawler, O.F.M. Cap. He taught the great life. And lived it every day.

My family, of course, shares much of the responsibility, though not the blame, for this book. I was blessed with three brothers, a sister, grandparents, aunts, uncles, and a swarm of cousins, all of whom are a part of this book though they may not know it.

And then there is the Old Man. This book is for him.

But it would never have been written without my teacher—my mother, who passed away just a few days shy of ninety and a few months shy of seeing this work completed. She's the one who told all the stories in the first place.

My son and daughter, Ryan Lockwood and Theresa Ruppert, despite the busiest times in their lives, cajoled and encouraged their Old Man all along the way. And, finally, there is my wife, Cindy. She's really to blame for all this. Without her faith, hope and love, I could never do a thing.

And for all my fellow Baby Boomers, let's start and finish with a simple prayer: *Credo, sed adiuva incredulitatem meam.* You can look it up.